Deep Deuce was still a thriving strip in the 1960s when a civil rights march wound its way past the Aldridge Theater. However, Deep Deuce never regained the height of popularity it enjoyed in the 1920s and 1930s. *Courtesy Oklahoma Publishing Company.*

(12) Dorothy

Best wishes,
Denyvetta Davis

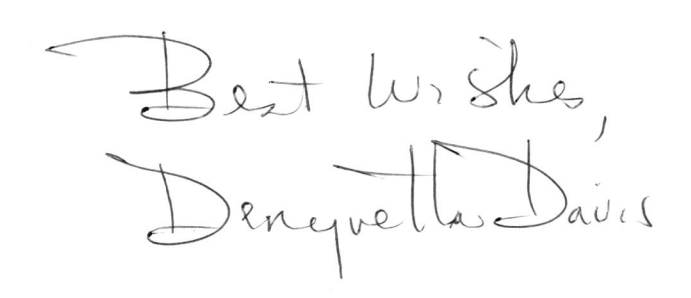

Ralph Ellison

**FOREWORD BY
JOHN F. CALLAHAN**

SERIES EDITOR
KENNY A. FRANKS

ASSOCIATE EDITOR
GINI MOORE CAMPBELL

Ralph Ellison
a biography

by Bob Burke &
Denyvetta Davis

OKLAHOMA TRACKMAKER SERIES

Copyright 2003 by Oklahoma Heritage Association

All rights reserved. No part of this book may be reproduced or utilized in any form or by any means, electronic or mechanical, including photocopying and recording, by any information storage and retrieval system, without permission of the publisher.

Printed in the United States of America.
ISBN 1-885596-30-8
Library of Congress Catalog Number 2002112813
Designed by Sandi Welch/2W Design Group

OKLAHOMA HERITAGE ASSOCIATION
PUBLICATIONS COMMITTEE

Everett E. Berry, Chairman, Stillwater
W.R. "Dick" Stubbs, Vice Chairman, Henryetta
Ann Simmons Alspaugh, Oklahoma City
Sharon Bell, Tulsa
Jean Berry, Stillwater
Edwin C. Boynton, Durant
Bob Burke, Oklahoma City
Don Ferrell, Chandler
LeRoy H. Fischer, Stillwater
Fred C. Harlan, Okmulgee
John Hefner, Oklahoma City
Pat Henry, Lawton, ex-officio
David V. Hume, Enid
William E. Humphrey, Pauls Valley
Hon. Vicki Miles-LaGrange, Oklahoma City
B. Chesley Montague, Lawton
C.D. Northcutt, Ponca City
Ann Woolley, Ada

OKLAHOMA HERITAGE ASSOCIATION
201 NORTHWEST FOURTEENTH STREET
OKLAHOMA CITY, OKLAHOMA 73103

Contents

FOREWORD BY JOHN F. CALLAHAN **5**
ACKNOWLEDGMENTS **7**
PROLOGUE **9**

CHAPTER 1: MEAGER BEGINNINGS **15**
CHAPTER 2: MUSIC AND BOOKS **41**
CHAPTER 3: SEARCHING FOR A FATHER FIGURE **61**
CHAPTER 4: THE INFLUENCE OF DEEP DEUCE **77**
CHAPTER 5: FINISHING HIGH SCHOOL **97**
CHAPTER 6: LEAVING HOME **107**
CHAPTER 7: POLISHING THE TRUMPET **121**
CHAPTER 8: SEPARATE BUT NOT EQUAL **133**
CHAPTER 9: DISCOVERING THE WASTELAND **143**
CHAPTER 10: HEADING NORTH **155**
CHAPTER 11: DETOUR TO OHIO **167**
CHAPTER 12: PERFECTING HIS CRAFT **179**
CHAPTER 13: MASTER STORYTELLER **191**
CHAPTER 14: COOKING ON THE HIGH SEAS **203**
CHAPTER 15: BIRTH OF A NOVEL **213**
CHAPTER 16: A CLASSIC **225**
CHAPTER 17: PROFESSOR IN RESIDENCE **239**
CHAPTER 18: SHADOW AND ACT **253**
CHAPTER 19: TAKING THE HIGH ROAD **273**
CHAPTER 20: INDELIBLE INK **293**

BIBLIOGRAPHY **317**
NOTES **319**
INDEX **327**

Foreword
BY JOHN F. CALLAHAN

"You have to leave home to find home," Ralph Ellison scribbled on one of the manuscript pages of his never finished novel-in-progress, and the line is an apt description of his rediscovery of the Oklahoma of his youth in other times and places. His affinity for the Territory in which he was born and passed the first 19 years of his life seemed to intensify as the year of his departure—1933—receded farther and farther into the past.

Although he returned to Oklahoma only once before his masterpiece of a first novel, *Invisible Man*, was published in 1952, and thrice thereafter, Oklahoma remained for Ellison what F. Scott Fitzgerald, another brilliant American writer from the provinces, referring to the middle-west, called "the warm center of the universe."

Emotionally, Oklahoma City and fields and woods surrounding the town provided the one comforting point of reference for the 23-year-old Ellison after a physician's incompetent diagnosis triggered the unexpected, sudden death of his mother in Ohio in October of 1937. Two days after her death he writes a desolate letter back to Oklahoma addressed simply, "Dear Folks," in which, with a trembling, stiff upper lip, he reveals his grief and his determination to overcome his sense of emptiness and loss. From Dayton, he soon writes Richard Wright, his close friend of a few months, that the streets of Dayton "are very much like those of Oklahoma City, home."

Intellectually, Ellison developed his ideas about the fluidity and complexity of American culture and personality from the range of his experience in Oklahoma. He more than held his own among American writers and thinkers by virtue of the "mammy-made" pragmatism engendered by virtue of his faithfulness to what he called his "cold Oklahoma Negro eye." In the last few years of his life, he wrote long reminiscences in the form of letters to old friends from Oklahoma, and, when asked to account for the strain of optimism and patriotism in his reading of America, he cited early experiences in Oklahoma as sources of that "sanity-saving comedy" and tragicomic sensibility he saw as the birthmark of American possibility.

In one of his last public appearances, an address at the Whiting Foundation on October 23, 1992, Ellison used a recurring incident from his Oklahoma boyhood as a parable for the successes and failures of American conscience and consciousness. "Our national tendency," he said, "to ignore or forget important details of our past reminds me of the philosophical stance of certain adults with whom I hunted during my boyhood in Oklahoma. After bringing down a rabbit or quail, men would proclaim in voices that throbbed with true American optimism, 'A hit, my boy is history!' But if they missed and the game got away, they'd stare at the sky or cover and say, 'A miss, my boy, is a mystery.'" Ellison went on to speak of the successes of "our democratic ideals" as hits, the failures to "achieve our democratic commitments" as misses. In the on-again, off-again integrated/segregated Oklahoma of his youth he saw enough hits and misses to both justify his lifelong faith in American democratic possibility, and keep him on guard against betrayals of the "new birth of freedom" called for by Abraham Lincoln in the Gettysburg Address.

For Ellison, Oklahoma, the country of memory, remained the very crucible in which the American covenant was tested. It is fitting that Bob Burke and Denyvetta Davis have devoted much of their biographical ink to Ellison's Oklahoma ties. Their attention to Oklahoma public records and the testimony of those acquainted with Ellison gives the volume an inimitable flavor of southwestern cooking. As time passes, and Ellison's legacy to American literature and letters only continues to grow in importance and intensity, I expect Oklahoma to figure more and more prominently in scholarly accounts of the sources of his talent.

JOHN F. CALLAHAN

Acknowledgments

We are grateful to many people for their help in paying proper tribute to Oklahoma's great author, Ralph Ellison.

John F. Callahan not only graced us with his foreword, but gave great encouragement to the project. Our editors, Dr. Kenny Franks and Gini Moore Campbell, were helpful and understanding as the manuscript took form.

Eric Dabney and Stephanie Graves Ayala developed needed research and were always ready with editing and content suggestions. Debbie Neill, Shelley Irby Dabney, Anna Hubbard, Mike Irby, and Amy Burke Nicar provided technical assistance. Jeff Reese at Fairlawn Cemetery helped locate Ellison's father's grave.

Linda Lynn, Melissa Hayer, Mary Phillips, Robin Davison, and Billie Harry at the Oklahoma Publishing Company, and Chester Cowen at the Oklahoma Historical Society (OHS) provided photographs. Also at OHS, Bill Welge, Rodger Harris, Judith Michener, and Bill Moore helped in research—as did Kitty Pittman, Adrienne Butler, Melecia Caruthers, Marilyn Miller, and Mary Hardin at the Oklahoma Department of Libraries.

Thanks to Sandi Welch for her interesting and delightful design of the book and the dustjacket and to the Oklahoma Heritage Association, including its president, Richard Ratcliffe, and chairman of the board, Pat Henry, for its commitment to preserve Oklahoma's incredible story.

Finally, we are grateful to the brave souls who reviewed the manuscript—The Honorable Vicki Miles-LaGrange, The Honorable Hannah Atkins, David Draper Clark, B.J. Williams, The Honorable Steven Taylor, George and Marcia Davis, Tia Jones Bibbs, Mike Irby, Fred McCann, Scott Carter, and Jeanne Devlin.

BOB BURKE
DENYVETTA DAVIS

Prologue

To understand the true meaning of the Renaissance writings of Ralph Ellison, one must first inquire into the sociological climate of the Oklahoma in which he matured. Ellison was born in 1914, when the struggle for equality for blacks was in its infancy. Oklahoma was only seven years old as a state—only on paper were blacks free and equal.

President Abraham Lincoln took the first step to abolish slavery when he signed the Emancipation Proclamation in 1863 during the Civil War. Over the next few years of healing in the war-torn land, the Thirteenth, Fourteenth, and Fifteenth amendments to the United States Constitution were ratified, giving full citizenship to blacks.

After the Civil War, there was a substantial population of blacks in what would become Oklahoma—remnants of families of former slaves, called freedmen, who had accompanied the Five Civilized Tribes to the eastern part of the state known as Indian Territory.

Continuing patterns of racial segregation in the Old South caused many blacks to look toward the western frontier for economic hope. The vast stretches of fertile lands in Indian Territory and the undesignated areas of what would later be Oklahoma Territory and western Oklahoma acted as a strong magnet for black families who believed they could find their "place in the sun" in the new land.

When a large section of Unassigned Lands in central Oklahoma was opened for settlement in a dramatic land run in 1889, many blacks came—taking advantage of the fact that the government did not officially permit any discrimination. On April 22, 1889, at the sound of gunfire announcing the mad dash for free land, the color of a man's skin did not hamper his ability to set out in a wagon, on a horse or bicycle, or run toward a homestead to call his own.

Oklahoma Territory was forged from the plains of western Oklahoma in 1890. During territorial days, blacks were a healthy part of the electoral process. Blacks voted regularly and some ran for public office. The "free" atmosphere resulted in trainloads of blacks coming to Oklahoma—both families of means and those who came with only the clothing on their backs.

Black boosters such as Edward P. McCabe had visions of establishing an all-black state. On April 22, 1890, he founded an all-black town, Langston City, named for John Mercer Langston, a black congressman from Virginia. Langston was billed as "the only distinctively Negro city in America."

In his newspaper that was distributed in black communities in the older states, Langston passionately pleaded for "moneyed Negroes" to settle in Langston. He wrote, "What will you be if you stay in the South? Slaves, liable to be killed at any time, and never treated right; but if you come to Oklahoma you have equal chances with the white man." The *Kansas City Times* reported on efforts to have 100,000 blacks in Oklahoma by the end of 1890. Even the *New York Times* referred to Langston as a "black Mecca."

A growing number of whites feared McCabe and others might actually succeed in carving an all-black state from the newly settled territories. The fear bred hostility from the much larger white population. White reaction to rumored mass migrations of blacks ultimately killed McCabe's idea of becoming governor of Oklahoma Territory—even though he was appointed deputy territorial auditor, the first black to occupy a major political office in the West.

The plight of blacks in Oklahoma and in all of America suffered in 1896 when the United States Supreme Court declared in the case of *Plessy v. Ferguson* that separate but equal facilities for blacks did not violate the federal constitution's guarantee of equality and freedom for all Americans. Tragically—because whites controlled the territorial legislature and most city councils and school boards—black schools, parks, and other public facilities were never allocated sufficient funds to be "equal."

During talk of joining Oklahoma and Indian territories into a new state of Oklahoma, President Theodore Roosevelt let it be known that he would not allow Oklahoma to join the Union if its constitution did not reflect equality of races. In fact, Article I, Section 6 of the proposed Oklahoma constitution read, "The State shall never enact any law restricting the right of suffrage on account of race, color, or previous condition of servitude."

The hollow "paper" victory for blacks was tempered by the true feelings of white leaders who called for constitutional segregation of the races. Segregation was a key issue for whites who insisted that blacks be kept apart in schools, on railroads, in waiting rooms, and in other public facilities. The Democratic Party became the champion of the effort to make segregation part of the constitution. When Democrats won all but 12 seats in the constitutional convention, it was a victory for white supremacy.

Constitutional Convention Chairman William H. "Alfalfa Bill" Murray, of whom Ellison later wrote in discourses on his early years in Oklahoma, told convention delegates, "We must provide the means for the advancement of the Negro race, and accept him as God gave him to us and use him for the good of society."

In a cruel and bigoted speech, Murray said of blacks, "As a rule they are failures as lawyers, doctors, and in other professions. He must be taught in the line of his own sphere, as porters, bootblacks, and barbers…it is an entirely false notion that the Negro can rise to the equal of a white man in the professions or become an equal citizen to grapple with public questions."

Blacks vigorously fought against the approval of the new state constitution. Protest groups called the document "a Jim Crow constitution," a term derived from a comedy act in the 1830s when a white comedian painted his face black and called the character "Jim Crow."

Blacks despaired when the constitution was approved. Historian Jimmie Lewis Franklin noted, "They again dug in for another intense fight to prevent the new state from erecting a Jim Crow system to limit their rights. They would fail. Their children, and their children's children, would have to drink from the bitter cup of discrimination and segregation for many years to come."

With the vision of an "all-black" state evaporated, some blacks still had hope that when Oklahoma became a state on November 16, 1907, they could enjoy all rights of citizenship. However, attempts to make blacks second-class citizens continued.

The first bill considered by the new Oklahoma legislature required separate railway cars and waiting rooms for black and white passengers. The law called for "conspicuous" signs in "plain letters" indicating the race for which the public facility was set apart.

Subsequently, the legislature approved bills that prohibited marriages between whites and blacks and prohibited black children from attending white schools. From the beginning, black schools were under funded, falling woefully short of the constitutional mandate for "separate but equal" educational facilities.

The election of a black Republican, Albert Comstock Hamlin, to the Oklahoma House of Representatives from Logan County in 1908, frightened white segregation leaders. Their answer was State Question 17, an overt move to follow the lead of other southern states to disenfranchise blacks.

Oklahoma voters approved the state question in 1910, amending the state constitution to provide a literacy test for all voters. Essentially, the new law required that any voter must be able to read a section of the state constitution, but exempt any person whose ancestors could legally vote before January, 1866, the year that blacks were granted the right to vote. It was called the "grandfather clause" and was seen by black leaders as an open and obvious attempt to grandfather in white voters and shut blacks out of the electoral process.

Many of the nation's constitutional scholars agreed with black leaders. However, the first few efforts to overturn the grandfather clause in the Oklahoma Supreme Court fell on deaf ears. Oklahoma City newspaper editor Roscoe Dunjee took up the cause in 1914 after two Logan County Election Board officials were indicted for violating a federal law that made it illegal to refuse to register a potential voter on the basis of race.

In June of 1915, the United States Supreme Court, in *Guinn v. United States,* upheld the convictions of the two election officials and threw out Oklahoma's grandfather clause as an unconstitutional attempt to abridge the right of a citizen to vote on the ground of ancestry. The Guinn case was the first national victory for a fledgling black organization known as the National Association for the Advancement of Colored People (NAACP).

Within weeks, Oklahoma leaders looked for new ways to circumvent the United States Supreme Court decision. In a special session of the legislature that was marked by a near riot with the hurling of inkwells, paperweights, and books when

Republicans and Socialists accused the Democrats of racism, Oklahoma legislators passed a new law that required all unregistered voters in the state to register in a 12-day period beginning April 30, 1916.

There was a widespread conspiracy by registrars to refuse to register blacks who again were locked out of the electoral process. That law was not successfully challenged until the United States Supreme Court struck it down 18 years later, in 1934, in the case of *Lane v. Wilson*.

In 1914, black children attended classes in rickety school buildings—cold in winter and hot in spring and fall. Most black adults had virtually no say in the election of local and state officials. They lived in segregated rows of shacks in the poorest parts of town. Both black men and women were relegated to the worst and dirtiest jobs and were paid wages far inferior to their white brothers and sisters. Equality, as guaranteed by the federal and state constitutions, was an empty promise for blacks who called Oklahoma their home.

Thus was the state of affairs in Oklahoma City as Ralph Ellison prepared to enter the world in 1914.

Meager Beginnings

CHAPTER 1

> The Negroes were forced to live their humble existence in shanties built on the unstable sands along the North Canadian River and in groups of tenements and quickly put-up houses near Second Street.
>
> —JIMMY STEWART

Oklahoma City was born grown. Unique among all land settlements in history, nearly 2,000,000 acres in central Oklahoma were opened in the Land Run of 1889. Soldiers held back thousands of modern pilgrims standing in rows 20-feet deep, separated from the Promised Land "not by an ocean, but by a line scratched in the earth with the point of a soldier's bayonet."[1]

Writing in *Harpers,* Richard Harding Davis later pieced together the moment, "The long row toeing this line are bending forward, panting with excitement, and looking with greedy eyes toward the New Canaan, the women with their dresses tucked up to their knees, the men stripped of their coats and waistcoats for the coming race."[2]

Thousands of men, women, and children—in buggies and buckboards—on bicycles, horses, mules, and oxen—and by foot, leapt from the starting line at the sound of cannons and rifles at noon on April 22, 1889. Some prospective homesteaders even dived from the windows of slow-moving trains. Most of the hearty souls were armed only with wooden stakes with which to mark a parcel of land that would be their new home.[3]

By nightfall, Oklahoma Station—the early name of the Atchison, Topeka, and Santa Fe railroad stop on the prairie that became Oklahoma City—had 12,000 inhabitants. Groups of men gathered under trees to form governing bodies and commercial clubs. There was bedlam. No one really knew who owned what piece of land. Tents and shanties were thrown up by settlers to prove they owned that location. If forced off by someone bigger and more vociferous, they moved on to find another poor soul more timid and less possessive of their claim.[4]

One water well near what later was the corner of Main Street and Broadway Avenue constituted the city's water supply. The owner briefly sustained a brisk business of selling water for a nickel per cup until self-appointed authorities stopped the practice for humanitarian reasons. Everyone was thirsty after dashing at least 15 miles from boundary lines to the choice land along the North Canadian River.[5]

Even though Oklahoma City instantly became the largest city in Oklahoma Territory, the territorial capital was established at Guthrie, 25 miles to the north. When Oklahoma became a state in 1907, Guthrie served as the state capital until state voters approved a move of the seat of government to Oklahoma City in 1910.

There was a housing and population boom in Oklahoma City after statehood. As far as the eye could see, houses and businesses sprang up. New immigrants arrived in the city daily.

But there is another side of the story of early-day Oklahoma City—the rarely told history of black families that made the Run of 1889 and came later to establish their homes.

Hard and fast rules of segregation forced blacks to live in groups on land others did not want. Black families built small, shotgun houses in places labeled Sand Town, West Town, Walnut Grove, and South Town—and the authorities made them stay there. Within a decade of statehood, the City Council of Oklahoma City passed an ordinance that made it a crime for blacks to build schools, churches, or community

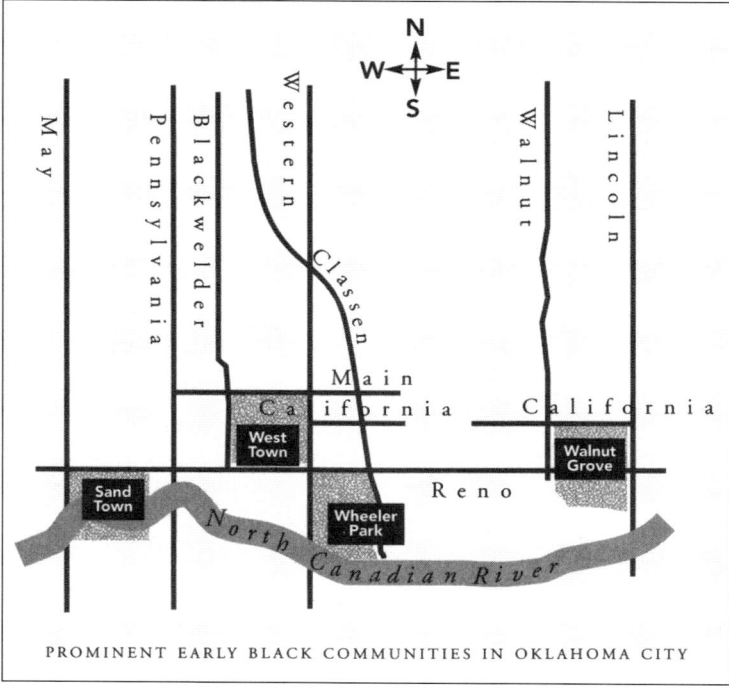

PROMINENT EARLY BLACK COMMUNITIES IN OKLAHOMA CITY

In early Oklahoma City, black families lived in one of four neighborhoods and in a narrow strip around Second Street just east of downtown. *Courtesy Oklahoma Heritage Association.*

centers in any ward of the city that was at least 75 percent white.[6]

Intolerable were the living conditions in the black villages when spring rains flooded houses and washed away garden spots from which families were fed and sustained for the year. But the blacks held on to their spots, hoping for better times.[7]

That tinge of hope in the air was what brought Lewis Alfred Ellison and his wife, Ida Milsap Ellison, to Oklahoma City in 1910. Lewis was the son of a South Carolina former slave, Alfred Ellison, and his wife, Harriet Ellison. Ida also grew up in the deep South, in White Oak, Georgia, in a family of sharecroppers. The two met in Lewis' hometown of Abbeville, South Carolina, when the Milsaps came calling on relatives.[8]

After working on farms and on new railroad construction, Lewis enlisted in the 25th United States Colored Infantry in 1898. The 25th was part of the famed black Indian fighters called "Buffalo Soldiers." While stationed in what is now southwestern New Mexico, Lewis had access to the fort library in which he read magazines, newspapers, and poetry.

Lewis spent three years in the cavalry and left with a sour taste in his mouth after being court-martialed over a misunderstood incident involving an alleged refusal to drill properly. Without income and dishonored by his government, he returned home to Abbeville.

Lewis and Ida married in 1909 and moved to Chattanooga, Tennessee, where Lewis worked in a restaurant, as a construction worker, and in a candy kitchen. They heard stories about opportunities in the new state, Oklahoma, "the promised land." Soon they traveled by train to Oklahoma City and rented a house east of Stiles Avenue at 407 East First Street. They moved into an apartment built onto a rambling, two-story house owned by Jefferson Davis Randolph, a man who later would serve as a friend and role model for their son, Ralph. The First Street apartment was home to the Ellisons for four years.

Lewis and Ida Ellison's first son died as an infant. But their hopes of having a family were buoyed in the fall of 1913 when Ida became pregnant. A second son, Ralph Waldo Ellison, was born in the humble Ellison home on First Street on March 1, 1914.[9] A third son, Herbert, was born in 1916.

Lewis made a living for his family by selling coal and ice to residents of the black section of Oklahoma City. Although a common laborer, he loved poetry and insisted that his second son be named after the 19th century writer and philosopher Ralph Waldo Emerson—although Ralph Waldo Ellison abhorred his name because of constant kidding about who he really was—Emerson or Ellison. In fact, he later shortened his name to Ralph W. Ellison and pledged early in life that he would never read Emerson's works.[10]

The Ellison family prospered enough to move into a house on North Byers Avenue—a section that was mixed with black and white families. The new home had a large yard where Ida raised guineas and chickens. The family budget was apparently sufficient to buy Ralph a tricycle. One of his earliest memories is of "pedaling like mad" with a small lard bucket hanging on the handle bars to put out a fire he had set in the backyard trash can. As he played fire department, Ralph made the sound of a fire engine "to the best capabilities of my high, shrill voice."[11]

The Ellisons lived next door to the family of Dr. Ezelle W. Perry who came to Oklahoma City in 1915 with his wife and six children to become pastor of the Tabernacle Baptist Church. He was president of the Oklahoma Baptist

Just outside the shade of a fruitless mulberry tree, Lewis Ellison's gravestone glimmers in the afternoon sun at the Fairlawn Cemetery in Oklahoma City. The stone was placed by Ralph Ellison decades after his father's death. Ida had no money to purchase a marker in 1916—a similar fate of the hundreds of other unmarked graves in the colored section of the cemetery. *Courtesy Eric Dabney.*

Convention for more than 40 years.[12] Ellison remembered one of the Perry's fighting roosters attacking him as a child—setting in motion Ellison's lifetime curiosity of birds.[13]

On June 19, 1916, tragedy struck Lewis Ellison and his family. While delivering ice to a dirt cellar of a grocery store, he slipped and a heavy block of ice punctured his stomach. As was often the custom, young Ralph was with his father on his ice delivery route. A bystander took Ralph home as Lewis was rushed to nearby University Hospital.

Massive infection set in and Lewis remained in the hospital—even while his wife was giving birth to their second son, Herbert Maurice Ellison. By the middle of July, Ida consented to an experimental surgery for Lewis—a final effort to save his life, to thwart the infection that had control of his body. On July 19, 1916, one day after the experimental surgery, Lewis died.

Forty years later, Ralph remembered the final time he saw his father alive:

> We had said good-by and he had made me a present of the tiny pink and yellow wild flowers that had stood in the vase on the window sill, had put a blue cornflower in my lapel. Then a nurse and two attendants had wheeled in the table and put him on it. He was quite tall and I could see the pain in his face as they moved him. But when they got him covered, his feet made little tents

of the sheet and he made a joke about it, just as he had many times before. He smiled then and said good-by once more, and I had watched, holding on to the cold white metal of the hospital bed as they wheeled him away. The white door closed quietly and I just stood there, looking at nothing at all.[14]

Lewis' body lay in the back room of a local funeral parlor for days until Ida could raise sufficient money to pay for the funeral. Finally, Lewis was buried in the colored section of Fairlawn Cemetery in an all-white area of north Oklahoma City.

After Lewis' death, Ida took her two sons to Abbeville, South Carolina, to visit their grandfather, Alfred Ellison, a former slave who worked as a local government marshal during Reconstruction. But after a visit with Lewis' family, she traveled back to Oklahoma to be close to friends who had lent their prayers and support to her after the death of her husband.

Left to earn a living for her sons, Ida worked as a nursemaid and housekeeper. But while short of material things, Ida gave her sons something far more valuable—the desire to learn and achieve. She brought home discarded books, opera recordings, and magazines such as *Vanity Fair* from the homes of the affluent families for which she worked.[15]

The discarded trappings of white families enlarged Ralph's life. He once mused, "You might say that my environment was extended by these slender threads into the worlds of white families whom personally I knew not at all."

"These magazines and recordings and the discarded books," he continued, "spoke to me of a life which was broader and more interesting, and although it was not really a part of my own life, I never thought they were not for me simply because I happened to be a Negro. They were things which spoke of a world which I could some day make my own."16

Formal education for Ralph began in a kindergarten class in the basement of the Avery Chapel African Methodist Episcopal (AME) Church—then at the Frederick Douglass Elementary School near Reno Avenue and California Street. The segregated school was the center of social, civic, and educational activities for most black families in the area.

Because of segregation, Ralph was forced to walk by a brand new school, Bryant Elementary, where only white children could attend. Instead, he walked eight blocks to Douglass. It was not a safe route for children who were required to climb flights of stairs to a viaduct that arose over the tracks of the Chicago, Rock Island, and Pacific Railroad. Ida told Ralph to never talk

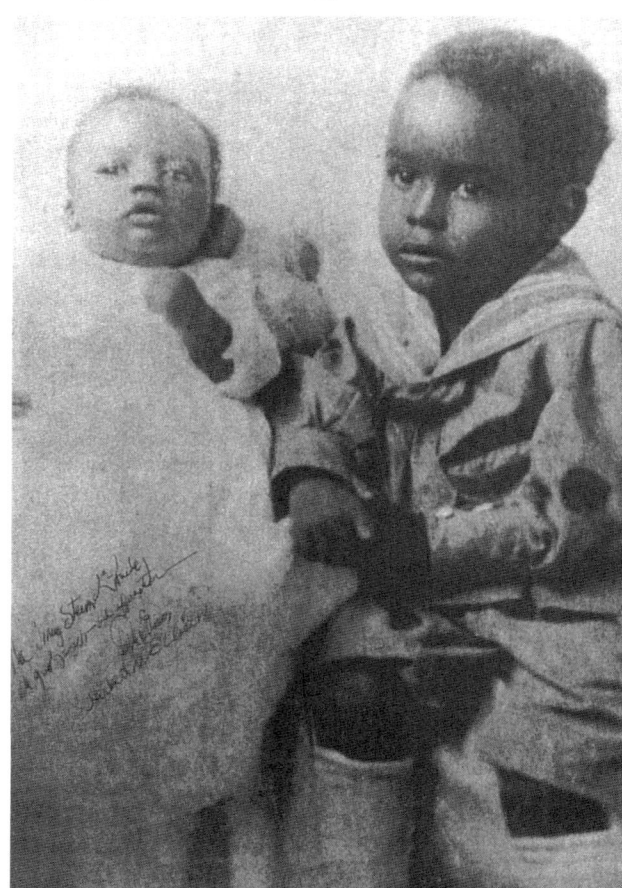

With the death of her husband in 1916, Ida Ellison was left alone to raise her two sons—Ralph, right, and his younger brother, Herbert. *Courtesy Jimmie Lewis Franklin, Jr.*

Ralph Ellison's childhood home at 419 North Stiles in Oklahoma City—as it appeared in 1990. *Courtesy Ernestine Jennings.*

to strangers, especially as he walked past factories, warehouses, and the city's notorious red light district.

In his black world, Ralph became aware of the cruelty of segregation. If he and his mother rode a streetcar, they were forced to sit in the rear. By 1921, there were 12,000 blacks in Oklahoma City, and most relied on the street car system for transportation to distant points in the city because they could not afford a car or truck.

Each streetcar was equipped with a long, adjustable bar that divided white and black passengers. Oklahoma City's black newspaper, *The Black Dispatch*, often printed complaints from blacks who had to stand in the aisles, "packed like sardines," even though there were plenty of vacant seats in the area of the cars reserved for whites. The newspaper said, "When a Negro sits on a vacant seat in the white section, the trouble starts."[17]

But at least the streetcar could take Ralph and his mother and brother to distant places such as the Oklahoma City Zoo. That is, until local officials passed a law making it illegal for blacks to visit the zoo, unless they were accompanied by white people. Ralph wondered, "Had someone black done something bad to the animals? Had someone tried to steal them or feed them poison? Could white kids still go?" His mother said, "Quit asking questions, it's the law…only because some white folks are out to turn this state into a part of the South."[18]

Once, Ida decided to test the crazy law. She dressed herself and her sons in their finest and rode the streetcar to the zoo on a Saturday afternoon. They slipped into the zoo amidst a sea of white families. But trouble arose when they were leaving. A white man dressed in a black suit and a white straw hat met them at the gate and demanded, "Girl, where are your white folks?" Ida replied, "What white folks? I don't have any white folks. I'm a Negro."[19]

With the sound of anger in her voice, Ida stood her ground. She said, "I'm here because I'm a taxpayer, and I thought it was about time that my boys had a look at those animals. And for that I didn't need any white folks to show me the way."[20]

As long as Ralph Ellison could remember, he believed Oklahoma to be different for black children and their opportunity to succeed. He never dwelled on his family's meager possessions or status in a majority-white city or the problems associated with visiting his favorite animals at the zoo. Instead, he focused on the positive things about growing up in Oklahoma. In *Shadow and Act*, he recalled, "Oklahoma had no tradition of slavery, and while it was segregated, relationships between the races were more fluid and thus more

Looking north on Broadway from Grand Avenue in downtown Oklahoma City—the world that Ida Ellison took her sons to on Sunday afternoons to gaze into store windows and hope for a better day. *Courtesy Oklahoma Historical Society.*

MEAGER BEGINNINGS

human than in the old slave states. My parents...had come to the new state looking for a broader freedom and had never stopped pushing against the barriers...It made for a tradition of aggressiveness and it gave us a group social goal which was not as limited as that imposed by the old slave states."[21]

Ida Ellison gave her two sons hope for the future—emphasizing the possibilities of what they might become. On Sunday afternoons she took them on walks through the wealthy white sections of Oklahoma City and by shop-window displays of fine clothing, furniture, and elegant Lincoln automobiles. The intrinsic thought planted in young Ralph's mind was, "For me none of this was hopelessly beyond the reach of my Negro world...because if you worked and you fought for your rights...you could finally achieve it."[22]

Even though he was black, Ralph knew many white people. He worked for them and bought from them. Whites owned the grocery stores. There was a Jewish family that lived around the corner from the Ellisons and were friends of his mother. There was even a family from England that owned the Blue Front Grocery across the street from the Tabernacle Baptist Church.

Ralph learned to deal with whites:

> One had to be careful...They treated you or could treat you as though you had no personal identity—you were part of a mass...On the other hand, for your own safety, or for your own chicanery, or for your own amusement, if you were black, then you looked at the individual. You looked for nuances of voice or for nuances of conduct and interrelationships, and that's how you survived. And very often you wore a mask, very often pretending to be what you were not just to survive or to keep out of trouble.[23]

By early adolescence, the idea of Renaissance Man was firmly entrenched in the minds of Ralph and a half-dozen of his friends. One of his playmates and fellow dreamers was James Edward "Jimmy" Stewart, who lived a few houses from the Ellisons for a while and went to Orchard Park Elementary School, on North Peach Avenue. The Orchard Park School was housed in the bottom two rooms of a two-story house.

Stewart, two years older than Ralph, identified with Ralph because he also had lost his father while young. Stewart became Ralph's lifelong friend and correspondent and was a leading figure in the civil rights movement for a half-century in Oklahoma. In the foreword to Stewart's biography, former United States Ambassador to the United Nations Andrew Young called Stewart "a powerful player in the movement toward change in this United States."[24]

With Stewart, Ralph explored his local environs and beyond. They often visited Ralph's cousins in a black area known as West Town—rows of shanties built along the shifting North Canadian River, a few blocks west of downtown Oklahoma City.

Boys of the era had to search its riverbed looking for deep enough holes in which to swim. The river was filled with only slivers of water during the dry season but often left its banks and did massive destruction during heavy rains. More than once residents were hauled to safety in boats when floodwaters crept around the foundations of their rickety houses.[25]

Youngsters from West Town learned to swim at Sandy Bend on the river, just north of the present Exchange Avenue Bridge, and at a popular picnic spot known as Gargoly, the only public swimming area for blacks in early Oklahoma City.[26]

Near Sandy Bend was the old Western League baseball park. From a nearby hill, Ralph, Stewart, and other friends

Jimmy Stewart lived for a time on the same block with Ralph Ellison and they became lifelong friends. Jimmy was seldom seen without a hat. Stewart later became a national leader of the National Association for the Advancement of Colored People (NAACP). *Courtesy Oklahoma Publishing Company.*

watched games from afar. Admission price was only a nickel but a nickel was scarce and was better used by the family for a loaf of bread. Ralph expanded his world by attending carnivals that were featured at the old show grounds between Exchange and Reno avenues.[27]

Ralph often asked his mother about the origin of his name. He discovered that his father read a lot and enjoyed Ralph Waldo Emerson, a literary name that was quite popular with pre-World War I blacks eager to show off their knowledge of a hoped-for world. Ralph could not understand why he was not named for his father—although he discovered his older sibling who died as an infant was his father's namesake. Ralph asked, "But why hadn't he named me after a hero, such as Jack Johnson, or a soldier like Colonel Charles Young, or a great seaman like Admiral [George] Dewey, or an educator like Booker T. Washington, or a great orator and abolitionist like Frederick Douglass? Or again, why hadn't he named me (as so many Negro parents had done) after President Teddy Roosevelt?"[28]

For a time, Ida and her boys moved from Byers Avenue into a white middle-class neighborhood where she was custodian for some apartments. Ralph was intrigued with the mystery of radio and built crystal sets and circuits consisting of a few tubes from instructions found in radio magazines.

Once while searching for round ice-cream containers which radio enthusiasts used for wrapping wire to form a coil, he met a white boy, the son of the pastor of Oklahoma City's

Ralph Ellison worked at Randolph's Drug, right, on Second Street. This photograph of the building was taken during World War II. *Courtesy Oklahoma Historical Society.*

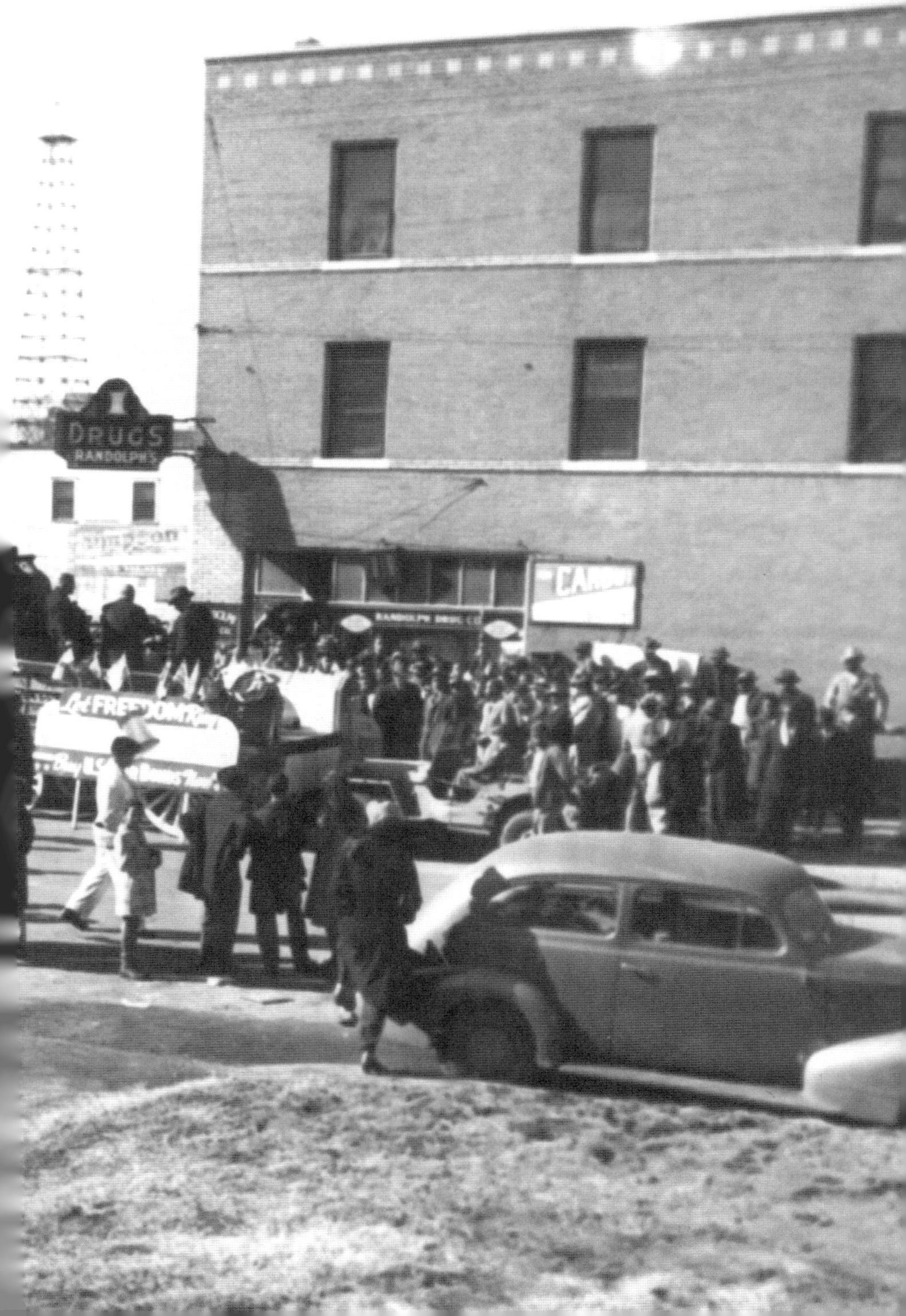
DRUGS
RANDOLPH'S

leading Episcopal church, who shared his interest in radio. Ralph gave Henry Bowman Otto "Hoolie" Davis some of the discarded cartons and they became friends. Interestingly, for decades, Ralph never knew Hoolie's real name until an associate at Yale University put him in touch with a historian for the Episcopal diocese of Oklahoma and traced Hoolie down and solved the mystery of his childhood friend.[29]

Hoolie had been stricken with rheumatic fever and was tutored at home. In his spare time, he constantly took apart and reassembled his parents' radio and built radio circuits of his own. Starved for company, Hoolie's parents encouraged Ralph to play with their son—so the radio experiments flourished for a while. Ralph remembered, "I moved back into the Negro community and began to concentrate on music, and was never to see [Hoolie] again, but knowing this white boy was a very meaningful experience." "It had little to do with the race question as such," he continued, "but with our mutual loneliness (I had no other playmates in that community) and a great curiosity about the growing science of radio. It was important for me to know a boy who could approach the intricacies of electronics with such daring and whose mind was intellectually aggressive. Knowing him led me to expect much more of myself and of the world."[30]

Ida tried hard to give her sons a good life. When Ralph was five, she moved into the vacated parsonage of the Avery Chapel AME after the pastor moved into a new home. In exchange for the free rent, Ida cleaned the church.

That Christmas was a memorable one for Ralph. His mother bought him a small roll-top desk, a tiny straight chair, and a toy typewriter. However, Ida was straightforward with her boys about their economic plight. She explained they could not have bicycles like other boys in the neighborhood.

Instead, Ralph and his brother made their own toys, fished and hunted, listened to music, and "spent a great amount of time reading and dreaming over books."[31]

Ralph's imagination was not always good for his pets. In one of his stories, he mimics the real-life story of when he and his brother took baby chickens and made small parachutes for them. Then, they climbed to the top of the chicken house and dropped the chicks to the ground below. A neighbor lady told Ida—and the boys were in great trouble with their mother.[32] Ralph's first remembered treasure in life was found in an alley—a large photographic lens that gleamed "with crystal mystery and it was beautiful."[33] Ralph used the lens to burn holes through newspapers and could pretend that it was the barrel of a cannon, a telescope, or the third eye of a monster. He constantly played with the lens, "looking through it with squinted eyes, holding it in shafts of sunlight, and trying to use it for a magic lantern."[34]

Older boys offered Ralph other treasures such as agate marbles, knives, tops, grass snakes, and even horned toads for his lens. But Ralph held on to his treasure. In *Shadow and Act*, he recalled, "No one, not even the white boys I knew, had such a lens, and it was my own good luck to have found it. Thus I would hold on to it until such a time as I could acquire the parts needed to make it function. Finally, I put it aside and it remained buried in my box of treasures, dusty and dull, to be lost and forgotten as I grew older and became interested in music."[35]

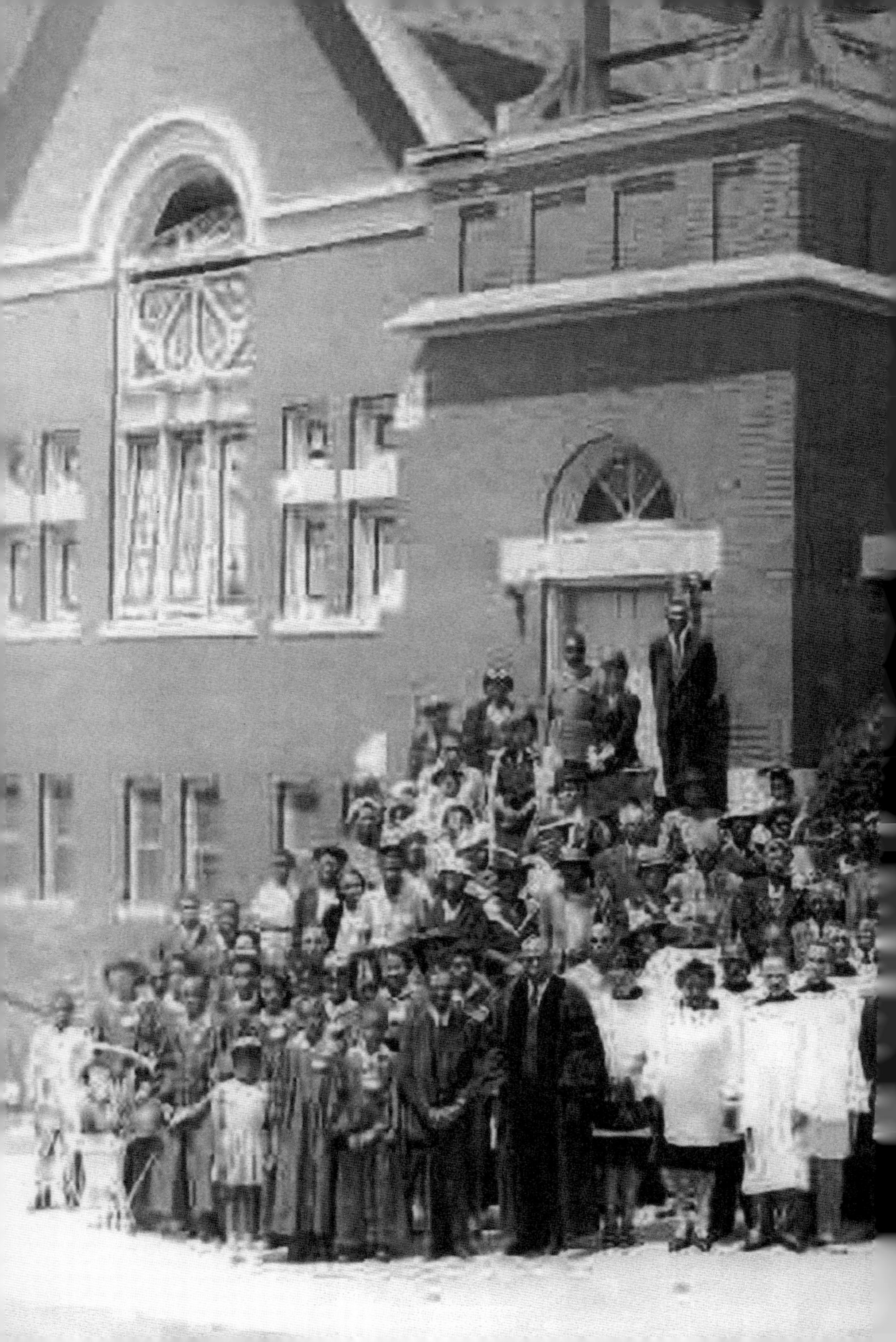

The Avery Chapel AME Church was located at 429 Northeast First Street in Oklahoma City. It was there that Ralph Ellison was introduced to Handel's "Messiah" and other religious music. After his father's death, Ralph, his brother Herbert, and his mother moved into the vacant parsonage of the church. *Courtesy Avery Chapel AME Church.*

Music and Books

CHAPTER 2

> *In the swift whirl of time, music is a constant, reminding us of what we were and of that toward which we aspire. Art thou troubled? Music will not only calm, it will ennoble thee.*
>
> —RALPH ELLISON
> IN *LIVING WITH MUSIC*

Ralph was drawn to music as children are drawn to ice cream. From his first introduction to opera and big band recordings brought home by his mother, he recognized the importance of music and determined that he would spend his life in some musical arena. At age two, he learned his first song, "Dark Brown, Chocolate to the Bone." His older cousins taught him to dance the Eagle Rock and introduced him to their player piano that spewed out a variety of music.[1]

While living in the church parsonage, a neighbor, Joseph Meade, taught Ralph how to play an old brass alto horn. Ida was so impressed with her son's musical prowess that she bought him a cornet in a nearby pawnshop.[2]

Even Sunday morning church services gave him appreciation for music. In the spirited Avery Chapel AME church, a local dentist, William Haywood, led the choir and disdained spirituals—opting instead for more formal music. The church had an organ, an orchestra, and a fair sized choir which performed even the music of George Frederic Handel. In the dimness of young Ralph's mind was the memory of his father playing drums during one church orchestra rehearsal.[3]

Young Ralph did not cherish activities of the youth group at his church, but he liked its music, even though choir director Haywood discouraged any love for music outside the "high" music performed by his church choir.

Ralph's real appreciation for music began in the second grade, largely due to the magic created by Zelia N. Breaux, supervisor of music for Oklahoma City's black schools. One day in 1922, Ralph was being the most active of the eight-year-olds dancing and singing to the nursery tune, "Oh busy squirrel with bushy tail and shiny eyes so round/Why do you gather all the nuts that fall on the ground?" In a moment of fate, Mrs. Breaux's eyes fell upon the slim Ralph and she immediately picked him out for special attention. Ralph later said, "It began one of the most important relationships in my life."[4]

For the next decade, Mrs. Breaux, who played trumpet, violin, and piano, was like a second mother to Ralph. When he and his mother disagreed on subjects, and he needed someone to talk to, he turned to Mrs. Breaux. But it was her uncharacteristic fervor for music that caused Ralph to bond so closely with his music teacher. Ironically, Mrs. Breaux discouraged Ralph from playing jazz, his favorite music.

On May Day, children from all the local black schools assembled at the Western League baseball park—the girls in their white dresses and the boys in blue serge knickers and white shirts. To the music of the Douglass High School band, the students competed in wrapping dozens of maypoles and performed mass versions of European folk dances.

Sometimes, sideline critics accused Mrs. Breaux of trying to teach the children to be white—to like dances of other cultures. But Ralph disagreed, writing, "We were being introduced to one of the most precious of American freedoms, which is our freedom to broaden our personal culture by absorbing the culture of others."[5]

Mrs. Breaux's expertise was felt far outside the black schools where she taught music. She was a leader in the national movement to enrich and broaden the country's musical culture. She taught musical theory, insisted that students learn to sight-read, and trained incredible marching bands. She organized school orchestras and choral groups and introduced opera to black school children in Oklahoma City who lived what seemed like an eternity from the stages where opera stars stood before the footlights in New York City and Chicago.[6]

When not filling the classroom with the sounds of all kinds of music, Mrs. Breaux was one of the owners of the Aldridge Theater, for years the only black theater in Oklahoma City. Before the era of sound movies, she employed a pit orchestra made up of the finest local musicians. On the Aldridge stage were the great blues singers, comedians, dancers, famous jazz orchestras, and repertory drama groups such as the Lafayette Players. "In other words," Ralph said, "just as she taught the Negro spirituals along with [Johann Sebastian] Bach and Handel, she provided a cultural nexus in which the vernacular art forms could be encountered along with the classical."[7] Much later, Ralph discovered that Mrs. Breaux's agenda helped clear away the "insidious confusion between race and culture which haunts this society."[8]

Ralph worked as both a musician and actor in Mrs. Breaux's productions. In his first role, he played one of the

BELOW: Zelia N. Breaux brought a "high" music experience for the black community in Oklahoma City. This is a 1930s production of an operetta at Douglass High School. *Courtesy Oklahoma Historical Society.*

ABOVE: Zelia N. Breaux was born in 1880 and died in 1956. Her love for music made a great impact upon young Ralph Ellison. *Courtesy Oklahoma Historical Society.*

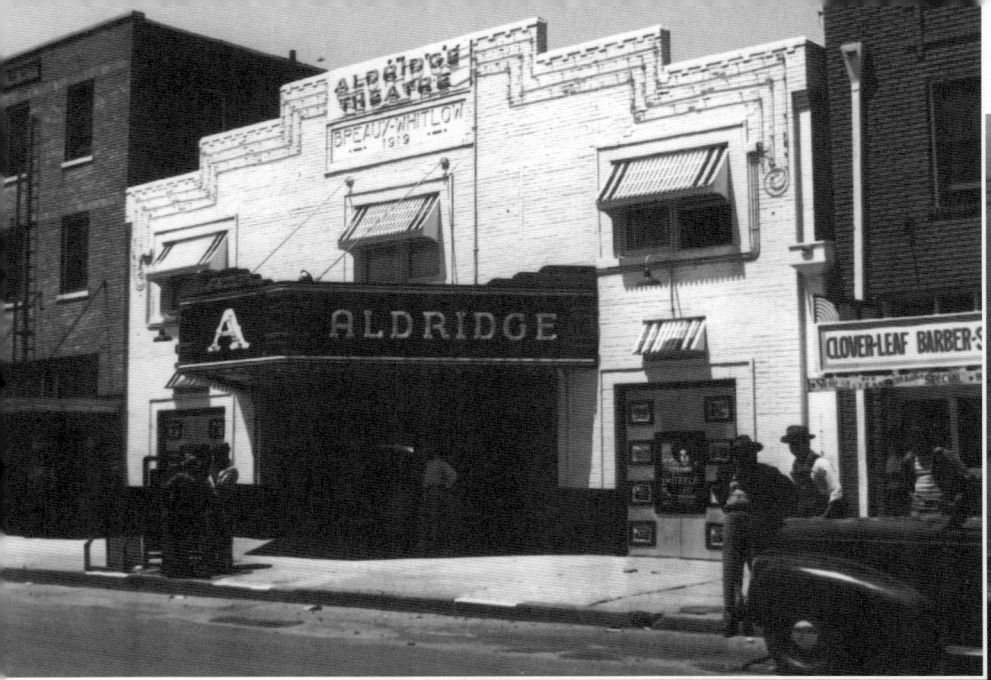

ABOVE: The Aldridge Theater was located at 303 Northeast Second Street in Oklahoma City—Deep Deuce. It was built in 1919 and was a showcase for musical and dramatic talent. *Courtesy Oklahoma Historical Society.*

The interior of the Aldridge Theater where young Ralph Ellison saw and heard the great jazz stars of the era and learned to appreciate dramatic presentations and opera. *Courtesy Oklahoma Historical Society.*

children in "The Gypsy Rover." Later, he was taught a tap dance routine for an operetta whose name he never remembered.[9]

But it was the trumpet that inspired Ralph at a very early age. When he was old enough to mow lawns, he traded his labor for trumpet lessons from Ludwig Hebestreit, who worked with the local symphony and was music instructor at the all-white Classen High School.

When his mother worked as a maid in a home near Northwest 17th Street and Classen Boulevard, Ralph went to the German-born Hebestreit's home to practice the trumpet. However, the youngster received something far more valuable. Ralph remembered, "[I]nstead of really teaching me trumpet, he'd take a score of [Richard] Wagner, for instance, and sit at the paper and dissect it and play out parts of it because he knew that's what I was interested in."[10] Hebestreit even invited Ralph to be his guest at the local symphony concerts, the "only brother of color who got into those concerts in those days."[11]

Ralph's trumpet practice sometimes disturbed his neighbors. After heavy suppers of "black-eyed peas and turnip greens, cracklin' bread and buttermilk, lemonade, and sweet potatoes," Ralph began to blow his horn.[12]

"Such food oversupplied me with bursting energy," he recalled, "and from listening to Ma Rainey, Ida Cox, and Clara Smith, who made regular appearances in our town, I knew exactly how I wanted my horn to sound."[13]

Ralph admitted that his playing caused "whole blocks of people to suffer."[14] During summer vacation he "blew sustained tones out of the windows for hours, usually starting—especially on Sunday mornings—before breakfast." He sputtered whole days through double and triple-tonguing exercises, "with an effect like that of a jackass hiccupping off a big meal of briars."[15]

On hot summer afternoons he tormented the ears of "all not blessedly deaf" with imitations of the latest popular solos of the day of Oran "Hot Lips" Page, a local musical hero; Earl "Fatha" Hines; and Louis Armstrong. Ralph's skill on the trumpet later helped him in an office job for a dentist who was interested in his progress on the instrument. Often with "some poor devil with his jaw propped open in the dental chair," Ralph was called upon to play Franz Schubert's "Serenade." When the dental drill reached a state of high revolution, or the forceps used by the dentist disturbed the tender gums of the patient, Ralph "blew real strong."[16]

During the school year, he played "Reveille" before leaving for class and entertained his neighbors with a slow version of "Taps" at bedtime, or as he called it, "a farewell to day and a love song to life and a peace-be-with-you to all the dead and dying."[17]

Ralph tried other instruments. Mrs. Breaux loaned him her soprano saxophone and he picked up a working knowledge of the instrument. However, when asked about other instruments, he always proudly answered, "Trumpet was my instrument."[18]

Ralph's first instrument in the school band was the mellophone—which sounded somewhat like a French horn. Instruments for school bands were usually supplied by the Oklahoma City Board of Education but uniforms were purchased with funds raised by black and white citizens of the community. Ralph and other members of the school band accompanied the Douglass football team on road trips. Because Ralph played on the varsity football squad, he often did double duty—playing the first half of a game, quickly changing into his band uniform, and marching in the enthusiastic halftime show. Back under the stands, he changed into his football uniform and shoulder pads and sprinted for the sideline before the whistle blew, announcing the start of the second half.[19]

In addition to sporting events, the school bands of which Ralph was a member traveled to Wichita and Topeka, Kansas, for music and marching competitions. Mrs. Breaux's bands were professional and entertaining, and she and Douglass officials took advantage of every opportunity to display their students' talents.

Wherever Ralph went, he was surrounded by music. The back alleys he traveled as a delivery boy were filled with the echoes of blues from somebody's phonograph. Watermelon men "with voices like mellow bugles, shouted their wares in time with the rhythm of their horses' hoofs." Washerwomen sang slave songs as "they stirred sooty tubs in sunny yards."[20]

"We learned some of it all," was the way Ralph described his music education in Oklahoma City. Jazz, blues, and spirituals were learned by everyday experience—the more formal music was learned in the classroom.

"Thus musically at least," Ralph wrote, "each child in our town was an heir of all the ages...While it might sound incongruous at first, the step from the spirituality of the spirituals to that of the Beethoven of the symphonies or the Bach of the chorales is not as vast as it seems. Nor is the romanticism of a Brahms or Chopin completely unrelated to that of Louis "Satchmo" Armstrong."[21]

Satchmo's visit to Oklahoma City in 1929 left a lasting impression upon 15-year-old Ralph. He was surprised to see the segregated dance hall suddenly filled with white women. "They were wild for his music and nothing like that had ever happened in our town before," he remembered, "His music was our music but they saw it as theirs too, and were willing to break the law to get to it."[22]

Ralph saw music transcending racial lines. Radio broadcasts of Earl Hines and the Mills Brothers were popular for whites and blacks alike. Ralph said, "Listening to songs such as 'I'm Just Wild About Harry' and knowing that it was the work of Negroes didn't change all our attitudes but it helped all kinds of people identify with Americanness or American music."[23]

Even in high school, Ralph studied musicians and their art. He recognized the style of Louis Armstrong—then he was introduced to Duke Ellington. He wrote:

> It was as though Ellington had taken the traditional instruments of Negro American music and modified them, extended their range, enriched their tonal possibilities. We were studying the classics then, working at harmony and the forms of symphonic music. And while we affirmed the voice of jazz and the blues despite all criticism from our teachers because they spoke to a large extent of what we felt of the life we lived most intimately, it was not until the discovery of Ellington that we had any hint that jazz possessed possibilities of a range of expressiveness comparable to that of classical European music.[24]

Ralph never forgot the time Ellington brought his band to Oklahoma City and Slaughter Hall, "with their uniforms, their sophistication, their skills; their golden horns, their flights of controlled and disciplined fantasy; came with their art, their special sound, came with Ivy Anderson and Ethel

Duke Ellington was Ellison's early musical hero. When Ellington was in Oklahoma City on his 75th birthday, he was presented a "pass" to the city by Ellison friend Jimmy Stewart. *Courtesy Oklahoma Publishing Company.*

Waters singing and dazzling the eye with their high-brown beauty."[25]

Ellington became a culture hero to Ralph—even Ralph's mother thought it would be great if her son could grow up to have a band like that someday. That very supportive thought surprised Ralph about his mother, "who shouted in church but...allowed me nevertheless to leave sunrise Christmas services to attend breakfast dances."[26]

Ralph was puzzled over his mother's approval of him listening to the "strangely familiar timbre of [Ellington] orchestral sounds issuing from phonograph records and radio." He said, "Now I suspect that she recognized a certain religious

54 RALPH ELLISON: A BIOGRAPHY

element in Ellington's music—an element which has now blossomed forth in compositions of his own form of liturgical music. Either that, or she accepted the sound of dedication wherever she heard it and thus was willing to see Duke as an example of the mysterious way in which God showed his face in music."[27]

During the trying times of the Great Depression in the 1930s, Ralph's morale was lifted when Ellington's "East St. Louis Toodle-oo" came on the air. There was "something inescapably hopeful in the sound. Its style was so triumphant and the moody melody so successful in capturing the times yet so expressive of the faith which would see us through them."[28]

The musical training of young Ralph's life never became burdensome but enlarged his appreciation of various cultures and ways of life. He said, "Perhaps in the swift change of American society in which the meanings of one's origins are so quickly lost, one of the chief values of living with music lies in its power to give us an orientation in time. In doing so, it gives significance to all those indefinable aspects of experience which nevertheless help to make us what we are."[29]

Ralph did not spend all his time with his trumpet or doing odd jobs to make extra money to supplement his mother's meager income—he loved to read. He started with the fairy tales and moved through junior fiction, the Westerns, and detective novels before discovering the classics. He read magazines—both of the pulp variety and leading publications of the day—*Vanity Fair* and *Literary Digest*. Ralph digested heavy doses of literary criticism while his playmates read comic books.

One of Ralph's teachers at Douglass was Lamonia McFarland, an aficionado of the Renaissance of the 1920s who brought to class the poetry, writings, and short stories of

Claude McKay, Countee Cullen, and Langston Hughes. Mrs. McFarland was so enthralled with such writers, her students felt like they knew them personally.

The importance of books was the focus of Ralph's answer to a television interviewer on the occasion in 1975 of the dedication of the library in Oklahoma City named for him:

> It was a mysterious craft, but hearing narrative gave me great pleasure. And all of us had plenty of prior conditional: after all, there are nursery rhymes, bedtime stories, biblical stories, sermons when projected by a really eloquent minister of which we had quite a number in this city. So it was a matter of transferring all of these oral forms and your love for them, your ardor for them, to the printed word. When you've got a person who read to you and who read with some expressional eloquence, you began to increase and intensify your love of reading.[30]

For a while in Ralph's youth, there was no library available for blacks in Oklahoma City—that is until a determined minister invaded the white library and demanded at least an equal facility for blacks. City officials quickly rented two large rooms in a black office building, most recently used as a pool hall, and installed shelves and dumped every book possible onto them.[31] However, the disorganization of the newly stocked library was an advantage for Ralph. He was not directed to a children's section, as in modern libraries. Instead, he was sent searching in the stacks that had Freud mixed in with cowboy stories. There was no one there to say, "You're too young to read that," so Ralph read them all.

Then came what Ralph thought was surely a miracle—the Paul Laurence Dunbar Branch Library. Morris McCorvey described the oasis for blacks, "A clean, well-lighted, one-room, red brick haven in the midst of a segregated intellectual desert known colloquially as the 'whores' stroll.' A hallowed place of peace and quiet set in the warm, rich, shine of polished hardwood and golden lamplight, midst the turmoil and constant noise of my childhood world."[32]

Besides reading books, Ralph was introduced to great oral storytellers—at church, in the schoolyard and barbershop, and especially at Randolph's Drug Store on Second Street where he was employed. On rainy days and in the midst of winter, older men would sit and drink their Coca-Colas and tell stories and yarns. Ralph wrote in "Hidden Name and Complex Fate:"

> It was here that I heard stories of searching for buried treasure and of headless horsemen, which I was told were my own father's versions told long before. There were even recitals of popular verse, "The Shooting of Dan McGrew," and, along with these, stories of Jesse James, of Negro outlaws and black United States marshals, of slaves who became the chiefs of Indian tribes and of the exploits of Negro cowboys. There was both truth and fantasy in this, intermingled in the mysterious fashion of literature.[33]

Ralph also was enthralled with his 11-year-old neighbor, Frank Meade, who drew cartoon characters and acted out visual narratives that Ralph found "far more interesting than those provided by the newspaper comic sections." Ralph found Meade's work enjoyable because "[the stories] were about us, about Negro boys like ourselves. He filled his notebooks with drawings which told stories of Negro cowboys and rodeo stars like Bill Pickett, of detectives and gangsters, athletes, clowns, and heroes."[34]

The "hero of my childhood" was the accolade given Meade later when Ralph wrote, "[H]e created such a variety of characters and adventures that our entire neighborhood took on a dimension of wonder."[35]

The lure of Africa for American blacks reached a peak during Ralph's childhood. His mother told him of the Marcus Garvey movement to mobilize American blacks to look to their roots on the African continent through his Universal Negro Improvement Association. Ralph said, "The people I knew thought this was very amusing, going back to a place they had never been."[36]

The association with Africa was often unpleasant for young Ralph. At the time, most literature portrayed Africans as lazy people, living in the sun. He knew he was "partially descended from African slave stock" and he recognized Negroes were black and that blacks came from Africa. He also ran into African villains in jungle movies so he, like all other children in the community, identified with the white heroes.[37]

One childhood activity that Ralph despised was the ever-popular field drilling, thrust upon black children by local lodge members and veterans of the Spanish American War and World War I. The veterans believed drilling was "good for the soul." But young Ralph lost any future love for the military before it had a chance to flourish in him. He remembered:

> Sometimes we'd be there marching in the moonlight, and sometimes we'd be there to watch the men dressed in Knights of Pythias uniforms, going through their maneuvers on nights so dark that you saw hardly more

than their plumed hats, their silverex belts, steel scabbards, and the gleaming shapes of their swords."[38]

"Those old guys were mad for drill," Ellison said, "and no kid of a certain height was safe from their enthusiasm." [39] By the time Ralph was 13, he had been drilled "wrong side out" and knew so many fancy formations and had been "threatened, cursed, and cajoled" so much, that his group could have posed for a West Point squadron on dress parade. Ellison later reflected that it may have been his utter disgust—and pains from corns on his feet and muscle-aches in his legs—that caused him to forsake the drill field and concentrate more on the trumpet.[40]

When Ralph was not playing music, or listening to the latest in vernacular stories at the drug store, he searched the shelves of the Dunbar Library—searching for some thought or profession of faith that would undeniably add to the volumes of conflicting values and expressions of life that swirled in his head.

All of the experiences in Ralph's young life led him to one conclusion:

> There was a world in which you wore your everyday clothes on Sunday, and there was a world in which you wore your Sunday clothes every day—I wanted the world in which you wore your Sunday clothes every day. I wanted it because it represented something better, a more exciting and civilized and human way of living; a world which came to me through certain scenes of felicity which I encountered in fiction, in the movies, and which I glimpsed sometimes through windows of the great houses…in the wealthy white sections of the city.[41]

Searching for a Father Figure

CHAPTER 3

> *We were forced into segregation, but within that situation we were able to live close to the larger society and to abstract from that society enough combination of values—including religion and hope and art—which allowed us to endure and impose our own idea of what the world should be.*
>
> —RALPH ELLISON

Even with a loving mother, caring teachers, and a passion for music and books, Ralph was still missing something in his life—his father. The loss of his father in 1916 affected Ralph so traumatically that he began stuttering, especially in moments of anguish.[1] Though he never publicly admitted the severity of the void left by Lewis' death, Ralph frequently wrote of the significance of men in his young life. There were at least four role models, or heroes—Roscoe Dunjee, Jefferson Davis Randolph, Inman Page, and Johnson Chestnut Whittaker.

West Virginia-born Dunjee was editor of *The Black Dispatch*, the powerful voice of blacks in Oklahoma. He began publishing the newspaper on November 5, 1914, the same year Ralph was born. At first, Dunjee was criticized for using the word "black" in the title of his newspaper. But, in his independent and thoughtful manner, he shrugged off the

Roscoe Dunjee, editor of *The Black Dispatch*, urged demonstrations by blacks who wanted quality city parks for their children. The leader of this march holds a sign that reads "Criminals are made in alleys—not parks."
Courtesy Oklahoma Publishing Company.

criticism as coming from people who were ashamed of their color and did not like to be reminded of their race.[2]

Dunjee sensed and observed the discrimination his people endured in Oklahoma since he arrived in Oklahoma Territory in 1891. Blacks had little representation at any level

RIGHT: Roscoe Dunjee published Oklahoma's most prominent black newspaper and led the struggle for civil rights in the state for decades. He recruited plaintiffs in cases that ultimately ended up in the highest court in the land and changed the legal status of blacks in Oklahoma and across the nation.
Courtesy Oklahoma Publishing Company.

of government and they suffered greatly from discrimination in public transportation, education, housing, and in facing criminal law prosecutors.

From the time he "was barely able to talk," until his teenage years, Ralph delivered *The Black Dispatch* to subscribers and hawked them on the street corners in the black sections of Oklahoma City. After he completed his route, he read each week's edition from front to back. The newspaper prodded its readers to organize and fight for civil rights. Its circulation would someday climb to 24,000 and be read in every state and in many foreign lands.[3]

Sometimes Ralph lingered at the office of the newspaper to hear Dunjee talk about his latest fight with authorities—or more interesting to a youngster, stories about past fights against injustices in Oklahoma's capital city. Ralph especially liked the true tale of the fight for city parks for blacks.

For many years the only park available for blacks in Oklahoma City was Riverside Park, described by Dunjee as "an undeveloped, unlighted, unsupervised tramp rendezvous in a red light district where no decent black man would want to send his children or go himself."[4]

Primarily because of pressure from the editorial pages of *The Black Dispatch*, the city built for blacks the Booker T. Washington Park in the 1920s. However, the city soon took back the acreage because it was in the middle of an active oil field and the city wanted revenues from oil wells drilled on the property. City leaders made promise after promise—but still there was no park for black families.

It was after Ralph graduated from high school that the city council passed an infamous "segregation ordinance" that set aside residential districts for blacks and provided for three "Negroes Only" parks—Washington, Hassman, and

Riverside. When the council went back on its promises to improve the parks to the level of similar parks for white citizens, Dunjee called race prejudice "Public Enemy No. 1."[5]

Ralph also looked to Dunjee to explain a race riot in Tulsa, Oklahoma, in 1921, when Ralph was only seven. Just before the riot, Ralph and his mother and brother visited Tulsa on their way to Gary, Indiana, where Ida expected to find a more promising job. She was tired of moving in and out of apartments and rooming houses every few months as she changed jobs or no longer could afford her present quarters. They stopped to visit relatives in the Greenwood section of Tulsa that was destroyed in the 1921 race riot.

Within a few months, after promises of jobs evaporated in Indiana, Ida moved her boys back home to Oklahoma City, and she again took her children to visit relatives in Tulsa. Young Ralph saw the terrible destruction, described by the *New York Times*, "The entire black belt of Tulsa is now only a smoldering heap of blacked ruins. Hardly a Negro shanty is standing throughout the area that housed upward of 15,000 blacks."[6]

Incidents such as the Tulsa race riot and the daily discrimination resulted in Ralph having little respect for the law. But, Dunjee cautioned him against giving up on the American dream of justice for everyone—after all he had faith in the Constitution, the Bill of Rights, and federal and state laws to protect equal rights. Dunjee's influence birthed hope in young Ralph, who later wrote, "There was optimism within the Negro community and a sense of possibility which, despite our awareness of limitation (dramatized so brutally in the Tulsa riot of 1921), transcended all of this."[7]

The images of riot-scarred Tulsa never left Ralph's fertile mind. John F. Callahan, the literary executor of Ralph's estate, said that scenes from *Juneteenth*, written four decades after viewing the carnage, were obviously inspired by his memories of Tulsa:

> Up there on Brickyard Hill the octagonal tents shimmered white in the sunlight. Below, my God, sweet Jesus, lay the devastation of the green wood? Ha! And in the blackened streets the entrails of men, women and baby grand pianos, their songs sunk to an empty twang struck by the aimless whirling of violent winds. Behold! The charred foundations of the House of God![8]

Callahan theorized that, "Ralph may have literally remembered 'the charred foundations of the House of God' from what he and his mother and brother witnessed in 1921. Just eight weeks before the riot, the blacks of Tulsa had dedicated Mt. Zion Baptist Church, a splendid new brick edifice that would soon become a cherished target for the rioting white mob."[9]

In his essays, Ralph refers to one white Oklahoma political leader who served as governor during Ralph's teenage years—William H. "Alfalfa Bill" Murray, the former chairman of the constitutional convention, who expressed anti-black sentiment on the campaign stump and in his writings. Ralph's dim view of Murray was enhanced by his conversations with Dunjee who called the Democratic governor a "demagogue" and said his four years as governor of Oklahoma turned the cause of the black man backward at least a quarter century.[10]

It was from Dunjee's editorials that Ralph and other young blacks of the day learned about the importance of voting. Everywhere he went, Dunjee admonished listeners, "Do not be intimidated by any man...do not lose your temper, be sober, firm and determined, look the election official squarely in the eye and tell him you want to vote and should you be denied, go into the federal court and let that court tell us in legal language what sort of a state it is that calls on man to die without permitting them a chance to live."[11]

Dunjee said black citizens who did not exercise their right to vote were "disgusting" and "senseless." When he was accused of selling out fellow blacks by being active in politics, Dunjee wrote, "The same Negro who thinks like that is always the first man to hide out when the mob comes. He never owned a gun in his life, for he does not know the value of it any more than he does the value of his suffrage rights."[12]

During the first half of the 20th century, Dunjee used the power of the press to right many wrongs and, with the help of young NAACP lawyer and later United States Supreme Court Justice Thurgood Marshall, brought several Oklahoma racial discrimination cases to the front of the national struggle for civil rights. The United States Supreme Court used Oklahoma cases supported by Dunjee to make it the law of the land that all-white juries would not be tolerated in criminal cases and that state higher education institutions were legally bound to admit black students.

The uniqueness of another of Ralph's childhood heroes began with his name—Jefferson Davis Randolph. What black family would name their son after the president of the Confederacy? When Ralph was 11, he worked as a custodian's assistant at the Oklahoma State Capitol under the tutelage of Randolph who was the caretaker of the State Law Library. It was in Randolph's extended house that Ralph had been born.

Randolph was the teacher of the first school for black children in Oklahoma City in 1891. He had been one of the leaders of a group of hope-searching blacks who walked to Oklahoma Territory from Gallatin, Tennessee. Ralph described Randolph as "a tall man, as brown as smoked leather, who looked like the Indians with whom he'd herded horses in the early days."[13]

Legislators called Randolph, "Jeff," and Ralph was overwhelmed by the knowledge of the law that the black janitor had in his head. Ralph was not shocked that Randolph, only because of the color of his skin, was not higher in the State Capitol hierarchy. But the situation made Ralph think. "I only knew that Mr. Randolph appeared to possess a surer grasp of law than certain of the legislators," he recalled, "and my youthful sense of justice led me to see his exclusion from the profession as an act of injustice."[14] Ralph never heard Randolph complain but the youngster knew there was something shameful about such a state of affairs and something "rotten in the lawyers if not indeed in the law itself."[15]

Ralph's early impression of discrimination, at least in the case of his revered Mr. Randolph, was short and to the point, "Nor was it possible for me to ignore the obvious fact that race was a source of that rot, and that even within the mystery of the legal process, the law was colored and rigged against my people."[16]

While Dunjee was open and public with his opinions and beliefs, Randolph quietly and invisibly went about his business—surely impressing upon young Ralph to write someday about an invisible black man.

And, in the notes of the unfinished *Juneteenth*, Ralph surely had his friend Randolph in mind when he penned:

> Forget the name of that State Negro with the Indian face...a schoolteacher, tall man, always smoking Granger Rough Cut in his pipe and talking politics and the Constitution? From Tennessee, walked all the way from Gallatin leading a whole party of relatives and friends

and no preachers either. That scar on my skull to this day from going to the polls with ax handles and pistols, some whites and Indians with us, and battling for the right.[17]

Ralph's third hero was Inman Page, born a black slave on a Virginia plantation. When he was ten, he ran away from his master's home and worked his way through Civil War battle lines to end up in a private school for black children in Washington, D.C. He was the first black to graduate from Brown University in Providence, Rhode Island, and launched a long and distinguished career in education.

In 1898, Page became the first president of the Colored Agricultural and Normal University, later Langston University, at Langston, Oklahoma—a post he held for 17 years. In 1924, after serving as president of three other black colleges, he became the supervising principal of black schools in Oklahoma City. It was as principal of all-black Frederick Douglass High School that Ralph came to know Page.

Page, the father of Ralph's inspiring music teacher, Zelia N. Breaux, served as a representative figure for Ralph. In *Going to the Territory*, Ralph chronicled the

Inman Page was the first president of Langston University. Later, he was supervising principal of blacks schools in Oklahoma City. *Courtesy Oklahoma Historical Society.*

SEARCHING FOR A FATHER FIGURE **71**

worth of Page's influence, "He inspired the extremes of ambivalent emotion: love and hate, admiration and envy, fear and respect. He moved many of his students to secret yearnings to possess some of his implicit authority, some of his wisdom and eloquence."[18]

Ralph was somewhat intimidated by Page, "due to his personal style, his quality of command." Page was an eloquent orator and often read Saint Paul's Letter to the Corinthians to his students during daily chapel exercises. Ralph remembered, "Just listening to him taught one the joy and magic of words."[19]

Ralph usually preferred to avoid direct contact with Page. However, on one occasion, his best-laid plans failed. It was customary for the junior and senior boys to sit behind Page while he "preached" his chapel sermon of the morning. To get to the stage, the boys had to climb stairs on either side. The stairs—hidden from the view of teachers—was often the site of horseplay. On one particular day, Ralph decided that if he was pushed—he would push back.[20]

Ralph was pushed—and went into action. To his great surprise, it was not a student he was pushing—it was Principal Page. In an instant Page grabbed Ralph, grabbed the ropes of the stage curtain, and the two of them went swinging in what Ralph described as "a tight circle that carried us around and around over the platform and steps until I lost my grip and caused the two of us to fall—with me landing on top of Dr. Page."[21]

The shocked principal roared, "What do you think you're doing boy?" Ralph, who feared at the moment for his future, never remembered his reply. However, friends who watched the encounter with Page later said Ralph answered with high-pitched cries of "We fell, Mister Page! Mister Page, we fell!"[22]

In the long moment that followed, Ralph heard Page chuckling to himself. Then the irate principal chased Ralph up the aisle and out of the auditorium. As Ralph scampered up a flight of stairs, Page, right behind him, bellowed, "And don't come back! Don't you dare come back!"[23]

To lessen the humiliation suffered when the entire student body broke out in laughter, Page sent word the next day that Ralph was not permanently barred from the school. Ralph returned and never had official disciplinary problems with Page again.[24]

Johnson Chestnut Whittaker was Ralph's first principal in grade school. Whittaker was born a South Carolina slave, the property of the family of United States Senator James Chestnut, Jr.—thus the source of Whittaker's middle name.

Whittaker was one of the first black students admitted to the United States Military Academy but was court-martialed in his final year as a result of a false charge that he faked an assault on himself to make West Point look bad. The fair-skinned Whittaker—Ralph described him as a *white* black man—had done well at West Point until his classmates discovered his true ancestry, tied him to a cot, and beat him.

More than a century later, in 1995, President Bill Clinton granted Whittaker a commission from West Point and presented Whittaker's descendants with his second lieutenant bars.[25]

Professor Whittaker helped drill some of the school bands to which Ralph belonged. "He was a man of erect military bearing...with white hair, clear, piercing blue eyes, and a goatee," Ralph remembered. Whittaker, who was also a lawyer, introduced a certain element of the West Point style in his administration of Douglass School.[26]

It was Whittaker who took Ralph and his fellow band members to march in the 1926 Oklahoma City Boys Day

Parade, the first time black children were allowed to participate in the event.[27]

Adding to Ralph's burden of life without a father was his responsibility for his younger brother, Herbert. The younger Ellison sibling was not a quick learner and had a stuttering problem so bad that Ralph often had to interpret his babblings.[28] Ida frequently worked odd hours and Ralph was his brother's protector and caretaker.

In 1924, Ida picked up her family and moved to McAlester, Oklahoma, to take a servant's job. The trip to McAlester, in the southeast portion of the state called Little Dixie, because of its climatic and political similarities to the Old South, was a daylong train ride, an excursion that left a great impression on the ten-year-old.

A dozen years later, Ralph wrote a short story, "Boy on a Train," a tale certainly woven from Ralph's past. In the story, a fatherless boy with a younger brother, repeatedly "acting like a baby," was riding on a train to a town called McAlester and desired the world of his childhood—candy, bicycles, and trips to the zoo and concerts. But his mother insisted that he pursue freedom and much larger adult causes. In the story, the mother said:

> You remember this James...We came all the way from Georgia on this same railroad line fourteen years ago, so things would be better for you children when you came...We traveled far, looking for a better world, where things wouldn't be so hard like they were down South...Now your father's gone from us, and you're the man. Things are hard for us colored folks, son, and it's just us three alone and we have to stick together. Things is hard, and we have to fight...O Lord, we have to fight!...[29]

Ralph ended the short story with an autobiographical sense of the deep love he felt for his mother. He wrote, "James looked at his mother; she was through crying now, and she smiled. He felt some of his tightness ebb away. He grinned. He wanted very much to kiss her, but he must show the proper reserve of a man now. He grinned. Mama was beautiful when she smiled."[30]

After a short stay in McAlester, Ida and her boys returned to Oklahoma City, to a different house on East Fourth Street. She also met, was courted by, and married a Texan named James Ammons on July 8, 1924. She was 39—he was 10 years younger.

Ida's remarriage, eight years after her husband's death, produced a stark reality for Ralph—his father was never coming back. Since his childhood, he had a recurring fantasy of his father reappearing in his life, musing:

> [O]n my way to school of a late winter day I would emerge from a cold side street into the warm spring sun and there see my father…rushing toward me with a smile of recognition and outstretched arms. And I would run proudly to greet him, his son grown tall. And then I could awake at last from a tortuous and extended dream that was my childhood with my father gone. So urgent had been my need for a sense of familial completeness, to have our family whole and happy as it had been until shortly before I saw him placed at last into the earth, this thin fantasy had been made to serve for the man of flesh and blood, the man of the tales, the ghost stories, the gifts, and strength and love. From the age of three…, the processes of time and the cold facts of death alike were—in this special area of my mind, for I understood death and was eager for change and for my own manhood's attainment—held off by this recurring daydream.[31]

With a stepfather in the house, Ralph knew his father would never return.

Ralph got along well with Ammons, who taught his stepson to hunt, catch rabbits in the snow, and enjoy the out-of-doors. But the newfound joy was short-lived. Less than a year later, Ammons suddenly died.

Without the extra income generated by Ammons, Ida and her boys moved into a simple room of a house on North Stiles Avenue. Ralph plunged deeper into his library books, admitting later that he read *The Last of the Mohicans* ten times. For Ralph, the fiction of his beloved books was an escape from his nightmarish plight on the black side of Oklahoma City.

The Influence of Deep Deuce

CHAPTER 4

> *We have the Constitution and the Bill of Rights...*
> *and we have jazz.*
>
> —RALPH ELLISON

*t*o any reader of Ralph Ellison, there is little doubt that jazz was a major influence on his literature. It was not oppression of blacks or groping with his past in the poor sections of Oklahoma City that most influenced his soul—it was jazz. And the source of the jazz in Ralph's life was found only four blocks from his teenage home. He found Deep Deuce.

The center of black culture in Oklahoma City in the 1920s and 1930s was a strip along Northeast Second Street, just northeast of downtown. The area, filled with everything from hotels, pool halls, dance halls, theaters, jumping night clubs, and barber shops, was known as "Deep Second" or "Deep Deuce."

A variety of attractions drew Ralph and his friends to Deep Deuce. Nights were alive as strains of jazz and the blues somehow escaped the smoke-filled clubs out onto the sidewalks that were crowded with people.

ABOVE: Deep Deuce was still a thriving strip in the 1960s when a civil rights march wound its way past the Aldridge Theater. However, Deep Deuce never regained the height of popularity it enjoyed in the 1920s and 1930s. *Courtesy Oklahoma Publishing Company.*

RIGHT: Deep Deuce was rejuvenated with construction of multi-level apartments in 2001. This photograph is of the same block depicted in the above photograph taken 40 years earlier. *Courtesy Eric Dabney.*

It was the era before television, and with little radio, live entertainment was sought by teens such as Ralph. Slaughter Hall became the most popular dance hall for blacks in Oklahoma City. Often Ralph earned a few dollars from delivering groceries or other merchandise for community retailers and spent his earnings at world-class cafes like Ruby's Grill or the Midway Café. For a nickel, he could buy a large glass of tea. A quarter bought a plate lunch piled high with chitlins and peach cobbler.[1]

Deep Deuce was filled with apartments and an information center in 2002. It was adjacent to the Bricktown section of Oklahoma City, a thriving center of restaurants, one of the nicest minor league baseball stadiums in the country, and a canal that wove its way southward toward the North Canadian River. *Courtesy Eric Dabney.*

But it was the lure of jazz on Deep Deuce that made a huge difference in young Ralph's life. On most nights, outstanding musicians who sometimes moved onto the national and international jazz scene, could be found playing along Second Street. Charlie Christian, Claude "Fiddler" Williams, Buddy Anderson, and Jimmy Rushing started their careers in the dance halls there. Oklahoma served as a melting pot for both the New Orleans "Dixieland" jazz and East Coast music. If a national jazz band needed a musician, it was not uncommon for the leader to head to Oklahoma City to scout some new artist who was nightly displaying his talent. Even Count Basie recruited band members from Deep Deuce nightspots.[2]

William W. Savage, Jr., a music historian, called Oklahoma, and particularly Second Street, the "matrix whence came much of the best of American jazz."³ Hannah Atkins, the first black woman to serve in the Oklahoma legislature, had her own description of jazz:

> What became known as jazz had its genesis in work songs, field hollers, railroad crew chants, church shouts, spirituals, blues; all part of the folk heritage of a people subjected to slavery, then extreme poverty and hardship

Charlie Christian, left, and bandleader Benny Goodman, who crossed color lines and introduced Christian to America. Christian developed his talent in jazz clubs on Second Street and revolutionized the electric guitar as a solo instrument. The Charlie Christian Jazz Festival has been an annual celebration in Oklahoma City since 1985. *Courtesy Anita Arnold and BLAC, Inc.*

during and following emancipation and reconstruction. It was sometimes a matter of singing to keep from crying...jazz...is seen by some as a music of protest, of revolt against conformity to a hostile society.[4]

Deep Deuce was the Bourbon Street of Oklahoma City and home to Charlie Christian, a Texas native who learned to play the guitar from his father, a blind street singer who came to Oklahoma City after World War I. Some say Christian, who died at the alarmingly young age of 24 of tuberculosis blamed on a childhood spent in a wooden Oklahoma City slum apartment house, influenced many of the great jazz guitarists in the middle of the 20th century. Ralph said he was probably the greatest of the jazz guitarists.

Ralph had known Christian for a long time because the guitarist and Ralph's younger brother were in the same first grade class in 1923. Christian often joined his brothers, Clarence and Edward, and their father to stroll through the upper class white sections of Oklahoma—playing serenades upon request. They played the light classics and their contributions to music were far more valuable than the pennies and nickels they received for their street performances.[5]

Ralph, Jimmy Stewart, and Christian all attended manual-training classes at Douglass School. Ralph predicted that Christian would become a great guitarist because he spent much of his time in class building guitars out of cigar boxes. Ralph wrote of Christian in 1958 in *Saturday Review*, "With Christian the guitar found its jazz voice. With his entry into the jazz circles his musical intelligence was able to exert its influence upon his peers and to affect the course of the future development of jazz."[6]

Ralph enjoyed visiting the Christian musical home. In *Saturday Review*, Ralph described Christian's life in a slum in

Ralph Ellison's singing idol was Bessie Smith, whose title of Empress of the Blues was no exaggeration. She was a major record star and Negro vaudeville performer extraordinaire in the 1920s. She died in 1937 after being refused admission to a white Southern hospital after being injured in an automobile accident.
Courtesy Fanny Ellison.

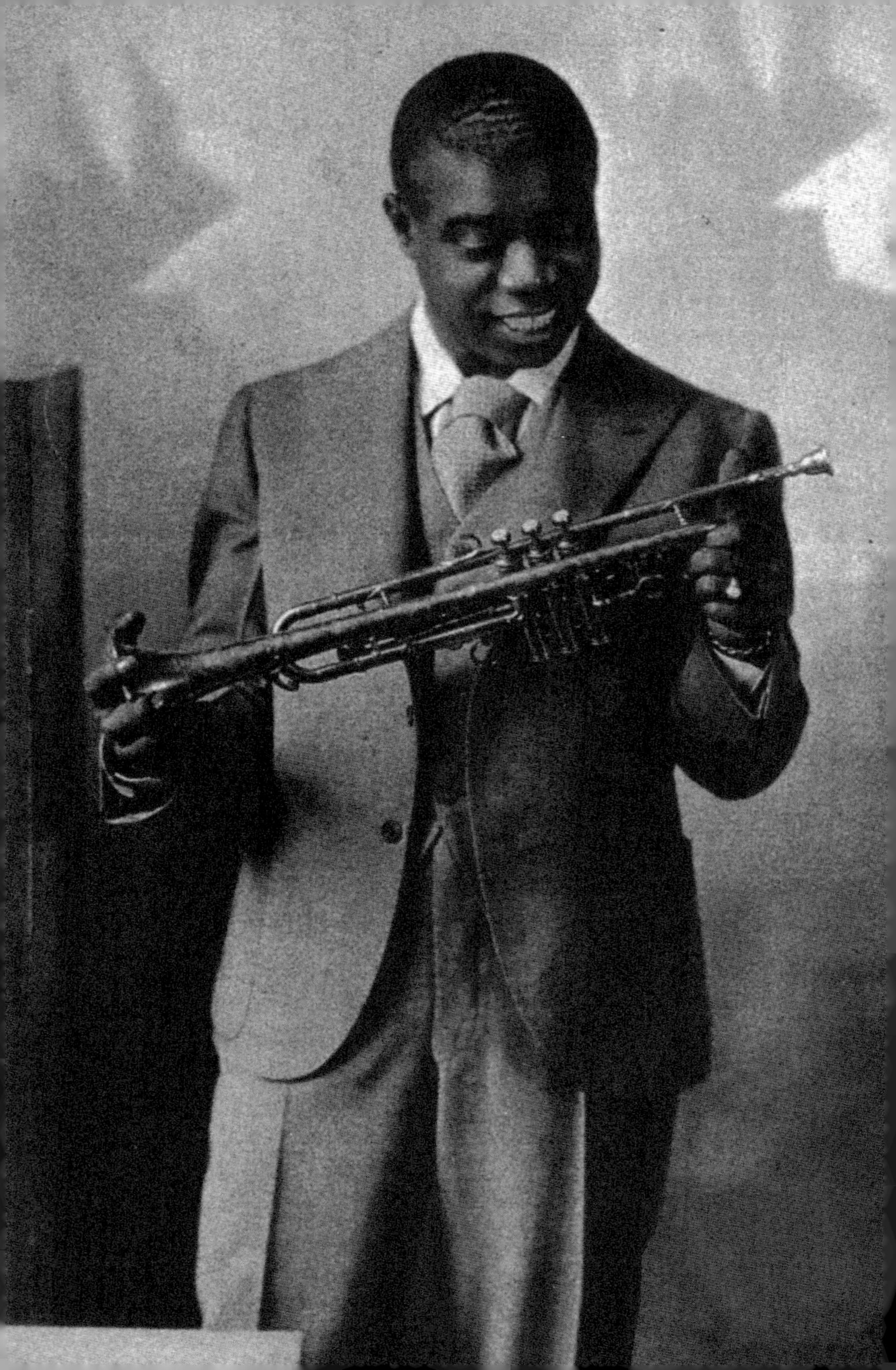

Ralph tried to blow the trumpet like Louis Armstrong whose raspy voice and personality made him an icon to lovers of jazz. "Satchmo" was billed as "The World's Greatest Trumpeter." *Courtesy Fanny Ellison.*

which all the problems associated with urban blacks in the 1930s ran rampant, "Although he himself was from a respectable family, the wooden tenement in which he grew up was full of poverty, crime, and sickness. It was also alive and exciting...for the people both lived and sang the blues."[7]

In his brief career, Christian was featured with the Benny Goodman Orchestra, the Metronome All-Stars, and with Lionel Hampton.

Christian was not alone in making a big splash on the national jazz scene. Oklahoma was fertile ground for the production of jazz artists because of its central location in the nation and because of the amalgamation of cultures in the young state. Professor George O. Carney wrote, "Within this Oklahoma cultural mosaic, music knew no color. Black, white, and red musicians borrowed freely from each other, exchanging repertoires and musical ideas and adopting new techniques and styles."[8]

Oklahoma-born jazz artists were members of the most prestigious ensembles of their day. Count Basie's band proved to be the most popular with nine, followed by Duke Ellington and Benny Goodman each with six, Lucky Millinder with five, and Woody Herman with four. Other Oklahomans played with Lionel Hampton, Cab Callaway, Charlie Parker, Miles Davis, and Louis Armstrong.[9]

Young Ralph was also privy to an intense musician who exerted a great deal of influence on Christian and Deep Deuce when he arrived in Oklahoma City in 1929. Lester Young, "with his heavy white sweater, blue stocking cap and up-and-out-thrust silver saxophone," took Oklahoma City by storm and motivated Ralph and many players of any instrument to join his flights of imagination. One of Ralph's friends gave up his instrument for the tenor sax and soon ran away from home to Baltimore, Maryland, to play in a blues club.[10]

His intense love for jazz put Ralph at odds with many of his mentors, the most respectable teachers and leaders of the black community. Many of them believed jazz was a backward, low-class form of expression. Of that struggle against popular opinion, Ralph said:

> There was a marked difference between who accepted [jazz] and lived close to their folk experience and those whose status strivings led them to reject and deny it. Charlie [Christian] rejected this attitude in turn, along with those who held it—even to the point of not participating in the musical activities of the school. Like Jimmy Rushing, whose father was a businessman and whose mother was active in church affairs, he had heard the voice of jazz and would hear no other. Ironically, what was perhaps his greatest social triumph came in death, when the respectable Negro middle-class not only joined in the public mourning, but acclaimed him hero and took credit for his development.[11]

Ralph preferred the music of two leading bands of the Deep Deuce era. The Ideal Orchestra and the famous Blue Devils played almost nightly at the Aldridge Theater, Ruby's Grill, or Slaughter Hall. When Ralph could get away from his house for the evening, he worked his way into the crowded cafes and grills where jazz flowed like molasses. If he had any money left after

The Blue Devils were featured in a 1997 issue of *Oklahoma* magazine. The band was one of Ellison's favorites. Eddie Christian and his musicians spread their message of jazz from Deep Deuce to jazz hotspots across the region. *Courtesy Anita Arnold and BLAC, Inc.*

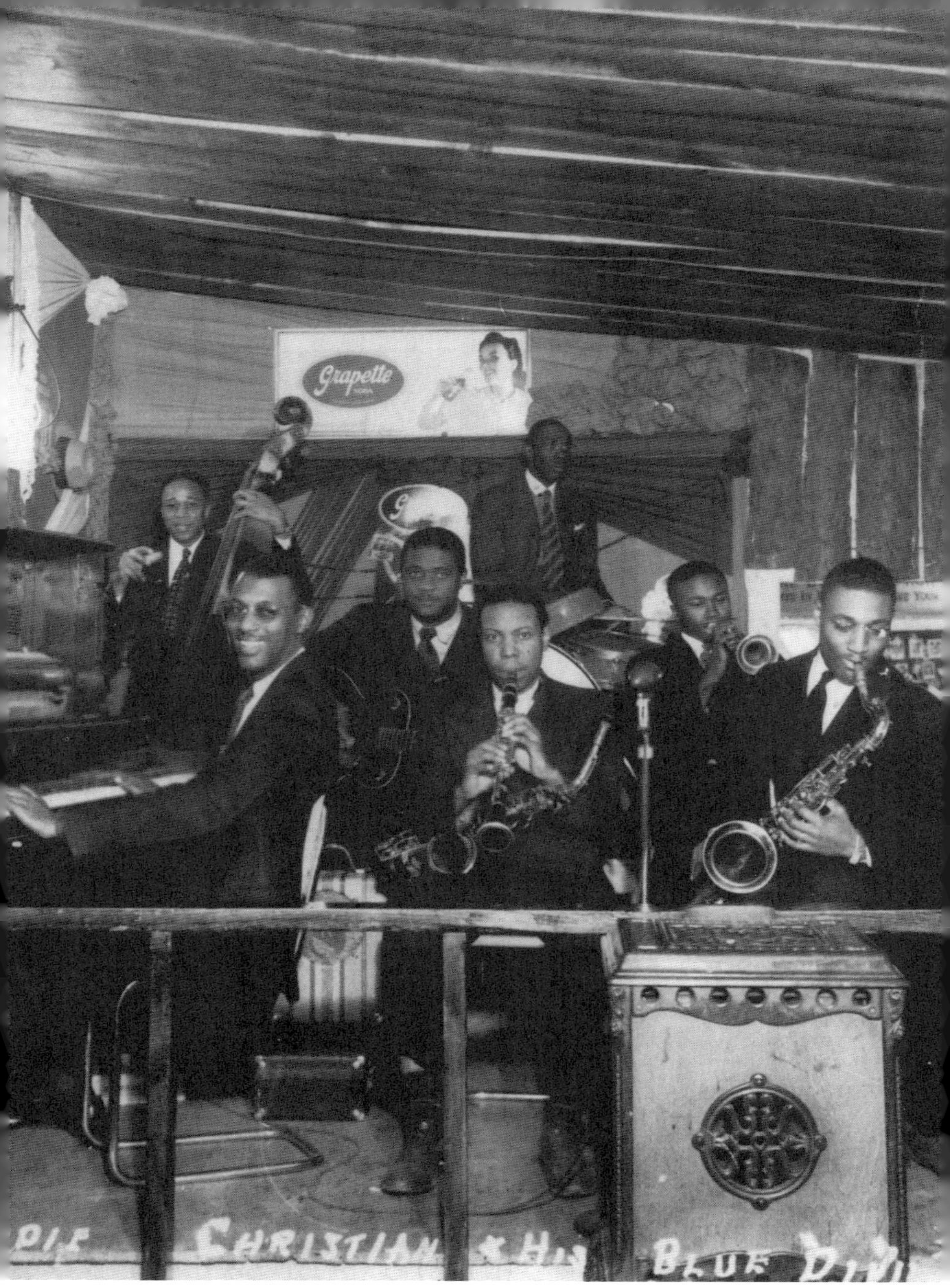
Grapette
CHRISTIAN & HIS BLUE

buying soft drinks to soothe his parched throat, he might trudge on down to Well's Chili Parlor to sit alongside the musical giants who had finished their gigs for the night to enjoy huge bowls of chili laced with hot sauce and onions.[12]

The Blue Devils became one of the Southwest's best-known jazz bands—turning out many excellent jazz musicians that moved on to national bands. There was the gifted pianist Willie Lewis and string bassist Walter Page. Edward Christian, Charlie's older brother, was an arranger and bandleader.

Ralph wondered why Walter Page named the band the Blue Devils. The term in the English language referred to a state of psychic depression—but during the cattle country range wars, recalcitrants who cut barbed wire fences were called "blue devils." Ralph opined that Page perhaps chose the name "Blue Devils" because of its outlaw connotation.[13]

In his younger years, Ralph's mother would allow him to go to Deep Deuce only on Saturday nights. However, he made friends with the musicians, often allowing some bandsman to use his mellophone in exchange for the right to sit in on a practice session. Such opportunities provided a music education that could not be obtained in any classroom.

Ralph's jazz vocalist hero was Jimmy Rushing, the son of local bandsman Andrew Rushing. Jimmy Rushing learned to play the violin and piano by ear and studied music at Douglass High School. He cooked and poured root beer while he sang at his father's lunchroom on Second Street. He was short and heavy, later to be known as "Mister Five by Five" when he gained worldwide fame as a vocalist for the Count Basie Band from 1935 to 1950.[14]

Many nights as young Ralph lay down for sleep, he heard Rushing's high, clear and "poignantly lyrical" voice ring over

Jimmy Rushing, known as "Mister Five-by-Five," sang his familiar tunes as a vocalist for the Count Basie Band for decades. In his later years, he lived in NewYork City and often had meals with Ellison and relived their early days in Oklahoma City. *Courtesy Oklahoma Publishing Company.*

the four-block expanse between Second Street and the Ellison apartment. Ralph remembered the singer's upper range as "steel-bright…possessed of a purity somehow impervious to both the stress of singing above a twelve-piece band and the urgency of…[his] own blazing fervor."[15]

On dance nights, Ralph and his friends could stand on the rise of the school grounds two blocks east of Second Street and hear Rushing's melodic notes "jetting from the dance hall like a blue flame in the dark; now soaring high above the trumpets and trombones, now skimming the froth of reeds and rhythm as it called some woman's anguished name—or demanded in a high, thin, passionately lyrical line, 'Baaaay-bay, Bay-aaaay-bay! Tell me what's the matter now'—above the shouting of the swinging band."[16]

Ralph called Rushing's voice "the essence of joy." In *Saturday Review*, Ralph bragged:

> And how it carried! In those days I lived near the Rock Island roundhouse, where, with a steady clanging of bells and a great groaning of wheels along the rails, switch engines made up trains of freight unceasingly. Yet often in the late-spring night I could hear Rushing…carrying to me as clear as a full-bored riff on "Hot Lips" Page's horn. Heard thus, across the dark blocks lined with locust trees, through the night throbbing with the natural aural imagery of the blues, with high-balling rains, departing bells, lonesome guitar chords simmering up from a shack in the alley—it was easy to imagine the voice as setting the pattern to which the instruments of the Blue Devils Orchestra and all the random sounds of night arose.[17]

Even before Ralph was old enough to attend night dances, he and his playmates gathered under the dim street lights east of Deep Deuce and interrupted their own conversation with the exclamation, "Listen, they're raising hell down at Slaughter's Hall."[18] Then the young men would turn their heads westward to hear Rushing's voice "soar up the hill and down, as pure and as miraculously unhindered by distance and earthbound things as is the body of youthful dreams of flying."[19]

Rushing was not only a great singer—he was an accomplished dancer, sometimes cutting "an old step from slavery days called 'falling off the log' for the sheer humor provided by the rapid, and apparently precarious, shifting of his great bulk."[20] Despite his size, Rushing was capable of graceful movement. Ralph fondly remembered:

> A nineteenth-century formality still clung to public dances at the time, and there was quite a variety of steps. Jimmy danced them all, gliding before the crowd over the polished floor, sometimes with a girl, sometimes with a huge megaphone held chest-high before him as he swayed.
>
> The evenings began with the more formal steps, to popular and semi-classical music, and proceeded to become more expressive as the spirit of jazz and the blues became dominant. It was when Jimmy's voice began to soar with the spirit of the blues that the dancers—and the musicians—achieved that feeling of communion which was the true meaning of the public jazz dance.[21]

Ralph's frequenting of Second Street somehow made his own poverty and the glum news of the Great Depression seem another world away. His friend, Jimmy Stewart, said, "The four-four beat on Second Street drove the feelings of hopelessness away—even if just for one night."[22]

It was on Second Street that Ralph met other interesting characters that he later wrote about in essays and articles for national magazines.

Hallie Richardson owned a shoeshine parlor and book and magazine store. Called "Fat Hallie" by friends and enemies alike, Richardson occasionally loaned Ralph and other customers a few dollars until payday but, more often than not, did not expect repayment. An open-air bootlegger, Richardson served as manager for several musical groups, putting together bands, and driving them to their gigs. As he matured as a trumpet player, Ralph was hired by Richardson for a few appearances at dances and parties.

Most importantly, Richardson, in his gruff manner, was a source of encouragement to Ralph and other young musicians—especially struggling jazz artists.[23]

Pioneer black physician W.H. Slaughter was a big man in Ralph's eyes. Slaughter, orphaned at age five and raised by an aunt who was a former slave, graduated from medical school in Tennessee, and arrived in Oklahoma in 1903. He was the first president of the Oklahoma Medical, Dental, and Pharmaceutical Association, the black medical society. Aside from healing the sick, Slaughter was an entrepreneur, building and operating Slaughter Hall on Deep Deuce.[24]

When Slaughter died in 1952, *The Black Dispatch* lauded him as "easily the outstanding citizen of his city and state."[25] Editor Roscoe Dunjee editorialized, "While he had an uncanny capacity and ability to drive a good business deal, his patients knew he would serve them without money and without price, and many a home of an early day settler in the Sooner capital city was saved for them through the big heart and neighborly assistance of Dr. Slaughter."[26]

Another of Ralph's friends on Second Street was James Brooks, known as "Doebelly," who had made his living shining shoes on the active sidewalks of the area since 1923. Doebelly got his nickname from eating raw cookie dough and was a delight to be around. He broadcast the news and gossip about black citizens and even had a snapshot or two for shoe shine customers.

Finishing High School

CHAPTER 5

> *For the Negro, there are no hiding places.*
> —RALPH ELLISON

Ralph's mother married a third time in December, 1929, and again wed a man more than a decade her junior. Initially, Ralph and Herbert had problems with their second stepfather. However, Ralph was busy with music and dancing—earning a spot playing with the Jolly Jugglers, Edward Christian's band.

Even though he spent a lot of time inside, with his books and his music, Ralph still admitted the human side of his status as a teenager. He said, "In high school, even in the off season, I would want very much to be out on the front lawn throwing and kicking a football, showing off in front of the girls."[1]

Ralph's first experience with writing came as a result of a lingering sickness. For weeks, a bad cold had "clung" to him.[2] When the school nurse saw him on the street one day and heard his hacking cough, she directed him to a nearby lung clinic. As he waited in the reception room, the gathered cadre of sick people horrified him—so he began to doodle, then write, his observations.

He thought he was doing it in the style of his syndicated columnist hero, O.O. McIntyre, whose columns Ralph regularly read in *The Daily Oklahoman*. Before he knew it, Ralph had set his thoughts to verse, influenced by the style of Southern writer Albion Tourgee. Ralph was proud of his work and presented it to his American literature teacher who was shocked because he had not shown a great deal of interest in studies in her class. The teacher, Ralph remembered, "looked at me as though I had gone out of my mind."[3] With no encouragement from his instructor, Ralph put aside, for the moment, any serious thoughts of writing.

In the spring of 1931, Ralph first met Melvin Tolson, English professor and poet whose latest academic post made him coach of the prestigious Wiley College debate team in Marshall, Texas. The occasion was the competition between the debate teams of Wiley and Langston University. Ralph thought it strange that Wiley's black debaters were not allowed to compete against Oklahoma's white colleges even though the Wiley team had defeated debaters from Oxford University in England. The news of Wiley's win over Oxford was a "sense of affirmation" for young blacks such as Ralph.[4]

Ralph left the orchestra pit for the stage in Mrs. Breaux's spring operetta, "Sonia: The Girl From Russia," in May of 1931. He played a villain named Boris and, according to *The Black Dispatch*, engaged in an intricate dance with another student, "the attractive Dorothy Cox." The star of the operetta was Alonzo Williams—who looked like actor Lon Chaney.[5] The greatest applause went to football quarterback McHenry Norman who was greeted with applause every time he appeared on stage at the Aldridge Theater.[6]

Possibly because of his late nights on Deep Deuce or spending too much time practicing for Mrs. Breaux's operetta, Ralph ran afoul of his Latin and math teachers and their assignments. He was shocked when he learned that he could not graduate with his class because of failing grades in the two classes.

History does not shed any further light on why Ralph appears in both the 1931 and 1932 Douglass High School class photographs although the official transcript shows him graduating a year later, in May of 1932. Perhaps he was allowed to appear in the photograph with his original graduating class to prevent major embarrassment.[7]

Toward the end of the 1931 school term, *The Black Dispatch* editor Dunjee launched a three-month-long community fundraising drive to send the 25 members of the Douglass High School band to Denver, Colorado, to march in an Elks Lodge convention parade. Dunjee saw the annual trip as an opportunity to widen the horizons of the young black bandsmen while galvanizing the community of 15,000 black citizens. He editorialized, "It will make their imagination more practical and elastic, add to their fund of knowledge and spur them on towards a more definite program in life."[8]

Band supporters planned a parade through the black sections of Oklahoma City. Ralph was now 18 and proudly marched in his Douglass uniform. Along with the band, the James Europe Post of the American Legion, the Ladies Drill Team of Victoria Temple, and the Boy Scouts marched in the parade. When the parade encountered a group of onlookers, pretty teenagers left a decorated car to ask for donations. The newspaper reported that the parade gathered $87 for the trip—$100 shy of the goal.[9]

Ralph and his fellow band members had a wonderful experience in Denver. Not only were they proud to lift high their school banner before a large crowd, they also witnessed Douglass student, Hilliard Bowen, win first place in the Elks oratorical contest with a speech titled, "The Constitution and Slavery."[10] The subject of Bowen's speech was influenced by Dunjee who later drove the lad to compete in another national oratorical contest in Philadelphia, Pennsylvania.

The Denver trip was closely followed by *The Black Dispatch*. The students swam in an indoor swimming pool for the first time at the Denver YMCA. The sparkling water of the indoor pool was a far cry from the muddy eddies of the North Canadian River. The only swimming pools in Oklahoma City were reserved for whites.[11]

No doubt during the long bus trip to Denver, Ralph mused about his future. He knew he would have to make up the two classes he had failed. He also realized his grades would not gain him any substantial scholarships at the leading black colleges. He assumed he would complete his course work at Douglass and then enroll the following year at Colored Normal and Agricultural Institute at Langston.

For the summer, Ralph looked for a better job than his occasional work at Randolph's Drug. A friend told him of a job opportunity at a car lot near Ninth Street and Broadway Avenue, north of downtown Oklahoma City. On a 100-degree-plus Oklahoma summer day, Ralph walked the mile to the car lot.

"Sir, I understand you need someone to work here," Ralph said to a white man sitting out under a tree. The man replied, "Yes, sit over here on this box and tell me about yourself." The man asked Ralph about his family and his grades. But at the moment that Ralph felt confident that the job was his, he felt an electric current shooting through his tailbone. He jumped up and landed in the dirt—while the car salesman bellowed.

As a practical joke, the man had rigged a coil from a Model T Ford to a battery. There was no job—just a moment of cruel merriment for the car lot owner.[12]

By fall, Ralph found a job at Lewinsohn's Clothing Store on Main Street—giving him the opportunity to upgrade his dress. With a light courseload at Douglass, Ralph had plenty of time to work and frequent the jazz halls of Deep Deuce. He spent a great part of every day blowing his horn.

Ralph finally received his high school diploma in May, 1932, at commencement exercises at the Tabernacle Baptist Church. With high school behind him, he had every intention of becoming a member of the band at Langston. By earning good money waiting tables at the Oklahoma City Golf and Country Club, he thought more and more about Langston—having been introduced to the campus by his music teacher, Zelia Breaux, who had directed the music programs at Langston before she came to the Oklahoma City black school system.[13]

Ralph made at least one trip to Langston to follow what he thought was a lead on a scholarship to the school. However, when he arrived, he found there was no scholarship and no position in the college band. Without a scholarship—even with the relatively inexpensive tuition at the state-run school—Ralph could not afford to go to college at Langston.[14]

With no possibility of attending college at the time, Ralph continued his employment at Lewinsohn's and practiced long hours on his music. Being a well-read 19-year-old, he was aware of the best music programs at American colleges—he knew about Oberlin College in Ohio and the Julliard Conservatory of Music in New York City.

Then—in December, 1932—fate dealt Ralph a good turn. On radio, he heard a stirring performance of the Tuskegee

Institute choir at the opening of the Radio City Music Hall in New York City. After conferring with Mrs. Breaux, he ordered a catalog from Tuskegee.

By 1932, Tuskegee was a half-century old. The Alabama state legislature appropriated $2,000 in 1880 to establish a college for blacks in Macon County, Alabama. A former slave, Lewis Adams, and a former slave owner, George W. Campbell, had lobbied the legislators and convinced them of the need for the education of the black population of Alabama. Governor Rufus Willis Cobb signed a bill that established Tuskegee Normal School on February 12, 1881. The school's purpose was to train black teachers.[15]

A three-man commission set out to recruit and hire a teacher. After great effort, they hired Booker T. Washington, who opened the school on July 4, 1881.

The man for whom hundreds of black public schools would be named over the next century was born into slavery as Booker Taliaferro in 1856 in Franklin County, Virginia. His father was a white man who took no responsibility for him. His mother married another slave and fled to West Virginia during the Civil War. In school, he knew only his first name until roll call one day as the students studied about the nation's first president, George Washington. When asked his name, he added "Washington" to Booker T. He was educated at Hampton Institute in Virginia and became convinced early in his career in education that practical, manual training in rural skills and crafts would save the black race—not "higher learning divorced from the reality of the black man's downtrodden existence."[16]

Thirty men and women from Macon and surrounding counties gathered for the first day of class at Tuskegee in 1881. The following year, Washington found 100 acres of prime land that became the nucleus of the present-day Tuskegee campus. The renowned educator began a program of self help that permitted students to live on campus and earn part or all of their college expenses by helping build the campus—including making their own bricks for campus buildings.[17]

In 1893, the name was changed to Tuskegee Normal and Industrial Institute—still the school's name at the time Ralph expressed interest in 1933. Booker T. Washington served as principal and president of Tuskegee for 34 years, until his death in 1915 when he was succeeded by Dr. Robert Russa Moton.[18] By 1915, the college had 1,500 students and had the largest endowment of any black higher education institution in the country. The university is now known as Tuskegee University.

By the 1930s, Tuskegee had grown from its humble beginnings in a one-room schoolhouse to a sprawling campus that served as a magnet to some of the nation's brightest black students. Because of the adverse effects of the Great Depression, the school was struggling—not unlike most other higher education institutions in the country that suffered from state and federal budget cuts.

Ralph was restless—spending the year after he graduated from high school going from one music gig to the other—in addition to working at the clothing store and earning eight dollars a week running an elevator in an office building.

He still believed he could obtain a music degree from a good college and become a symphonic composer—or at least a public school music teacher. He knew his future was in the world of his music.

In June, 1933, Ralph mailed his enrollment application to Tuskegee, along with a single letter of recommendation—from Zelia Breaux. His longtime teacher and friend had previously sent students to Tuskegee and knew exactly to whom to send her letter.

A few days later, the registrar at Tuskegee notified Ralph that he was admitted for the fall term of 1933—and he would be awarded a scholarship to the Tuskegee Music School. However, Tuskegee band director Frank Drye wanted Ralph to report within a few weeks to audition and become familiar with the Tuskegee music program that was in its infancy—having yet to graduate a student with a bachelor's degree in music.

The early arrival hindered Ralph's plan to earn as much money as possible working in Oklahoma City in the summer to pay off the debt on a new trumpet he had purchased from Jenkins Music Company and set aside money to help him make it through his freshman year at Tuskegee. He faced a crossroads. Should he go on to Tuskegee and worry about the financial considerations later? Or, should he delay his entrance into college yet another year?

Ralph's desire to move on to his dream—a college education in music—won out. He then looked at his next hurdle—how to get from Oklahoma City to Alabama. He thought he might hitch a ride with someone going east from Oklahoma City to the South—but that idea fizzled. He had not yet learned to drive, and he owned no car, so only one option remained—hop a freight train and head to his new life.

Leaving Home

CHAPTER 6

> *You have to leave home to find home.*
> —RALPH ELLISON

despite living most of his 19 years within earshot of railroad tracks, and knowing the meaning of the clang of uncoupling cars and the rumbling of slow-moving engines, Ellison had never illegally hopped a train. But, the pressing need to travel halfway across America to Macon County, Alabama, left him no option but to freeload a ride on one of the trains that passed through Oklahoma City to distant points in the land.

Ellison's first obstacle was his mother—she had heard of blacks being maimed and killed when discovered unlawfully riding trains in the South. But she gave her permission when Ellison turned to a family friend and relative, Charlie, who could pass for a white man. Charlie knew about hoboing and offered to ride to Tuskegee with Ellison and teach him the ins and outs of riding the rails free across the country. Charlie taught him how to get on trains, who to avoid, and how to protect himself. Ellison once recalled:

The world of Ralph Ellison when he left Oklahoma City in 1933. In the foreground is the Rock Island train yard where Ellison hitched a ride on a freight train when he left home. At far left is the east end of Deep Deuce. *Courtesy Oklahoma Historical Society.*

STEFFEN'S ICE CREAM

CARROLL, BROUGH & ROBINSON

You had to be able to read a manifest which was nailed to the side of the car to know where a train was going and when it was scheduled to be there. You had to know how to avoid railroad bulls (detectives). You had to know what to do when a train got into a town where there were difficult police or sheriffs. You had to know where you could buy things in a racial situation.[1]

First, Charlie suggested making a specific plan on what trains would take them to Tuskegee. At all costs, they knew they must avoid Arkansas, whose railroad workers did not take kindly to black men hoboing through their state. Charlie reasoned that they should first go north, to East St. Louis, Missouri, then to Evansville, Indiana, where they would leave the Chicago, Rock Island, and Pacific and take the L & N south toward Alabama.

With $32 in his pocket, Ellison kissed his mother and headed to Alabama with Charlie in July of 1933. They picked out a northbound Rock Island locomotive with trailing boxcars. Charlie taught his young friend how to cling to boards underneath the freight cars to avoid detection by railroad yard men. Ellison learned to squat flat-footed and put his weight on his palms to absorb the shock that resulted from the heavy freight cars bouncing on uneven sections of track.[2]

In those days, the Rock Island went straight north to Wichita, Kansas, then veered to the east to St. Louis. Charlie and Ellison ran into a problem on the outskirts of East St. Louis because railroad inspectors were kicking hobos off the train—suspecting they were headed for the World's Fair in Chicago, Illinois.[3]

Charlie made other arrangements while Ellison walked across the Mississippi River Bridge and convinced a bridge guard that he was not going to the World's Fair, but instead was on his way to college and had no other way to get there except aboard the freight. The guard believed Ellison and let him pass.[4]

Riding the rails with Charlie was an incredible learning experience for Ellison. Getting enough to eat was difficult. The normal meal in hobo jungles along the route was often bologna, mulligan stew, and cornbread. However, one older white couple who had arrived on hard times, shared their bountiful supply of meat and vegetables—a change of pace certainly welcomed by the travelers headed for Alabama.[5]

To Ellison, traveling on the rails was romantic and adventuresome. He said, "I…regarded hoboing as the next best thing to floating down the Mississippi on a raft. My head was full of readings of the *Rover Boys* and *Huckleberry Finn*."[6]

Ellison lost Charlie somewhere in Missouri or Illinois. In St. Louis, Charlie had found a bootlegger and bought a healthy supply of whiskey. Mixed with the hot, sweltering weather, the intake of whiskey caused Charlie to have a sunstroke and faint. Ellison retrieved some fresh water from a whites-only store in a small town, revived Charlie, and gave him $2.50 with which to seek medical attention. Ellison continued the journey alone.[7]

Transferring to the L & N, Ellison headed south through Tennessee and into Alabama. Still 200 miles from Tuskegee, two white railroad detectives brandishing nickel-plated .45-caliber revolvers suddenly halted the train near Decatur, Alabama. All 40 or 50 whites and blacks, including Ellison, were herded off the train and ordered to line up along the tracks. It was a frightening moment for Ellison because he knew he was near the town of Scottsboro, Alabama, where two years before, black hobos were convicted of raping two white women on a train.[8]

The tension of the moment appeared year's later in Ellison's writing:

> Not only was I guilty of stealing passage on a freight train, but I realized that I had been caught in the act in the town where, at that very moment, the Scottsboro case was being tried. The case and the incident leading to it were widely reported in the black press, and what I had read of the atmosphere of the trial led me to believe that the young men in the case had absolutely no possibility of receiving a just decision. As I saw it, the trial was a macabre circus, a kangaroo proceeding that would be soon followed by an enactment of the gory rite of lynching, that ultimate form of racial victimage."[9]

Ellison feared he might be the scapegoat of the railroad detectives because of the color of his skin. So when a group of white boys broke from the ranks and started running, he "plunged into their midst, and running far closer to the ground" than he had ever managed to do as a high school football running back, he kept running until he found a shed and scooted under a railroad loading dock. He hid there until dawn and caught another train, remembering, "I grabbed the first thing that was smoking and headed south."[10]

Ellison never talked much about his encounter with the train detectives in northern Alabama. However, the files of Tuskegee University contain a photograph taken of Ellison when he showed up at the administration building. The photograph shows two large, fresh head wounds, a heavy bandage on the left side of his head, and a gash to the side of his right eye. The registrar sent Ellison directly to the doctor's office.[11]

Even though it is pure speculation, Ellison's first short story written four years later about the brutality of railroad detectives he called "bulls," surely is an insight into what really happened on his own trip in northern Alabama. In "Hymie's Bull," Ellison wrote:

> From Birmingham we had swung up to the world's fair at Chicago, where the bull had met us in the yards and turned us around and knocked a few lumps on our heads as souvenirs. If you've ever had a bull stand so close he can't miss, and hit you across the rump as you crawled across the top of a boxcar and when you tried to get out of the way, because you knew he had a gun as well as a loaded stick, you've had him measure a tender spot on your head and let go with his loaded stick like a man cracking black walnuts with a hammer; and if when you started to climb down the side of the car because you didn't want to jump from the moving train like he said, you've had him step on your fingers with heavy boots and grind them with his heel like you'd do a cockroach and then if you didn't let go, beat you across the knuckles with his loaded stick till you did let go; and when you did, you hit the cinders and found yourself tumbling and sliding on your face away from the train faster than the telephone poles alongside the tracks, then you can understand why we were glad as hell we only had a few lumps on the head.[12]

Ellison could have been whipped by a railroad bull. But his description, vivid and real, could also have come from his rich imagination. "They have head-whipping down to a science," he said, "They know all the places to hit a guy to change a

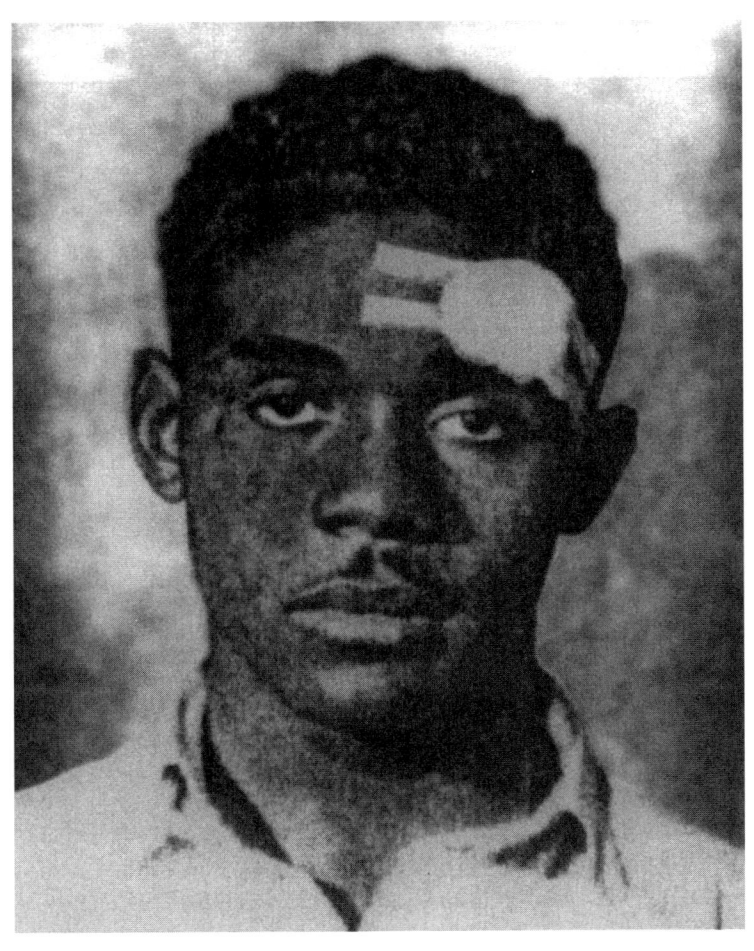

Ellison's official photograph taken by a photographer at Tuskegee on the day of his enrollment in July, 1933. *Courtesy Tuskegee University.*

bone into jelly...Once a bull hit me across the bridge of my nose and I felt like I was coming apart like a cigarette floating in a urinal."[13]

Ellison had passed his first test as an adult—a test in survival. He was very glad to be on the Tuskegee campus—traveling far from his home in Oklahoma City to make something of himself. He remembered the words of some drunk back home who had told him, "Raf, you don't want to get around and do like I do. You don't want to do like those sonsabitches here. You got a chance."[14]

He was assigned a room in Thrasher Hall where he quickly learned the house rules—no fighting and no ironing in the dormitory—and no urinating out the third-floor window rather than making the long trot to the outhouse behind the dorm in the middle of the night.[15]

Ellison must have been impressed with the meticulously kept Tuskegee campus that had sprouted new buildings even in the throes of the Great Depression. The Hollis Burke Frissell Library was only a year old and housed more books than Ellison had ever seen in one place. Logan Hall was a new, modern facility where music and drama performances were held.[16]

With an intimidating band audition out of the way, Ellison quickly became acquainted with musicians on the Tuskegee campus. Before the fall semester began, he was playing trumpet in a band headed by Shorty Hall. They played dances for teachers and students and for medical personnel at the veterans' hospital on the Tuskegee campus. They also played dances in nearby towns such as Columbus, Georgia, and Montgomery, Alabama.[17]

Playing with Hall was fun, profitable, and a wonderful education in jazz. Hall had been trained by Captain Frank Drye, an old Tenth Calvalry bandmaster who was director of the Tuskegee band and later taught Ellison trumpet. Hall was famous for teaching John "Dizzy" Gillespie in North Carolina.[18]

Hall was called "Shorty" for a good reason—he was hardly four feet tall. But, Ellison said, "[H]e could blow the hell off of a big-bore symphonic trumpet. And I mean that he played all the difficult variations and triple tonguing. He had the facility of Al Hirt."[19] Ellison had enough money left from the $32 he had when he began his journey in Oklahoma to buy his Tuskegee school uniform, a sharp-looking blue serge suit with a cap, belt, white trousers, black tie, and black shoes.

Tuskegee, in many ways, was like a military school. The male students were required to drill in uniform three days a week. Freshmen students faced a mandatory study hall on weeknights and had to get permission slips from dormitory monitors to visit the tiny cafes and shops along a strip across the street from the campus. Freshmen were not allowed to venture to downtown Tuskegee.[20]

Ellison spent much of his time in the music rooms of Huntington Hall, Rockefeller Hall, and the Chapel under the tutelage of William L. Dawson, the chairman of the Tuskegee music department, who was best known for composing the Negro Folk Symphony. Dawson, who personally selected Ellison as a music scholarship student, was an accomplished and masterful choir director. However, David L. Johnson, in his dissertation on the life of Dawson, found that many students believed Dawson was pushy and often embarrassed and humiliated students when they arrived late for rehearsal or missed a note. Dawson was "self-centered" and "inclined to polish the halo he wore."[21]

But Ellison saw another side of Dawson, even though Dawson once threw a piece of crayon at him for missing a note. Ellison learned from Dawson that "life was real, life was honest, life was ambiguous."[22]

When Dawson stood before a band, choir, or orchestra, Ellison had the sense that he was "dealing with realities" beyond himself, that he was being asked to give himself to meanings that were not capable of definition except in terms of music and musical style. In a tribute to Dawson much later, Ellison said, "But you also had the sense that with his elegance and severity, with his grasp of the meaning of verse, the value that he could draw out of a word and make you draw out of it, the way he could make your phrase, could teach you to grasp the meaning of a line of verse which sometimes he had set to music—sometimes Handel—all this gave you a sense that through this activity and dedication to the arts, you were going beyond and were getting insight into your other activities."[23]

Ralph was in heaven at Tuskegee—the small campus was one of the major musical centers of the South. It was to Tuskegee that the great philharmonic orchestras of the day came. And it was where Ralph sat with the finest black music instructors of the period.

Polishing the Trumpet

CHAPTER 7

> *Here, I'm teaching you to use your lips and fingers and you want to go out there on the football field and get the shit kicked out of you.*
>
> —CAPTAIN FRANK DRYE

Ellison had a great working knowledge of the trumpet when he arrived at Tuskegee and began taking trumpet lessons under the watchful eye of Captain Frank Drye, the ex-Calvary bandmaster. Drye, unlike Ellison's high school music teacher, would not allow his music students to play football, fearing they would be injured in battle, and endanger Tuskegee's scholarship investment in the musically talented students.[1]

Drye believed in Ellison—giving him the nickname "Sousa" in his freshman year. Drye had enough confidence in the abilities of Ellison to occasionally leave him in charge of the marching band when he was out of town. Ellison was a proud music major and had every aspiration of becoming a classical composer.

Drye discouraged Ellison from playing jazz—his theory was that jazz would interfere with the instrumental techniques and methods of Jean Baptiste Arban and Louis A. Saint-Jacome that he taught his trumpet students.[2] Drye also believed that the trumpet was an instrument of dignity and preached the historical evolution of the instrument.

Ellison, not a frequent churchgoer during his final two years in Oklahoma City, was faced with a Tuskegee requirement that he attend chapel every morning for a religious service. Then at night, as a member of the orchestra, he sat at the front of the auditorium where President Robert Russa Moton delivered a Southern sermon. Moton, one of the leading black educators of his time, was a direct link with Tuskegee's founder, Booker T. Washington, and exhorted Washington's belief that blacks could excel in any forum. As the commandant of Hampton Institute for 25 years before arriving at Tuskegee, Moton had traveled to the North to persuade philanthropists to contribute to black colleges. At Tuskegee, Moton established a new college department to train black teachers.[3]

Moton, in his autobiography, said he realized early in life that blacks and whites had the same drive—that the "Negro…is cheerful and buoyant, emotional and demonstrative, keen of apprehension, ambitious, persistent, responsive to authority, and deeply religious."[4]

Ellison did not share Moton's deep religious beliefs. Ellison had been baptized at the Avery Chapel AME Church in Oklahoma City as a teenager but had drifted from any serious study of the Bible or its teachings after ceasing regular Sunday School attendance.

Ellison received music instruction from four members of the faculty at Tuskegee who had studied music in Europe. Abbie Mitchell was head of repertoire and voice culture; Andrew Fletcher Roseman, a violinist, directed the concert orchestra; and Booker T. Washington's daughter, Portia Pittman, taught choir and piano. Orrin Clayton Suthern was a superb organist and orchestra conductor.[5]

In addition to Captain Drye, pianist Hazel Harrison had a great deal of influence on Ellison. Having studied in Berlin, Germany, Harrison was a single lady in her fifties who generously welcomed Ellison to the Tuskegee campus when he introduced himself to her. She was a close colleague of composer Sergey Prokofiev and displayed original Prokofiev scores on an immaculate Steinway in her office.

Harrison was the new Zelia Breaux in Ellison's life—a confidant who understood his desire to learn. But, like most of the European-trained music teachers at Tuskegee, Harrison discouraged jazz, a propensity that Ellison thought was acceptable:

> To an extent it was fortunate that not everyone tried to teach the blues because they were not of its spirit, and it was not part of their background. We have to recognize that there are various cultural backgrounds and levels…Some people knew nothing about the blues…I think it fortunate that jazz wasn't taught because it has developed its own unique body of techniques through its free-swinging, improvisational, irreverent attitude. Teaching it formally might well have imposed too many thou-shalt-nots and imposed stability upon a developing form.[6]

Unlike many of his professors, Ellison had been introduced to every kind of music—he heard the spirituals in his native Oklahoma City, had been introduced to "high" music like Handel at the Avery Chapel AME church, and, most precious to him, he had learned the blues on Deep Deuce.

For the most part, Ellison got along well with the professorial staff at Tuskegee. However, the great black inventor, George Washington Carver, often ran Ellison out of Rockefeller Hall where he had gone to work out harmonic exercises on the piano. Ellison mused, "My investigations into the mysteries of harmony interfered with his investigations of the peanut, and to me harmony was more important."[7]

Carver was born a slave in Kansas Territory and was kidnapped, along with his mother, by night riders. While in captivity, his mother died, and the baby was ransomed for a $300 racehorse from a German farmer. After educating himself, he earned his master's degree in agriculture from Iowa State University in Ames.[8]

Booker T. Washington hired Carver to teach at Tuskegee in 1896. It was a unique offer. Washington said, "I cannot offer you money, position, or fame. The first two you have. The last from the position you now occupy you will no doubt achieve. These things I now ask you to give up. I offer you in their place: work—hard, hard work, the task of bringing a people from degradation, poverty, and waste to full manhood. Your department exists only on paper and your laboratory will have to be in your head."[9]

Accepting the challenge, the black scientist achieved international stature. He developed nearly 150 products from the peanut; 60 products from the pecan; and nearly 100 products from the sweet potato. He never earned more than $125 a month in his 40 years at Tuskegee. At the dedication of a building in his honor at Simpson College in Indinola, Iowa, Nobel Prize winner, Dr. Ralph Bunche, called Carver "the least imposing celebrity the world has ever known."[10]

Carver, who some blacks called "Uncle Tom," was always a role model for Ellison. In a 1976 interview with Robert B.

Stepto and Michael S. Harper, later published in *Massachusetts Review*, Ellison defended Carver's success in an all-white world. Ellison was disturbed by the fact that not many blacks were succeeding in winning prizes in science, architecture, biology, and

Morteza Sprague was an English professor at Tuskegee who opened Ellison's eyes to great literature. Ellison later dedicated *Shadow and Act* to Sprague. *Courtesy Tuskegee University.*

electronics. He said, "Sheer militancy isn't enough, and when used as an excuse to avoid study, it is disastrous. Today we're in a better way to learn and participate in the intellectual life of this country than ever before, but apparently we're taking fewer advantages of our opportunities than when we were limited to carrying bags and waiting tables."[11]

Ellison's first public recital at Tuskegee was in the Chapel on October 28, 1933. The school newspaper, the *Tuskegee Messenger*, reported that Ellison played "Must We Then Meet as Strangers," by J.R. Thomas, as the sole cornet soloist at the recital. Other students performing were Mabel Hayes, Victoria Howard, and James Barr.[12]

A non-music professor who became an intimate intellectual friend to Ellison was Morteza Sprague, head of the Tuskegee English department. Sprague was 24, only four years older than Ellison, and had taken over the reins of the department at the age of 21. Ellison, as a freshman, took Sprague's senior course on the nineteenth century English novel.

Later, Ellison recognized the importance of his relationship with Sprague by dedicating to him his 1964 collection of essays, *Shadow and Act*. At the beginning of the book, he called Sprague "a dedicated dreamer in a land most strange."[13]

Sprague talked endlessly with Ellison outside the classroom—not the norm for professors at Tuskegee. Ellison secretly resented the fact that most of his instructors would not speak to him outside the formal class setting. Because of that policy, Ellison never could take some of his professors seriously. He said, "One of the worst things for a teacher to do to a Negro child is to treat him as though he were completely emasculated of potentiality."[14] Ellison classified his professors' unwillingness to converse with students outside of class as a "fatal noise…introduced into the communication."[15]

Being with "his people" on the Tuskegee campus caused Ellison to think deeply about the segregation policies of the nation. As a member of a jazz orchestra that played gigs in Columbus, Georgia, he and his fellow bandsmen had to pass through Phenix City, Alabama, on the 40-mile route. It was a "brawling speed-trap of a town" through which it was impossible for black students to either drive slowly enough or fast enough to satisfy the demands of the town's white policemen. "The police lay in wait for us, clocked our speed by a standard known only to themselves, and used any excuse to delay and harass us," Ellison recalled.[16]

The trip through Phenix City was worth it to Ellison and his colleagues. He wrote, "[E]ach time we reached Columbus and returned safely to Tuskegee, it was as though we'd passed through fire and emerged, like the mythical phoenix bird (after which, presumably the town was named), from the flames. Still we continued to risk the danger, for such was our eagerness for the social life of Columbus—the pleasure of parties, dances, and picnics in the company of pretty girls."[17]

Even the fun trips to Columbus did not cancel out the unpleasantness or humiliation suffered by Ellison and other young blacks. Back on campus, they were "compelled to buffer the pain and negate the humiliation by making grotesque comedy" out of the extremes to which whites went to keep them in their place. Once safe at Tuskegee, Ellison and friends would become "fairly hysterical" as they recounted their latest adventures and laughed as much at themselves as the harassing police officers. Ellison mocked the officers' modes of speech and styles of intimidation. He said, "It was a wild, he-man schoolboy silliness but the only way we knew for dealing with the inescapable conjunction of laughter and pain."[18]

Even during his first year at Tuskegee, Ellison began to wish for the day when he could leave the South. He was surrounded by whiteness—Southerners who were true to their beliefs that blacks were inferior—a caste system that thrived on violence and sought endlessly for victims. "It didn't care whether its victims were guilty or innocent," Ellison said, "for guilt lay not in individual acts of wrongdoing but in non-whiteness, in Negro-ness."[19]

Ellison saw whiteness as a form of manifest destiny which designated blacks stereotypically because of coloration, hair texture, and speech. It denied blacks individuality. Not all whites were bad, Ellison discovered, but safety was a fragile commodity for a young black man in Alabama in 1933. In "An Extravagance of Laughter," he opined:

> Your safety demanded a careful attention as to detail and mood of any social scene, because you had to avoid even friendly whites when they were in the company of their fellows. Because it was in crowds that the hate, fear, and blood-madness took over. And when it did it could transform otherwise friendly whites into mindless members of mobs. Most of all, you must avoid them when women of their group were present. For when a Negro male came into view, the homeliest white woman became a goddess, a cult figure deified in the mystique of whiteness, a being from whom a shout or cry or expression of hand or eye could unleash a rage for human sacrifice. And when the ignorant, torch-bearing armies assembled by night, black men burned in the fire of white men's passions."[20]

Occasionally, Ellison faced adversity within the confines of his Tuskegee world. After one monthly recital, he was heavily criticized by faculty members who harshly judged his performance of pieces from Pytor Tchaikovsky, Felix Mendelssohn, Johann Sebastian Bach, and Claude Debussy.[21] The professors did not like his style, a criticism that stung to his very soul. Hurt, still dressed in his rented tuxedo, and with his ears burning from the harsh criticism, Ellison turned to his friend and mentor, Hazel Harrison.

In her basement studio, Harrison was less than sympathetic, "But, baby," she said, "in this country you must always prepare yourself to play your very best wherever you are, and on all occasions." Ellison knew that, but Harrison made her point, "You must always play your best, even if it's only in the waiting room at Chehaw Station, because in this country there'll always be a little man hidden behind the stove."[22]

At first, Ellison thought Harrison was joking about Chehaw Station, a nearby lonely whistle-stop where swift north- or southbound trains paused with haughty impatience to drop off or take on passengers or, on homecoming weekends, where special coaches crowded with alums and supporters were coupled to a waiting switch engine and hauled to the Tuskegee railroad siding.[23]

But Harrison was not joking—warning that some critic would always be in the wings. She said, "There'll always be the little man who you don't expect, and he'll know the music, and the tradition, and the standards of musicianship required for whatever you set out to perform." Ellison was still in shock, trying to understand his teacher. Chehaw Station was the last place he would expect to encounter a connoisseur "lying in wait to pounce upon some rash, unsuspecting musician."[24]

Miss Harrison's riddle was a thoughtful learning experience for Ellison—momentarily depressed because of his recent criticism. Years later, he understood Harrison's metaphor for the complexity of life with a mere whistle-stop:

> Chehaw Station functioned as a point of arrival and departure for people representing a wide diversity of tastes and styles of living. Philanthropists, businessmen, sharecroppers, students, artistic types passed through its doors. But the same, in a more exalted fashion, is true of Carnegie Hall and the Metropolitan Museum; all three structures are meeting places for motley mixtures of people. So while it might require a Melvillean imagination to reduce American society to the dimensions of either concert hall or railroad station, their common feature as gathering places, as juncture points for random assemblies of sensibilities, reminds us again that in this particular country even the most homogenous gatherings of people are mixed and plurastic.[25]

Ellison made decent enough grades in his first year to sustain his music scholarship. However, with his first year at Tuskegee behind him, he prepared to work at the Frissell Library for the summer as an assistant to Walter Williams. Even though his scholarship covered the comparatively inexpensive tuition at Tuskegee, he needed extra money to support any kind of extracurricular life—even a simple pleasure like taking in a movie or paying admission to see some traveling troupe making its way to Macon County. Life for Ellison at Tuskegee was good—and rewarding.

Separate but Not Equal

CHAPTER 8

> One of the most insidious crimes occurring in this democracy is that of designating another, politically weaker, less socially acceptable, people as the receptacle for one's own self-disgust, for one's own infantile rebellions, for one's own fears of, and retreats from, reality.
>
> —RALPH ELLISON

At Tuskegee, Ellison's appetite for reading was generously satisfied from the 40,000 volumes in the Frissell Library. He was frequently seen strolling about the campus with an armload of books of the great writers of the day. He was under the spell of literature, gained from moments stolen from endless hours of practicing the trumpet. *Wuthering Heights* caused him "agony of unexpressible emotion." *Jude the Obscure, Crime and Punishment*, and the works of Ezra Pound, Ford Maddox Ford, Sherwood Anderson, Gertrude Stein, Ernest Hemingway, and F. Scott Fitzgerald titillated his senses.[1]

Even though he had no idea of writing stories like he was reading, he was "moved to a great admiration of the art of fiction." He said, "And the fact that they could so take me out of myself and transport me to a more intense world of feeling and acting, yes, and thinking, intrigued me more than I realized at the time."[2]

Frankly, Ellison believed had he attended a white university, his intellectual curiosity may have been stifled by the customary teachings of writers he considered to be "over taught"—Mark Twain and Herman Melville.

Learning something of the craft and intention of fiction and modern poetry began a transition in Ellison's life—one that would eventually lead him to a craft as a writer. Years later, he reflected:

> Having given so much attention to the techniques of music, the process...seemed quite familiar...The more I learned of literature in this conscious way, the more details of my background became transformed. I heard undertones in remembered conversations which had escaped me before, local customs took on a more universal meaning, values which I hadn't understood were revealed; some of the people whom I had known were diminished while others were elevated in stature. More important, I began to see my own possibilities with more objective, and in some ways, more hopeful eyes.[3]

As he sought to improve his intellectual capabilities, Ellison was painfully aware that he still lived in a Southern white society. He could not eat in most white restaurants and certainly could not relax in city parks built for whites.

However, one area where the concept of separate but equal actually worked was in the double movie houses in the town of Tuskegee. Blacks and whites were accommodated in parallel theaters, entering through separate entrances on the same street level. The black side showed the same movie shortly after the film for the white customers began. Ellison observed, "It was a product of social absurdity and, of course, no real relief from our resentment over the restriction of our freedom, but the movies were just as enjoyable or boring...I went to the movies to see pictures, not to be with whites."[4]

Ellison did not feel disadvantaged by attending a black college in the deep South. Working in the campus library for a year caused him to believe he was getting a well-rounded education. He said, "A few of us used to talk about how nice it would have been, if we could have attended Harvard, and to have studied under such teachers as Kittredge, but the sense of being disadvantaged was nothing that bothered me. You got there to study music and you studied music. It wasn't any easier because you were at a Negro college."[5]

"When you're in the classroom," Ellison reasoned, "you're thinking about the specific problem that is before you, not the larger sociological problem—even though you are quite aware that you are Negro, and that in leaving the sanctuary of the college you're likely to run into possible discomfort, discourtesy, and even violence."[6]

Ellison tried his hand at writing poetry while at Tuskegee—especially after delving into T.S. Eliot's essays. He never wrote a poem that he considered decent and was surprised years later when some of his poems appeared in a book. Literary criticism intrigued him and he began reading books of criticism by Harriet Monroe and Edmund Wilson.

In Eliot, he found imagery and overtones "of a sort of religious pattern" with which he could identify with his own background. He also saw a style of improvisation—that reminded him of the improvisation in his beloved jazz. In literature, it is possible that Ellison found a hiding place from his accepted position in society—much like the hiding place he had found in reading after the loss of his father.[7]

While Ellison was at Tuskegee, his mother, Ida, became an activist for black causes in Oklahoma City. She was one of the most vocal and visible members of a band of blacks that began to militantly protest local housing segregation laws in Oklahoma City in the 1930s. Ellison took great pride in the fact that his mother was jailed on several occasions. He said, "But every time they arrested her, Roscoe Dunjee would go down, bail her out, and send her right back out to break the restrictive covenants again."[8]

Ida's activism waned after Ellison's younger brother, Herbert, beat up one of the white housing inspectors who was harrassing his mother. She decided her protest days were over—"before she got shot." Ellison appreciated his mother's perseverance in the housing desegregation battle in Oklahoma City, writing, "She had that kind of forthrightness, and I like to think that that was much more valuable than anything literary that she gave me."[9]

Ellison kept up with events in his hometown by reading copies of *The Black Dispatch* sent to him by his mother. The eyes of the nation were on Oklahoma City when Governor William H. "Alfalfa Bill" Murray, at the request of a group of white citizens, proposed a definitive boundary line between white and black residential areas. The purpose was to keep blacks out of white neighborhoods. One white leader charged that the Negroes were the aggressors invading white neighborhoods and whites just wanted the Negroes to "stay in their own districts and let white people alone."[10] The segregation ordinance, after a two-year legal battle, was struck down in the Oklahoma Supreme Court case of *Onie Allen v. Oklahoma City*. The decision, released November 26, 1935, and written by Justice Fletcher Riley, was probably the first denunciation of segregation ordinances by a Southern court.[11]

Ellison read, with a chuckle, Dunjee's latest editorials on segregation in Oklahoma City. In one particular case, Dunjee criticized city officials for maintaining two swimming pools—five feet apart—for white and black children. Dunjee observed the absurdity of the separation, "While the kids were separated in the two pools as to race, there was under the trees nearby an indiscriminate playing of mumble-peg and other childish games. With utter abandonment white and black kiddies were piled under the big tree, totally oblivious to any thought of who was who."[12]

In Ellison's sophomore year at Tuskegee, he began to feel a sense of restlessness. He believed that his learning suffered from a lack of tutorial imagination and was an education lacking in aggression and courage. He said, "You didn't do certain things because you were going to be frustrated...there were things that you didn't do because the world outside was not about to accommodate you."[13]

Part of the problem may have been Ellison's age. He was two years older than most members of his class—and the two years he spent in an unstructured life, playing jazz on Deep Deuce, left him uncomfortable with the rigid practice and study schedule of college. And, on top of his discomfort with the lifestyle, his relationship with principal conductor Dawson grew cold. Ellison could not overcome his feelings about Dawson because the bandleader was one of those Tuskegee professors who would not form any relationship with his students outside of class.

Ellison did not blame his professors for all of his problems. He recognized that the changing world in which he lived made him feel lonely and isolated. Attitudes and values in society were slowly changing—black students were able to compete for certain jobs which were never available before.

Ellison believed it was a period of desperation "where many young blacks became separatists because they were frightened by the need to compete."[14]

Nevertheless, Ellison persevered, made above average grades, and endlessly practiced on his trumpet. At the end of his second year, he looked forward to graduation week—a special time at Tuskegee. He remembered, "Countless high-powered word artists, black and white, descended upon us and gathered in the gym and the chapel to tell us in high-flown words what the Negro thought, what our lives were, and what our goals should be. The buildings would be packed with visitors and relatives and many guardians of race relations—Northern and Southern."[15]

Graduation week at Tuskegee was a time of festival and celebration for the blacks who lived in the area. While the "big-shot word artists" were pontificating inside the chapel or gym, the farm people were having picnics, dancing square dances, and playing baseball on the old athletic field—activities that Ellison preferred over the intellectual exercises indoors.[16]

Ellison recalled, "I found their celebrations much more attractive than the official ceremonies and I would leave my seat in the orchestra and sneak out to watch them; and while my city background had cut me off from the lives they led and I had no desire to live the life of a sharecropper, I found their unrhetorical activities on the old football field the more meaningful."[17]

Having grown up in the urbane Oklahoma City, Ellison had often wondered about farm life as a child. Many of his classmates in his early years were pulled from school during harvest time to pick cotton in the fields south of Oklahoma City where cotton was still king of the rich Oklahoma soil in the 1920s. His only knowledge of farm life was from his mother who had spent her formative years on tenant farms in Georgia.

Always one to expand his knowledge, Ellison became disenchanted with the gradual pace in which society was being integrated. Even his campus was segregated. Officials at Tuskegee still maintained a separate dormitory for white students attending the college. More and more, he tried to make connections between his own background and the world of ideas—connections that he was not being taught by Tuskegee professors.

He knew the connections existed in real life:

> As a musician, I had no problem in seeing connections between European and Afro-American music, so why not between my segregated condition and the world of ideas? So, I was groping. [Karl] Marx and [Sigmund] Freud were the dominant intellectual forces during that period, and I had been aware of Freud even before finishing high school. Marx, I encountered at Tuskegee—but how did you put the two together? I didn't know, so I read, talked, I asked questions, and I listened. Such ideas concerned me as I turned from music to literature.[18]

Ellison returned home for the first time in two years in the summer of 1935. He worked for a few weeks at Lewinsohn's Clothing Store and renewed his acquaintances with past mentors and friends. He and Jimmy Stewart looked for blues on Deep Deuce, even though the Blue Devils had disbanded. Ellison spent a lot of time with his mother—happy that she was comfortable living in a new house on Stonewall Avenue with John Bell—even though her militancy in the housing desegregation fight caused her friction with her husband.

Secretly, she harbored thoughts of moving to Ohio where she had many relatives and there was a more tolerant attitude toward blacks.[19]

Ellison was introduced to Ernest Hemingway while waiting to get a haircut in a barbershop on Deep Deuce. Looking at old copies of *Esquire*, Ellison became a Hemingway admirer and depended upon the writer for a list of books to read during his spare time.[20]

His encounter with "Papa" Hemingway, and his increasing interests in sculpture and the arts, caused Ellison for the first time to question his life's work—did he still want to be a composer or music teacher—or was there something else out there for him?

Discovering the Wasteland

CHAPTER 9

> *The pleasure I derived from reading had long been a necessity, and in the act of reading, that marvelous collaboration between the writer's artful vision and the reader's sense of life, I had become acquainted with other possible selves—freer, more courageous, and ingenuous.*
>
> —RALPH ELLISON

The climate at Tuskegee changed in the fall of 1935 as poor health caused President Moton to retire. He was replaced by his son-in-law, Tuskegee's third president, Frederick D. Patterson.

Ellison remained on a music scholarship and continued as first chair trumpet—but began to distance himself from the music school—even though he led the marching band at half-time performances at Tuskegee football games. Instead, he turned his attention to his non-music activities, especially literature courses and reading into the wee hours of the morning.

There is no doubt he was under the influence of Hemingway whose statement of moral and aesthetic purpose focused Ellison's search to relate himself to American life through literature.[1]

Ellison closely identified with the feelings Hemingway expressed in *Death in the Afternoon*. In describing his thought process as an infant writer in Spain, Hemingway wrote:

> [I] found the greatest difficulty, aside from knowing truly what you really felt, rather than what you were supposed to feel, and had been taught to feel, was to put down what really happened in action; what the actual things were which produced the emotion that you experienced.[2]

Adding to Ellison's despair at Tuskegee was a humiliating experience in a sociology course in which the professor, Ralph Davis, taught that blacks represented the "lady of the races." Ellison was angry, spouting, "This contention the Negro instructor passed blandly along to us without even bothering to wash his hands, much less his teeth. Well, I had no intention of being bound by any such humiliating definition of my relationship to American literature. Not even to those works which depicted Negroes negatively. Negro Americans have a highly developed ability to abstract desirable qualities from those around them, even from their enemies, and my sense of reality could reject bias while appreciating the truth revealed by art."[3]

Professor Davis' teachings apparently came from his association at the University of Chicago School of Sociology, co-founded by Dr. Robert E. Park, whose textbook, *Introduction to the Science of Sociology*, was being used in the Tuskegee sociology course. Even though Ellison later praised Park, a white sociologist, for making positive contributions to the understanding of race, he strongly disagreed with Park's theories such as:

> [The Negro] has always been interested in expression rather than in action; interested in life itself rather than its reconstruction or reformation," or "The Negro is, by natural disposition, neither an intellectual nor an idealist, like the Jew; nor a brooding introspective, like the East Indian; nor a pioneer and frontiersman, like the

Anglo-Saxon. He is primarily an artist, loving life for its own sake. His métier is expression rather than action.[4]

Ellison described Park's theory as a "descriptive metaphor so pregnant with mixed motives as to birth a thousand compromises and indecisions." He said, "Imagine the effect such teachings have had upon Negro students alone!"[5]

Such experiences gave Ellison a deep insight into the history of the American black, the part of history he considered most intimate. He said, "Through the very process of slavery came the building of the United States. Negro folklore, evolving within a larger culture which regarded it as inferior, was an especially courageous expression. It announced the Negro's willingness to trust his own experience, his own sensibilities as to the definition of reality, rather than allow the masters to define these crucial matters for him. His experience is that of America and the West, and is as rich a body of experience as one would find anywhere."[6]

During a trip to Chicago to lead the Tuskegee marching band at halftime at a game at Soldier Field against Wilberforce College of Ohio, Ellison surely mused about the relationship of Northern whites, philanthropists who supported black schools such as Tuskegee. He recognized that much of the North's interest in black education grew out of a philanthropic impulse and ignored the real contribution to the understanding of blacks made by social science.

Ellison's somewhat cynical view of the moral consciousness of Northern whites was explained later in a review of *An American Dilemma* by Swedish writer Gunnar Myrdal:

> At the end of the Civil War, the North lost interest in the Negro. The conditions for the growth of industrial

capitalism had been won and the Negro stood in the way of a return to national solidarity and a development of trade relations between the North and the South...In order to deal with this problem, the North did four things: it promoted Negro education in the South; it controlled his economic and political destiny, or allowed the South to do so; it built Booker T. Washington into a national spokesman of Negroes with Tuskegee Institute as his seat of power; and it organized social science as an instrumentality to sanction its methods.[7]

A major benchmark in the life of Ralph Ellison occurred in 1935 when he discovered among the stacks at the Tuskegee library a T.S. Eliot poem—"The Waste Land." The poem seized Ellison's mind. In digesting the poem, he truly began a transition from music to writing. Within days of reading "The Waste Land," he tried his hand at writing verse and took his work to Professor Sprague, who had not taught Eliot's work in his classroom, but had encouraged Ellison to reach beyond the normal literature chosen for focus in the formal class setting.

Eliot's poem changed Ellison's thinking. He was intrigued by the selection's power to move him "while eluding" his understanding. He said, "Somehow its rhythms were often closer to those of jazz than were those of the Negro poets, and even though I could not understand them, its range of allusion was as mixed and varied as that of Louis Armstrong. Yet there were discontinuities, its change of pace, and its hidden system of organization that escaped me."[8]

Ellison's conscious education in literature formally began when he meticulously looked up references in the footnotes to Eliot's poem. It was the beginning of his transformation or metamorphosis from a would-be composer into some sort of novelist.

"The Waste Land" defied Ellison's powers of analysis and he wondered why he had never read anything of equal intensity and sensibility by an American black writer.[9] He did not understand why the poem was "working" on him in such an intense manner, but he knew he was moved—yet could not reduce the work to a logical system.[10]

Ellison's new, voracious appetite for literature rose to a new level toward the end of a period referred to by some literary critics as the New Negro Renaissance or the Harlem Renaissance. The term describes the literary and artistic explosion that occurred in black America between 1910 and 1940. Dr. Alain Locke popularized the idea of "The New Negro" in a collection of essays published in 1925.

Ellison read and re-read Locke's works, particularly references to strength of the black man. Locke wrote, "…the great masses are [not] articulate as yet, but they stir, they move, they are more than physically restless…In real sense it is the rank and file who are leading, and the leaders who are following. A transformed and transforming psychology permeates the masses."[11]

Ellison had favorite poets from the New Negro Renaissance. There was Countee Cullen's "For a Lady I Know:"

She even thinks that up in heaven
Her class lies late and snores,
While poor black cherubs rise at dawn
To do celestial chores.[12]

Cullen had become important to Ellison since high school. The New York City native graduated from New York University and Harvard University and then taught in the public schools while serving on the editorial staff of *The Crisis*. Also from Cullen came "She of the Dancing Feet Sings:"

And what would I do in heaven, pray,
Me with my dancing feet,
And limbs like apple boughs that sway
When the gusty rain winds beat?...[13]

Ellison especially revered the rhyme of Langston Hughes, one of the most honored poets of the era. Hughes had degrees from both Columbia University in New York City and Lincoln University in Pennsylvania and came into prominence with his poem, "The Negro speaks of Rivers," in 1921. In "Song for a Banjo Dance," Hughes wrote:

Shake your brown feet, honey,
Shake your brown feet, chil'
Shake your brown feet, honey,
Shake 'em swift and wil'—
Get way back, honey,
Do that low-down step.
Get on over, darling,
Now! Step out
With your left.
Shake your brown feet, honey,
Shake 'em, honey chil'.[14]

In "The Weary Blues," released by Hughes in 1926, Ellison found basis for his pride that he was an American Negro:

The night is beautiful,
So are the faces of my people.
The stars are beautiful,
So are the eyes of my people.
Beautiful, also, is the sun.
Beautiful, also, are the souls of my people.[15]

Harvard trained Sterling A. Brown was another black American poet with whose works Ellison religiously spent time with in his dormitory room, in the library, or under a large oak tree that shaded the library building windows. The black man's strength, following a heritage as a slave, was the theme of Brown's "Strong Men:"

> *They dragged you from homeland,*
> *They chained you in coffles,*
> *They huddled you spoon-fashion in filthy hatches,*
> *They sold you to give a few gentlemen ease.*
>
> *They broke you in like oxen,*
> *They scourged you,*
> *They branded you,*
> *They made your women breeders,*
> *They swelled your numbers with bastards...*
> *They taught you the religion they disgraced.*[16]

It did not take Ellison long to read all the novels written by American blacks. Only about 60 had been published by 1935—and half of them were released between 1853 and 1920. Many of them were about sad quadroons and often dwelled upon "passing," or death. Most were gentle in their approach to race relations. Only after 1920 did black novelists and poets begin to sing about "blackness" or "Negro-ness."[17]

With his newfound intrigue with Black novelists and poets, Ellison's favorite novel was still *Moby Dick* by Herman Melville. The classic reminded him of his beloved jazz. Ellison said, "Some of it is quite funny and all of it is pervaded by the spirit of play, like real jazz sounds when a master is manipulating it. The thing's full of riffs, man; no wonder the book wasn't understood in its own time, not enough moses were able to read it!"[18] Ellison often used the slang term "mose" to describe a black person.

Ellison dressed well—influenced no doubt by photographs of the latest styles he saw in *Esquire* Magazine. Noted black author Albert Murray, later one of Ellison's closest friends for decades, arrived on the Tuskegee campus during Ellison's junior year. Murray remembered, "Ralph impressed me. He dressed like a 'Joe College' right out of *Esquire*...I was looking at other people who were going to college and was looking for older people, upper-classmen, who represented the type of aspirations that I had been expecting for myself."[19]

Murray was not formally introduced to Ellison but only knew him from his job at the checkout counter at the Tuskegee library. However, Murray got to know the Ellison name well because it appeared on the checkout list in the backs of hundreds of library books Murray borrowed from the library.

Ellison delved into other arts at Tuskegee. He was given a leading role in a campus play and, in his third year, began to explore painting and photography. In a watercolor class, his instructor, Eva Hamlin, encouraged him to try sculpture.

As Ellison completed his third year at Tuskegee, a mix-up about his scholarship created a huge problem—he did not have the $40 needed for the next semester's tuition, much less any money to live on. He decided to go to New York City for the summer where he believed he could make more money than in Alabama.[20]

Although Hamlin knew Ellison's first love was music, she was intrigued by his potential as a sculptor. So she gave him a letter of introduction to famed black sculptor Augusta Savage in Harlem. Savage often took in young students and introduced them to the wiles of New York City from her studio on 125th Street.

Ellison, fully intending to return to school in the fall, headed north to New York City.[21]

Heading North

CHAPTER 10

> *Harlem was and still is a place where a Southern Negro who has a little luck, and who has a little talent, can actually make himself into the man or woman of his dreams.*
>
> —RALPH ELLISON

*I*n addition to traveling to New York City for the specific purpose of earning summer money, Ellison was drawn to the city by its glamour and promise of greater freedom and opportunity. The city "was one of the great cities prominent in the Negro American myth of freedom," he wrote.[1] In Negro spirituals Ellison learned as a child, Northern cities such as New York were the North Star and symbolized freedom.

Ellison arrived in the "Apple," his term for the city, on the day after Independence Day in July, 1936. The long bus ride from Alabama had left him tired—but the bustling skyline of Manhattan rejuvenated him as he took the subway to Harlem—the Black Mecca.

Harlem had become America's most famous black neighborhood—one of the densest concentrations of blacks anywhere on earth. In the previous 20 years, black churches had moved to Harlem, drawing post World War I migrants to the area. But as blacks coped with overpopulation and inadequate housing, the dream of early developers of a Utopia for blacks lost its brilliance. The summer before Ellison arrived, a full-blown riot had ravaged houses and tenements along 135th Street.

Ellison had learned from friends that he could stay at the Harlem YMCA on 135th Street. He made his meager room at the three-year-old facility his home base as he scouted the city where he would live out his life.

Harlem was full of the people from Ellison's recent past—the literary figures who occasionally spoke at Tuskegee or of whom Ellison had read in his quest to be current with modern literature. On his second day in Harlem, Ellison walked across the street from the YMCA Annex for breakfast and ran into the black philosopher Alain Locke, whom he had met just a few weeks before when Locke visited Hazel Harrison at Tuskegee.[2]

Locke was talking to another man when Ellison interrupted the conversation. It was another fateful moment in Ellison's life—the stranger with whom Locke was speaking was the famous black poet laureate, Langston Hughes, with whose poems Ellison had been familiar since the sixth grade. After an intense discussion about the latest black literature and even Eliot's "The Waste Land," Hughes put Ellison to work—returning two library books, *Days of Wrath* and *Man's Fate*, by Andre Malraux. Hughes said, "You can read these before you return them, if you like." And, of course, Ellison did.[3]

It was not the first time Ellison had read Marxism, the thoughts and teachings of Karl Marx. He was so excited, he asked Hughes if he knew a black writer by the name of Richard Wright—Ellison had happened to read a poem by Wright in the latest copy of *New Masses*. Hughes promised to

Ellison found he had much in common with Richard Wright who also had come to Harlem from the South. They were both descendants of slaves and wanted to put their experiences down on paper. *Courtesy Fanny Ellison.*

introduce Ellison to Wright when he came to New York the following week. Ellison was fraught with anticipation because he considered two poems by Wright, "I Have Seen Black Hands" and "Between the World and Me," the best ever written by a black writer.

Hughes wrote Wright in Chicago about Ellison's interest in him. Wright quickly sent Ellison a postcard that said, "Dear Ralph Ellison, Langston Hughes tells me you're interested in meeting me. I will be in New York on [a certain day]."[4]

Ellison and Wright immediately became friends. Even though his world was still music—he fully intended to return to Tuskegee in the fall—Ellison impressed Wright with his vast knowledge of writing and literature.

Wright, who migrated to the North from Mississippi, Ellison found common heritage. He later wrote, "While we both grew up in segregated societies, mine lacked many of the intensities of custom, tradition, and manners which 'colored' the institutions of the Old South...Both of us were descendants of slaves, but since my civic, geographical, and political circumstances were different from those of Mississippi, Wright and I were united by our connection with a past condition of servitude, and divided by geography and a difference of experience."

"And yet it was difference of experience and background," Ellison said, "which had much to do with Wright's important impact upon my sensibilities."[5]

Wright, six years older than Ellison, was in New York to work in the Harlem bureau of *The Daily Worker*, the official newspaper of the American Communist Party, and to edit a floundering magazine that had been called *Challenge* and now was labeled *New Challenge*. Wright and Ellison spent long hours over coffee and lunch talking about the similarities between the intense studies of both music and writing. In the magazine editorial offices, Ellison read many of Wright's unpublished stories and discussed ideas of literature and culture.

Ellison was puzzled about Wright's position with the Communist Party. Wright had been thrown out of Chicago's 1936 May Day parade by the communists but somehow ended up working on the party's newspaper in New York. Ellison saw that most of the loyal communists in the newspaper office treated Wright as an intruder and distrusted him because he was an intellectual. There was no doubt that many of his superiors sneered at Wright's intellectuality, ridiculed his writings, and dismissed his concern with literature and culture as an affectation.[6]

However, Ellison could care less about Wright's role with the Communist Party. Instead, he was "absolutely intrigued" with Wright's talent and felt privileged to be able to read writings that no one else cared for—writings that eventually became famous, two years later, in *Uncle Tom's Children*. Ellison said, "I'd never met anyone who, lacking the fanfare of public recognition, could move me with the unpublished products of the fictional imagination."[7]

Even better, Wright took the time to discuss his works with Ellison, an "exciting and inspiring experience" for the soon-to-be writer from Oklahoma.

Ellison worked over the sweltering steam tables in the dining room at the YMCA to pay his room and board. To help his young friend, Wright not only asked Ellison to become a part-time secretary, but also asked him to

Ellison's association with Richard Wright allowed him to read the writings that later became Wright's best seller, *Uncle Tom's Children*. Courtesy HarperCollins Publishers.

HEADING NORTH **161**

review a book for *New Challenge*. Ellison worked hard on the review of Waters Edward Turpin's novel *These Low Grounds*, but did not think it was very good.[8]

A few weeks later, Wright asked Ellison to write a short story for the magazine. Ellison said, "I don't know anything about writing a story." Wright replied, "You talk well about stories. Why don't you try? You've had some experiences." Ellison agreed. He had ridden on a freight train so he wrote a story about an incident occurring on a hobo trip. The story was called "Hymie's Bull."[9]

Wright and two women editors of the magazine accepted the story but before it could be published, the magazine folded. However, Ellison was now hooked on writing.

Ellison used his introductory letter to sculptor Augusta Savage. However, he did not like Savage's style and took Wright's recommendation of another sculptor, Richmond Barthe, in Greenwich Village. Ellison identified with Barthe who had arrived in New York City without fame or fortune and had become one of the great black American sculptors. Barthe accepted Ellison as his first pupil.

Ellison learned that exploring New York City was a "journey without a map." Everywhere he went he was introduced to a sea of exciting and interesting multi cultures. He quickly discovered how to fit in:

> How one was received by the natives depended more upon how one presented oneself than upon any ironclad rule of exclusion. Here the portals to many places of interest were guarded by hired help, and you approached with an uncertain mien, you were likely to be turned away by anyone from doormen to waiters to ticket agents. However, if you acted as though you were in fact

a New Yorker exercising a routine freedom, chances were that you'd be accepted. Which is to say that in many instances I found that my air and attitude could offset the inescapable fact of my color.[10]

In his words, Ellison called it "assuming a mask," to be conceived as a New Yorker. He used his spare time enjoying the city's many cultural possibilities, making new acquaintances, and "enjoying the many forms of social freedom that were unavailable to me in Alabama."[11] He enjoyed the art and history museums, art galleries, and the endless used bookstores where he could pick up reading materials for pennies. He also availed himself of the many libraries in Manhattan.

By mid summer, Ellison realized he would not be able to save sufficient money to return to Tuskegee for classes in September. He moved into a room near Barthe's sculpture studio on West 14th Street and concentrated on reading revolutionary writings such as those published by Malraux. Langston Hughes introduced him to Louise Thompson who was a prominent black communist who often had Ellison and other students to her home to participate in a Marxist study group.

Still a stranger in Harlem, Ellison spent "many a homesick afternoon" playing Duke Ellington's records on the jukebox in Small's Paradise Bar, asking himself why he was in New York and finding reassurance in the music that, "although the way seemed cloudy," he should remain there and take his chances. He had little money and even spent a few nights sleeping in the park below City College.[12]

On one of the great nights of his young life, Ellison was escorted to Ellington's apartment on Sugar Hill in Harlem. Much to Ellison's surprise, the Duke remembered meeting him at Tuskegee. When Ellison told him of the sad state of finances at Tuskegee, Ellington offered to give the school his extensive library of recordings. Ellison enthusiastically passed along the Duke's offer but, for some reason, it was rejected, possibly because the administrators of the Tuskegee Music Department still thought jazz was a lower-class form of music.[13]

Ellison worshiped Ellington's musical offerings. He later wrote, "Jazz styles have come and gone and other composer-conductors have been given the title 'King of Jazz' and Duke knew the reason why, as did the world—just as he knew the value of his own creation. But he never complained, just smiled, and made music. Now the other kings have departed, while his work endures and his creativity continues."[14]

A series of odd jobs kept Ellison alive. He worked in factories, as a free-lance photographer, a builder of record players and radios, and as a file clerk for a psychoanalyst, Harry Stack Sullivan.

Ellison was introduced to Broadway when Hughes invited him to see *Tobacco Road*, an adaptation of the novel by Erskine Caldwell. There, "in the darkness of a Broadway theater," Ellison was snatched back to rural Alabama, remembering the Southern Negroes' strategies for dealing with poor whites. His mind returned to the freight yard in northern Alabama, where he had his skull bashed in by railroad detectives, and to the over-anxious traffic cops in Phenix City, Alabama.[15]

Overcome with one love scene between characters Ellie May and Love, Ellison was "reduced to such helpless laughter" that he distracted the entire balcony and embarrassed both himself and his learned host. Ellison recalled, "It was a terrible moment, for before I could regain control, more attention was being directed toward me than at the action unfolding on the stage."[16]

The laughing convulsions in the blackened theater continued. "It was as though I had been stripped naked, kicked out of a low-flying plane onto an Alabama road, and ordered to laugh for my life," Ellison wrote in "Extravagance of Laughter," "[f]or now in my hypersubjective state, viewers around me…were getting to their feet to gawk at me. It was as though my personality was split in twain, with the lucid side looking on in wonder while the manic side convulsed my body as though a drunken accordionist was using it to belt out the 'Beer Barrel Polka.'"[17]

The theater was "rapidly becoming the scene of a virtual orgy of disgraceful conduct," so much so that Jeeter Lester, played by actor Will Geer, and other characters were shading their eyes and peering "open-mouthed" at the young black in the balcony.[18]

The mostly white audience began to despair, with patrons who had paid high dollar for front row seats standing and shaking their fists at Ellison. When Ellison quieted down, he realized he had learned something valuable from *Tobacco Road*:

> I couldn't have put into words at the time, but by forcing me to see the comedy of Jeeter Lester's condition and allowing me to react to it in an interracial situation without the threat of physical violence, Caldwell told me something important about who I was. And by easing the conflict that I was having with my Southern experience (yes, and with my South-Southwestern identity), he helped initiate me into becoming, if not a "New Yorker," at least a more tolerant American.[19]

Detour to Ohio

CHAPTER 11

> *I had to look at everything through my cold Oklahoma Negro eye.*
>
> —RALPH ELLISON

Ellison practiced his trumpet but increasingly spent more time each week on becoming a writer. His friend, Richard Wright, said candidly that Ellison had started too late in life, at 23, to be a serious writer—although Wright was impressed with Ellison's ability to talk about literature with the intellectual writers of the day.[1]

In the fall of 1937, Ellison received word that his mother was ill in Ohio, where she had moved the previous year. Ida had cracked her hip in a fall from a porch at her home in Dayton but did not get adequate care at the local antiquated segregated hospital. When tuberculosis settled in the hip, her sister moved her to nearby Cincinnati—hoping that better medical care would help her condition.

Ellison arrived in Cincinnati late in the afternoon of October 15. He immediately went to the hospital where his mother was in so much pain she failed to recognize him. She died the next day. It was the deepest emotional hurt of Ellison's life. For all his formative years, his mother had been by his side. As a fatherless youngster in Oklahoma City, his mother was his everything.

Without money, Ellison slept in a car at night until a relative invited him into her warm home. After the funeral, Ellison and his brother, Herbert, moved to Dayton with the intention of finalizing their mother's affairs. The extent of his remorse was contained in a long letter to Richard Wright:

> This is the end of childhood for both of us. I used to pretend this was so when I came to New York, but now I know it was just pretense and nothing more. This is real, and the most final thing I've ever encountered. I feel very sorry for my brother as he has never been away from her before and though he tries to hide it he is hurt very much. We spend a lot of time at the movies here eating candy like we did quite a while ago and then go along the streets that are very much like those of Oklahoma City, home. I say home because much from Oklahoma is here…
>
> It is terrible. He needs her very much and I am able to help so little. Too I know that as the pain which holds us becomes a little blunted the antagonism between us will come alive and then things will be very difficult to manage. We are so utterly different.[2]

Even though Ellison and his younger brother were different, they spent a lot of time together for the next few months in Ohio. As winter approached, he and Herbert frequently hunted with a friend's young hound and a .22-caliber rifle. Ellison wrote to Wright, "Most of the time it is very cold in the woods and rabbits stick very close to their beds making it very difficult to see them, so close do they merge into the fall scene."[3]

Ellison, surely born to be a legendary writer, described rabbit hunting in vernacular never previously explored:

> I walk along thinking, rifle ready, eyes supposedly looking for the cotton-tailed gents but lost in the color of leaves, the variations and designs from which I've been away a long time, then suddenly the sound of fast falling feet and mister rabbit is laying tracks up the hill to beat hell and the bullets which usually I'm unable to send into him. I lack the discipline which enables the eyes to pick the small live black eyes of mister rabbit out of the leaves and grass which are so like his coat, but in a week or so he'd better beware. And anyway the season will be open then. And I will be able to use my shotgun. But who knows, perhaps I'll be in New York by that time and someone else will bring these elusive dinners down to dust with metal sticks which roar and into flame do bust.[4]

With little money on hand, Ellison and his brother picked wild pears, walnuts, and butternuts to supplement the meals at their aunt's home. His mother's great-aunt filled his ears with stories of the old days when his grandmother "always spoke up to the white folks."[5]

For months, Ellison lived off the fields and woods, through the ice and snow—and through the loneliness. He had crossed "over into a new phase of living," later writing, "Shall I say it was in those February snows that I first became a man?"[6]

Always a thinker, Ellison sought out thinking black members of the Dayton community. He respected their ideas—

especially the grit and determination of a man he met at the local military base, Wright Field. Even though a janitor, the man was designing airplanes and entering his designs in contests. Ellison said, "He was working as a porter but his mind, his ambitions, and his attitudes were those of an engineer. He wasn't waiting for society to change, he was changing it by himself."[7]

The one positive for Ellison in Ohio was his "earnest" turning toward writing. During the long, endless, lonely nights, he studied James Joyce, Fyodor Dostoevsky, Gertrude Stein, and Hemingway, "especially Hemingway." He methodically analyzed Hemingway's sentence structure and story organization. He liked Hemingway's style and tried to emulate it.

In the light of dim lamps in his great-aunt's house, he drew on his past experiences and began to write pieces of stories. His descriptive words took on their own lives. About a town square torture of a black man in Phenix City, Alabama, Ellison wrote:

> God, it was a hell of a night…When the noise died down I heard the nigger's voice from where I stood in the back, so I pushed my way to the front. The nigger was bleeding from his nose and ears, and I could see him all red where the dark blood was running down his black skin. He kept lifting first one foot and then the other, like a chicken on a hot stove. I looked down to the platform they had him on, and they had pushed a ring of fire up close to his feet. It must have been hot to him with the flames almost touching his big black toes. Somebody yelled for the nigger to say his prayers, but the nigger wasn't saying anything now. He just kinda moaned with his eyes shut and kept moving up and down on his feet, first one foot and then the other.[8]

Ellison was befriended by William O. Stokes, one of the first black attorneys in Dayton. Stokes saw Ellison scribbling on a tablet while seated at a restaurant and gave the aspiring young writer a key to his office so he could work there. It was there that the earliest essays and short stories of Ellison were born.

John F. Callahan, the literary executor of Ellison's estate, places the time of writing of two short stories, "A Hard Time Keeping Up" and "The Black Ball," during the seven months Ellison was in Dayton. Neither was published during Ellison's lifetime. Much of Callahan's thesis is based upon the fact that early drafts of both stories were typed on old stationery of the Montgomery County Republican Executive Committee, Colored Section, of which Stokes was a member.[9]

In "The Black Ball," Ellison used a character by the name of John to narrate a story that presents Ellison's common theme of encouragement for blacks to suppress their hostility toward whites and join attempts at peace, tranquility, and brotherhood. Ellison painted the graphic story of John's meeting with a white man who had stuck to his alibi of a black friend who was accused of raping a white woman in Alabama. The white man said, "Well, I got them scars in Macon County, Alabama, for saying a colored friend of mine was somewhere else on a day he was supposed to have raped a woman. He was, too, 'cause I was with him. Me and him was trying to borrow some seed some fifty miles away when it happened—if it did happen. They made them scars with a gasoline torch and run me out the county 'cause they said I tried to help a nigger make a white woman out a lie. That same night they lynched him and burned down his house".[10]

It is even easier to assume that Ellison wrote the first drafts of "A Hard Time Keeping Up" while in Dayton. His frequent rabbit hunting trips, the snowy days, and memories of riding trains haunted the paragraphs of the story of two friends tramping through the snow to a good rooming house in the black quarters of town. Ellison began the story:

> The train pulled in town at 4 A.M. It had been snowing for thirty miles back, and the warm air in the diner made frost on the glass panes. Snow was piled along the window ledges.
> There had been few people in for the last meal, and looking out the car window I had seen five or six rabbits hopping along at leisure in the falling snow. It was very comfortable in the car. The jingle of silver and ice in the pitchers had been very cheerful. When we pulled into the station, we hated to leave the train, but the crew came up to switch the cars, so we decided to grab a trolley across town to the Negro section for a room. Ma Brown's would be swell if she could take us.[11]

Also in Dayton, Ellison wrote the first 100 pages of an unpublished novel he simply called *Slick*. For some reason, he later abandoned that novel although most literary experts believe his first published short story, "Slick Gonna Learn" is a substantial fragment of that novel in progress.[12]

By April of 1938, Ellison was unemployed, tired of reading, and weary of grieving the loss of his mother. "I'd gone into the woods to forget," he said.[13] He returned to New York, "flat broke," but settled on the idea that his creative energies would be directed toward becoming a "good" writer.

Ellison began to approach writing as he had approached music. At Tuskegee, he had gotten up early in the morning and blown sustained tones on his trumpet for one hour for breath control. Writing was the same—disciplined and consuming.

He wrote constantly, much of the material never submitted to anyone for critique or review.

He turned to Wright for help. The experienced writer suggested how to tighten and structure Ellison's writings. Ellison struggled with the problem of how to render black speech without resorting to misspellings. Some of his earliest attempts were embarrassing to him.[14]

Then a stroke of fortune came Ellison's way. He was hired by the New York City Federal Writers Project (FWP) to assist his friend, Wright, in gathering information on blacks in the City. The FWP was part of a make-work program instituted by the administration of President Franklin D. Roosevelt to move along the nation's recovery from the Great Depression. However, the historical value of the projects has proven incredibly valuable.

For the next four years, Ellison scraped out a meager living working for the FWP. He made $103.50 monthly—certainly enough for a small apartment and a relatively good life. Similar to the job of a cub reporter, Ellison went into the streets, talked to his people, and wrote their stories. He learned history he had never dreamed of. He called the experience "a rich harvest."[15]

Through the FWP, Ellison came in contact with writer-intellectuals in New York—many of them members of the League of American Writers. Ellison began to measure himself with the works of his newfound acquaintances. He tried to learn something from every black writer he met—although he discovered they did not know consciously what was going on in literature.[16] He discussed technique with them but the communist-inspired writers he often lunched with only shared ideology and could not talk to him about technical matters.

After his workday at the Federal Writers Project, Ellison began to arrange his life toward a career in writing. He toiled in perfecting his craft at night, writing and rewriting stories or dreams from his past. He gradually changed from thinking of himself as a musician to calling himself a writer. Courtesy Oklahoma County Metropolitan Library System.

He worked on a projected book of New York black folklore under the distant tutelage of B.A. Botkin. He collected children's rhymes and game songs and passed them along to superiors trying to place order to the massive infusion of information about the large black population in New York.[17]

When not collecting information for his day job, Ellison read with reckless abandon. Wright introduced him to the Henry James prefaces. He read Malraux, Russian authors, reread Mark Twain, and collected old copies of *Hound and Horn, International Literature,* and Eliot's works.[18]

What the FWP gave Ellison in the way of research—it lacked in training him to be a writer. He never did much of the finished writing, instead completing research and giving his interpretation of what he had learned from raw interviews. Eventually, the *Journal of the American Folklore Society* published some of the rhymes Ellison collected.

He wrote nearly 20 book reviews for radical periodicals such as *New Challenge, Direction,* and the *Negro Quarterly*. It was not uncommon to see an Ellison piece in almost every issue of *New Masses* by 1940.

As he matured, Ellison shifted his political perspective. For his first years in New York, he had associated with many Communist Party members and others sympathetic to their teachings. He had first been drawn to left-wing politics by his mother who had attempted to escape from the poverty and segregation in Oklahoma City by handing out leaflets for the Socialist Party.

From his intense readings, Ellison thought someone should step forward to redeem the world from war and depression—a promise the communists openly declared they could keep. His own experiences in New York had given him a leftist attitude. He wrote, "What happened to me during the thirties was part of a great swell of events which I plunged into when I came to town…The stimulus that existed in New York…was by no means limited to art; it was also connected with politics, it was part of the esprit de corps developed in the country after we had endured the Depression for a few years."[19]

Ellison himself was a sometimes activist. He joined labor picketers and circulated petitions for just causes. He was obviously influenced by his mentors—Wright, an active member of the Communist Party, and Langston Hughes—though never a member of the party, who often wrote of and spoke out in favor of Communist causes.

But with all the association with communists and left-wing publications, Ellison was his own man. He never accepted the ideology which the *New Masses* attempted to impose on writers.[20] He believed the communists lost support from Negroes because they thought one had to be more Russian than American.[21] He later reflected:

> For me, the party was not by any means a god…but at the time the party promised me the availability of association which was important not only to me but any number of young intellectuals, black and white—that part can't be denied. I knew all kinds of people and I got the chance to find out how they thought and to compare my own experience with theirs. And very often I found that their reactions came out of an experience which was far simpler than mine, and that their view of the United States and of culture was simplistic. I first questioned whether I wasn't wrong, and if there was something wrong with me, but finally I had to fall back on my own experience.[22]

Perfecting His Craft

CHAPTER 12

> *The thing that's forgotten is that everyone has to master his craft or profession. Without the mastery no one is free, Negro or white.*
>
> —RALPH ELLISON

In late 1938, Ellison became romantically involved with a professional dancer and actress named Rose Aramita Poindexter who had enjoyed a moderately successful career on the European stage. It was his first significant emotional relationship so it took no time for him to ask Rose to marry him. She said yes and they moved into a Harlem apartment.

When Ellison was not working on the Writers Project, he was struggling with his novel he had decided to call *Slick*. For whatever reason, the romance between Rose and Ellison cooled not long after they were married. They continued to live in the same apartment, but they shared nothing of their lives. Ellison later explained that one reason the marriage never flourished was that his in-laws were "disgusted" with him and thought he had no ambition because he did not want a regular job—such as a "job in the Post Office."[1]

During his separation from Rose, Ellison had a prolonged affair with Sanora Babb, an Oklahoma-born novelist living in California. They met at the 1939 meeting of the American Writers Congress. They became lovers and saw each other into the 1940s. When in New York, Babb stayed at the St. Moritz Hotel which did not allow entertaining—forcing Ellison to take the rear stairs to her room. Ellison cherished the relationship with Babb who became a successful writer of short stories.[2]

A veteran of publishing book reviews, Ellison's first short story, "Slick Gonna Learn," was published in *Direction*, a journal upon whose editorial board Ellison's friend Wright sat. Slick Williams was a black man who had migrated to New York City and searched for ways to support his white family. During a brawl, Slick was knocked unconscious by a black pimp who had insulted his wife. When Slick woke up, he promptly clobbered a white policeman staring him in the face. Ellison's descriptions of Slick's encounters with whites and blacks alike were rife with his insinuations that whites and blacks could coexist peacefully.

Feeling the need for intense practice in writing, Ellison began copying in longhand the works of Faulkner and Hemingway. He believed that if he copied their style, word for word, he would be learning their techniques. He related the exercise to the five-finger exercise he employed as he learned to play the trumpet.

Ellison began to write feverishly for *New Masses*. In August, 1939, he wrote an essay titled "Judge Lynch in New York," an outright attack on what he perceived as an increase in racially-based brutality in the City. He named names, attacking Catholic priest and radio star Father Charles E. Coughlin, who used anti-Semitic and anti-black statements in public speeches and on radio.[3]

As Ellison's focus changed from music to writing, the typewriter—not the trumpet—became his instrument of choice. *Courtesy Fanny Ellison.*

Possibly remembering his own migration from the South, he poignantly told the story of three black youths who had been accosted by white policemen and fell into the hands of an Irish mob that had been driven to do harm to blacks by Father Coughlin's racist preaching.[4]

Needing a more consistent flow of cash, Ellison became a regular reviewer at *New Masses*. After long hours of completing

Writers Project assignments, and writing reviews for the magazine, he wrote another 100 pages of *Slick* on sheets of notebook paper. Much of the novel was drawn from Ellison's experiences as a waiter at the all-white Oklahoma City Diner's Club and at special catering events in rich, all-white Nichols Hills, an exclusive suburb of Oklahoma City.

Ellison also worked on a short story, "A Coupla Scalped Indians," that would not be published for more than a decade. In the fiction piece, he returned to his childhood. On their way home from a carnival, his characters, Buster and Riley, fresh from being circumcised or "scalped," sneaked a look at a black woman named Aunt Mackie through her shadeless window. After a near sexual encounter, Riley ran from Aunt Mackie's vicious dog:

> I moved faster now and suddenly all my senses seemed to sing alive. I heard a night bird's song; the lucid call of a quail arose. And from off to my right in the river there came the leap of a moon-mad fish and I could see the spray arch up and away. There was wisteria in the air and the scent of moonflowers. And now moving through the dark I recalled the warm, intriguing smell of her body and suddenly, with the shout of the carnival coming to me again, the whole thing became thin and dreamlike...I stopped in the path and looked back, seeing the black outlines of the shack and the thin moon above. Behind the shack the hill arose with the shadowy woods and I knew the lake was still hidden there. All was real. And for a moment I felt much older, as though I had lived swiftly long years into the future and had been as swiftly pushed back again.[5]

In another Buster and Riley story, "Afternoon," published in *American Writing* in 1940, Ellison told the tale of the youngsters imitating New York Yankee baseball player Lou Gehrig while walking barefooted down a glass-infested alley—throwing apples and rocks. It was a veiled attempt to discuss human interaction on a higher and more complicated level than just the differences in white and black.

Ellison used childhood rhymes in many of his stories, including "Afternoon." Buster and Riley's stroll down the alley is given excitement by the chant:

Well I met Mister Rabbit
Down by the pea vine...
An' I asked him where's he gwine
Well, he said, Just kiss my behind
And he skipped on down the pea vine.[6]

Ellison's importance in the New York literary world rose on his 26th birthday, March 1, 1940, when his friend Richard Wright's latest novel, *Native Son*, reached American bookstores. The book sold 200,000 copies within a month and Wright became the toast of literary parties and functions. Everyone knew Ellison was Wright's frequent companion and associate—and the association brought Ellison new contacts. He spoke to groups all over town, explaining Wright's new book, its touches of Marxism and use of realism.[7]

In May, 1940, Ellison accompanied several friends to the third National Negro Congress (NNC) in Washington, D.C. The NNC was a black civil rights organization that had communists in key leadership roles.

Ellison wrote an essay about the convention and, for the first time, his piece appeared on the front page of *New Masses*. In "A

Congress Jim Crow Didn't Attend," Ellison told of his excitement about the NNC and his optimism that black struggles for equality were moving forward. He wrote of his disappointment in A. Phillip Randolph, the former leader of the Brotherhood of Sleeping Car Porters, who called for blacks to separate themselves from Communist-inspired unions.[8]

Ellison believed a broad-based group such as the NNC could bring about long-awaited unity for blacks. He wrote, "And in all Negroes at some period of their lives there is that yearning for a sense of group unity that is the yearning of men for a flag; for a unity that cannot be compromised, that cannot be bought." Ellison saw strength in the faces of the blacks who attended the NNC convention and in the whites in the audience, he said, "I saw the positive forces of civilization and the best guarantee of America's future."[9]

After writing a series of published essays, Ellison's third short story, "The Birthmark," was published in *New Masses* in July, 1940. "The Birthmark" was a descriptive piece about a man's search for his brother who has been lynched by a white mob—the only way he could identify his brother was by a birthmark just above his navel.[10]

The events of World War II in Europe in 1941 caused Ellison to further distance himself from communists and the leftwing *New Masses*. Communists and groups such as the NNC lost their appeal when the Soviet Union was overrun by the German army and began to look to the United States for a military ally. Black leaders such as A. Philip Randolph, who crusaded for an integrated war industry and military, quickly filled the philosophical void for many black Americans.

Ellison had published a dozen theater and book reviews in a 12-month period of 1940-1941 when his latest short story, "Mister Tousan," appeared in *New Masses* in November of

1941. Buster and Riley were back—continuing their flight from the protective covering of their mothers' nests, into the free world as would-be adults. In true Ellison fashion, an incredibly detailed story setting was woven:

> The two small boys...sat on the floor of the porch, their bare feet resting upon the cool earth as they stared past the line on the paving where the sun consumed the shade, to a yard directly across the street. The grass in the yard was very green, and a house stood against it, neat and white in the morning sun. A double row of trees stood alongside the house, heavy with cherries that showed deep red against the dark green of the leaves and dull dark brown of the branches. The two boys were watching an old man who rocked himself in a chair as he stared back at them across the street.
> "Just look at him," said Buster. "Ole Rogan's so scared we gonna git some a his ole cherries he ain't even got sense enough to go outa the sun!"
> "Well, them birds is gitting their'n," said Riley.
> "They mockingbirds."
> "I don't care what kind birds they is, they sho in them trees."[11]

No longer willing to write for *New Masses* for free, Ellison negotiated as much as $15 for future pieces written for the publication. By late 1941, his estrangement from Rose worsened and he moved to another apartment. They would never live together again.

In 1941, Ellison published "Recent Negro Fiction," his longest and deepest critical essay to that time. He waved the banner of his hero, Richard Wright, and his *Native Son*, calling the book "the first philosophical work by an American Negro," a book that possessed "an artistry, penetration of thought, and sheer emotional power that places it in the front rank of American fiction."[12]

The consuming act of learning to write fiction left Ellison little time to enjoy his life's first love—music. Once when a loud-singing neighbor caused him to sit and stare at his typewriter, he turned on his old Philco radio and heard Kathleen Ferrier singing the words from Handel's "Rodelinda," "Art thou troubled? Music will calm thee…"[13]

His past world of music flooded back into his mind. In *Living With Music*, he remembered, "It was ironic, for after giving up my trumpet for the typewriter I had avoided too close a contact with the very art which she recommended as balm. For I had started music early and lived with it daily, and when I broke I tried to break clean. Now in this magical moment all the old love, the old fascination with music superbly rendered, flooded back."[14]

In April of 1942, Ellison left his position at the Writers Project to become managing editor of the *Negro Quarterly*, a journal published under the auspices of the Negro Publication Society of America and a well-known black communist Angelo Herndon. The move was lateral—at about the same rate of pay Ellison earned at the Writers Project. However, it was advantageous for Ellison to be associated with a publication that was considered far more mainstream than *New Masses*—although *Negro Quarterly* had its leftist leanings also.

Another advantage for Ellison in his new position was the thrill he enjoyed asking leading writers of the time to review books or submit essays for publication. However, there was a disadvantage to Ellison's new job. In running the quarterly, he was responsible for keeping the lights on, editing manuscripts, and keeping abreast of what was happening in the literary world. In short, although he still had time to feed his insatiable appetite for reading—he had no time to write fiction.

Ellison did have time to comment upon increasing crime in his Harlem neighborhood. He wrote, "To live in Harlem is to dwell in the very bowels of the city; it is to pass a labyrinthine existence among streets that explode monotonously skyward with the spires and crosses of churches and clutter under foot with garbage and decay. Harlem is a ruin—many of its ordinary aspects (its crimes, its casual violence, its crumbling buildings with littered area-ways, ill-smelling halls and vermin-invaded rooms) are indistinguishable from the distorted images that appear in dreams, and which, like muggers haunting a lonely hall, quiver in the waking mind with hidden and threatening significance."[15]

Ellison had lost his early infatuation with Harlem's supposed romance as he learned its bad side from eking out a living in his world of black fiction. "Overcrowded and exploited politically and economically," he said, "Harlem is the scene and symbol of the Negro's perpetual alienation in the land of his birth."[16]

As Ellison completed the metamorphosis from musician to writer, he agonized over his written pieces, the result of "a crucial conflict raging deep within" him, the product of "an activity, dreamlike, yet intense," which was waxing on the dark side of his mind and assuming a major importance in shaping his life. He said, "In this sense, writing was an acting out, symbolically, of a choice which I dared not acknowledge."[17]

Writing, for Ellison, was a serious matter, "it was playing with the secret lore of a fascinating but less glorious art to which I owed, I believed, no prior dedication." Writing was a "reflex of reading, an extension of a source of pleasure, escape, and instruction."

The many hours at a typewriter or writing longhand caused Ellison's days to melt together. He could lose himself in his thoughts, his ideals, and his deep longing for success as a writer. Then, just as suddenly, reality could bolt him back into the real world. After all, even the most intellectual of artists had to pay rent and buy groceries.

The real world appeared early in 1943. The financial picture at the *Negro Quarterly* was bleak, he sometimes wondered if he would be paid—war was raging in many parts of the world—and because Ellison was separated, he was fair game for the local draft board.

Master Storyteller

CHAPTER 13

> By seeing and understanding the life stories of others, we understand better what motivates us. In our reading of these personal narratives we draw a clearer vision of our own personal search for what is unique about ourselves.
>
> —PROFESSOR STEVEN H. HOBBS

In February of 1943, Ellison escaped the national draft by joining the United States Merchant Marine. To sweep past others on the waiting lists of would-be seamen, he used his influence with officials of the National Maritime Union for which he had picketed for several years. There were two reasons Ellison wanted to avoid the draft—he had no desire to be an Army infantryman and he strongly protested the segregation of blacks in the American military. He wanted to contribute to the war effort, but did not want to be "part of a Jim Crow army."[1]

Illness plagued Ellison during 1943. He was fatigued, stricken by jaundice, and afflicted with nervous exhaustion.[2] He continued to manage the *Negro Quarterly* while he awaited assignment to a Merchant Marine vessel—until the journal's income dropped below a level to keep the doors open, and it closed.

In the summer, a new journal, *Common Ground*, published his short story, "That I Had Wings." Buster and Riley are the stars of a tale of the blacks' desire to fully participate in the American dream, as the characters compare their own aspirations with those of a young robin trying to make its first flight.

No doubt set in Oklahoma, Buster and Riley make cloth parachutes for two young chickens that desperately want to fly—a familiar exercise in which Ellison and his neighbors had participated as a child. When Buster tossed the chicks into the air, he said:

> "Riley! Catch 'em!"
>
> He turned, seeing the parachute deflating like a bag of wind and the chicks diving the cloth earthward like a yellow piece of rock. He tried to run to catch the chicks and found himself standing still and hearing Buster and Aunt Kate yelling. Then he was stumbling to where the chicks lay hidden beneath the cloth. Please God, please, he breathed. But when he lifted the chicks, they made no sound and their heads wobbled lifelessly. He dropped slowly to his knees.
>
> A shadow fell across the earth and grew. Looking around, he saw two huge black bunion-shaped shoes. It was Aunt Kate, wheezing noisily.[3]

As in so many of Ellison's stories, the events in the 1943 short story were hauntingly filled with exact details of stories from his childhood in Oklahoma City.

Being published in *Common Ground* was an important step for Ellison as a writer. The magazine was politically a middle-of-the-road journal, backed by the Common Council for American Unity, a broad-based group of celebrities and intellectuals interested in better race relations. No longer was he so closely tied with publishing his writings in leftist-dominated publications.

In July of 1943, editors at the *New York Post* hired Ellison to cover a riot in Harlem—the worst racial strife in the area to that time. Ellison tried to paint the human side of the rioters—their frustration and resentment over the high price of food and other necessities and the increasing police brutality at the hands of white policemen. He called the rioters' actions "a naïve, peasant-like act of revenge."[4]

Later, Ellison explained his reporting of the Harlem riots, "I certainly wasn't recommending that people burn buildings but was suggesting that that was a negative alternative to more democratic political action. When it was impossible to be heard within the democratic forum, people would inevitably be driven to other extremes."[5]

By fall, Ellison had still not heard from the Merchant Marine on what ship he would board for war service. In the waiting, he wrote the short story, "King of the Bingo Game," a third-person saga of a Southern black who arrived in Harlem and turned to the lure of bingo to win money to secure medical treatment for his sick wife. Spinning the bingo wheel became the man's life:

> When he saw the row of holes punched across the third card, he sat paralyzed and heard the man call three more numbers before he stumbled forward, screaming, "Bingo! Bingo!"
> "Let that fool up there," someone called.
> "Get up there, man!"
> He stumbled down the aisle and up the steps to the stage into a light so sharp and bright that for a moment it

blinded him, and he felt that he had moved into the spell of some strange, mysterious power. Yet it was familiar as the sun, and he knew it was the perfectly familiar bingo.[6]

Ellison wrote one final short story in the weeks before he sailed on a Merchant Marine ship. The story was "Flying Home," the narrative of a young man whose boyhood dream of learning to fly an airplane came true when he became one of the Tuskegee Airmen, the first group of black men allowed to train as pilots in the American military. The young pilot, Todd—out on a training mission—struck a buzzard and crashed into a racist landowner's field. Todd was aided by Jefferson, an elderly black man, who saved him from the white man and carried him to safety.

Ellison's own past and his innermost feelings emerged in "Flying Home:"

> He saw the old man watching, his torn overalls clinging limply to him in the heat. He felt a sharp need to tell the old man what he felt...He watched the old man, hearing him humming snatches of a tune as he admired the plane. He felt a furtive sense of resentment. Such old men often came to the field to watch the pilots with childish eyes. At first it had made him proud. They had been a meaningful part of a new experience. But soon he realized they did not understand his accomplishments and they came to shame and embarrass him, like the distasteful praise of an idiot...
>
> If I were a prize-fighter I would be more human, he thought. Not a monkey doing tricks, but a man...Somehow he felt betrayed, as he had when a child he grew to discover that his father was dead. Now,

for him, any real appreciation lay with his white officers; and with them he could never be sure. Between the ignorant black men and condescending whites, his course of flight seemed mapped by the nature of things away from all needed and natural landmarks.[7]

In "Flying Home," Ellison became a master user of black folklore, using images and storylines from Africa. Even the title of the short story came from the oral tradition of early Africans arriving on slave ships in America. There was a legend that a certain tribe of Africans had the ability to utter magic words, escape their slavery in the New World, and fly back to Africa.

Surely Ellison was following the tradition of "saltwater Africans," as slaves were called, who possessed the magic to fly. Ellison debunked the theory that blacks could not fly. The white landowner, Graves, has the attendants from an insane asylum put the young pilot in a straitjacket, and attacked his right to learn to fly:

> This nigguh belongs in a straightjacket, too boys. I knowed that the minnit Jeff's kid said something 'bout a nigguh flyer. You all know you caint let the nigguh git up that high without his going crazy. The nigguh brain ain't built right for high altitudes.[8]

"In his childhood stories," wrote Professor Steven H. Hobbs of the University of Alabama School of Law, "Ellison particularly captures the exuberance of boyhood with its fun and adventurous sense of play. Boys use their physical bodies to explore both the physical world around them and the world of pure imagination."[9]

Hobbs said one nearly hears Ellison's voice in reading his stories. "It is as if he is speaking off of the page, telling the tale to a live audience," Hobbs wrote, "He puts us in the middle of a sunny summer afternoon alongside two young boys finding their own amusement; or on a rolling freight train bouncing down the tracks; or looking over the shoulders of a father relating to his son."[10]

John F. Callahan described Ellison's storytelling as "radical in the familiar sense of going back to essentials, in this case the root meaning of narrative." Narrative comes from the word, *narrare*, to make known and to do so in the form of a story. Callahan opined, "So there is something of a distinction between narrative and story; in its stress on the act of storytelling, and the consequence of telling one's story on identity, narrative is a complicating form."[11]

Whatever the technique, whether intended or instinctive, Ellison expertly converted oral traditional concepts and stories into written words that jumped off the page with deep meaning and pure entertainment. Hobbs said, "His short stories are multilayered commentaries on social problems. Moreover, the stories offer insights and lessons on how our current problems are born from past social struggles. Through his storytelling, he reminds us of what our stated values are as a democratic, constitutional society and how we have not always lived up to those values."[12]

Ellison's short stories fall into four different categories: (1) tales from his childhood, featuring Buster and Riley; (2) hobo and train stories, drawn from his own experiences in illegally riding a series of freights to Tuskegee in 1933; (3) black fatherhood stories, often a comment upon the loss of his father at age two; and (4) stories of the struggle for equality, delving into the heart of racism.

Callahan wrote in his introduction to *Flying Home and Other Stories*, published in 1996 after Ellison's death:

The sequence I have chosen follows the life Ellison knew and imagined from boyhood and youth in the late thirties and early forties. Different faces look out from the stories. Sometimes tolerance and a wary solidarity break through the color line, while on other occasions unspeakable cruelty and violence disfigure the countenance of Ellison's America. The deceptive Jim Crow "normalcy" of the twenties is here; so are the jolt of the Depression and the opportunity and antagonism of black experience during the Second World War. Throughout the stories, Ellison experiments with narrative technique, point of view, and the impact of geography on personality.[13]

The power and lasting attributes of the stories woven by Ellison in the 1940s were based upon characters with vivid personalities who had dramatically experienced events and circumstances unique to the human condition. Heather Forest, in her book, *Wisdom Tales from Around the World*, explained the importance of telling stories, "A story can be a powerful teaching tool. In folktales far and wide, characters may gain wisdom by observing a good example."

Forest wrote, "A story's plot may inspire listeners to reflect on personal actions, decision making, or behavior. An entertaining story can gently enter the interior world of a listener. Over time, a tale can take root, like a seed rich with information, and blossom into new awareness and understanding."[14]

The characters in Ellison's stories used the physical characteristics of the human voice. In "Mister Toussan," Riley's mother sang a spiritual and calmed the entire neighborhood. In "That I Had Wings," Ellison combined the words of the old spirituals with a vibrant series of words of a childhood rhyme that engulf young Riley, "He bit his lip. But the words kept dancing in his mind. Lots of verses. *Amazin' grace, how sweet the sound. A bullfrog slapped his granma down.*"15

The reader vividly hears Aunt Kate's voice in "That I Had Wings" when she admonished the children to learn spirituals:

The Oklahoma County Metropolitan Library System honored Ellison in 2002 with a cover photograph taken by Fanny Ellison of the young writer deep in thought in his New York City apartment. *Courtesy Fanny Ellison.*

"Yuh chillun needs to learn some a the Lawd's songs," she beamed, singing:

Sing aaa-ho that
Ah had he wings of-vah dove
Ah'd fly to mah Jesus an'
Be at res.'

"Thass the kinda song fo yuh chillun to sing. Yuh needs the wings of the spirit to help yuh through this worl'. Lemme heah yuh try it erlong with me."

Sing aaa-ho that...[16]

With months of intensive writing behind him, Ellison prepared for service in the big war that had engulfed the world and dominated the day's headlines and the conversation in the barbershop and the coffeehouses Ellison frequented in Harlem. He was mentally prepared to continue perfecting his craft aboard a smelly freighter.

Before he left, he retained the services of a literary agent, Henry Volkening of the Russell and Volkening Literary Agency, to shop his stories to the finest periodicals and journals of the day.

Cooking on the High Seas

CHAPTER 14

> Coming ashore from the ship he had felt the excited expectancy of entering a strange land.
>
> —FROM "IN A STRANGE COUNTRY"

the American Merchant Marine had a storied past. In the Revolutionary War, without a Navy, the United States turned to experienced merchant seamen in privately owned boats and ships to protect its shores. One historian wrote, "The story of our nation would have been different were it not for the merchant seaman. He was on the sea with the first throb of independence. The navy, so hastily provided by the infant government, was made up of ordinary merchantmen pierced for guns. With Yankee merchant sailors upon their decks, they sailed jauntily to sea to confront the mightiest navy in the world, and just how well they acquitted themselves history amply records."[1]

In World War II, the Merchant Marine played a significant role in America's victory. Sailing through submarine-infested waters, ships dodged torpedoes and enemy bombers to deliver war munitions and other cargoes necessary for American servicemen to carry on the battle for freedom.

Ellison sailed from the docks of New York City aboard the S.S. *Sun Yat Sen* in late 1943. He was a third cook on the vessel owned by the North Atlantic and Gulf Steamship Company. For five months he labored over hot steam tables and cooked and served what seemed liked mountains of potatoes and beans.

But after the long hours in the ship's kitchen, Ellison turned his thoughts to his storytelling. Continuing the pattern of weaving stories from his own personal experiences, he wrote "In a Strange Country," which his agent Volkening would later sell to *Tomorrow* for $100—the most Ellison had ever received for a piece at that point in his literary career.

In the story, forty-five minutes into a visit to Wales, the seaman is drinking Welsh ale with a local, Mr. Catti, in a pub with a fireplace "with its grate of glowing coals." The seaman had come ashore expecting to see a strange land.

> Moving along the road in the dark he had planned to stay ashore all night, and in the morning he would see the country with fresh eyes, like those with which the Pilgrims had seen the New World. That hadn't seemed so silly then—not until the soldiers bunched at the curb had seemed to spring out of the darkness. Someone had cried, "Jesus H. Christ," and he had thought, "He's from home," and grinned and apologized into the light they flashed in his eyes. He had felt the blow coming when they yelled, "It's a goddamn nigger," but it struck him anyway. He was having a time of it when some of Mr. Catti's countrymen stepped in and Mr. Catti had guided him into the pub.[2]

As soon as his five-month tour with the Merchant Marine ended in the spring of 1944, Ellison delivered his writings to his agent. In May, Volkening informed him that he had been promised a $1,200 advance on a novel. Ellison had long given up on completing *Slick*, but was full of ideas for a full-length novel on a variety of topics.

Fanny McConnell was a beautiful young lady who shared Ellison's love for books and the finer things of life. Throughout his life, Ellison referred to Fanny's martinis as the best in the world. Ellison took this photograph of his wife. *Courtesy Fanny Ellison.*

Then, Fanny McConnell Buford entered his life. In June of 1944, Ellison was introduced to Fanny by Langston Hughes who had followed closely the breakup of Ellison's marriage to Rose. Fanny McConnell—she went by her maiden name—was a writer and sophisticated, well-educated woman. She studied drama and speech at the University of Iowa at Iowa City and directed drama presentations before marrying John Buford. Together, they managed the Negro Peoples' Theater company in Chicago in the 1930s.

Ellison and Fanny, who had a good job at the Urban League, were drawn together by their love for books. She wanted to see his library—which Hughes had told her was "magnificent." Their dates were filled with conversation about books and authors. Soon, Fanny was typing Ellison's longhand notes—usually after he had read aloud to her his latest rendering of a short story.[3]

By the end of the summer of 1944, Ellison's literary agent had struck a deal with Harcourt Brace to advance Ellison $1,500 toward a novel to be delivered in six months. The agreement was that Ellison would receive $250 for signing and $250 per month until the advance was paid.

His literary career was launched. Agent Volkening sold his story of the Merchant Marine in Wales to *Negro Digest*, the black sequel of *Reader's Digest*. Ellison also wrote several essays and book reviews while waiting on his next assignment at sea.

Ellison penned a lengthy review of Gunnar Myrdal's *An American Dilemma* to be published in *Antioch Review*, an academic journal headquartered in Yellow Springs, Ohio. Ellison's review was critical of the Swedish social scientist's analysis of American race relations. The review was too controversial—so the editors of the *Antioch Review* delayed plans to publish it.

In early 1945, Ellison began his second Merchant Marine assignment after failing in an attempt to avoid the draft completely with the help of a psychiatrist friend of Richard Wright. The doctor had written a report that said a young black man such as Ellison could not stand the mental pressures of racial prejudice often encountered aboard ships.

Aboard a supply ship headed for the Rhine River in Germany, Ellison performed his kitchen duties and spent his off-duty hours with pen in hand, transferring his fictional ideas to paper. The ship's officers were more concerned with timely delivery of war materiel for American troops fighting the Battle of the Bulge than routine flushing of its water tanks. Two months of drinking water, "so supersaturated with rust that it trickled from the taps as red as tomato soup," gave Ellison a kidney infection.[4]

As the ship neared the bombed-out harbor at Le Havre, France, Ellison's kidney infection became severe. Even though he had substantial free time on the ship, his physical condition prevented him from physically and mentally working on the novel which he had promised to deliver to Harcourt Brace.[5]

Staying healthy enough to keep his work completed, Ellison was on board an ammunition ship that sailed down the Rhine River. He saw the horror of the war—German Tiger Tanks burning out of control—and heard the rat-a-tat-tat of live fire from American machine guns.

Ellison returned to New York on April 6, 1945. He still felt ill and could not find work. He and Fanny renewed their relationship and fell deeply in love. They moved in together and talked of marriage, possibly in the next year. To earn a living, Ellison took a job installing high-fidelity stereo systems.

Looking for a way to survive while he completed his promised novel, Ellison applied for a Julius Rosenwald Fellowship. The fund had originally helped prepare teachers who studied at black colleges in the South. However, by 1945, the Rosenwald fund directors had broadened their criteria to fund annual support of writers who worked at their projects fulltime.

Ellison made an important literary contribution in the summer of 1945 with his review of Richard Wright's autobiography, *Black Boy*, in *Antioch Review*. In the review titled "Richard Wright's Blues," Ellison called Wright "perhaps the most articulate Negro American." He compared the work with Joyce and Doestoevsky and with his beloved blues. Ellison said of Wright's "song" of trouble and trial:

> [It is filled] with blues-tempered echoes of railroad trains, the names of Southern towns and cities, estrangements, fights and flights, deaths and disappointments, charged with physical and spiritual hungers and pain. And like a blues sung by such an artist as Bessie Smith, its lyric prose evokes the paradoxical, almost surreal image of a black boy singing lustily as he probes his own grievous wound.[6]

Ellison skillfully critiqued Wright's autobiographical description of his near-death beating by his mother after he set the house afire at age four. Of Wright's fear that gripped him under the heavy hand of his mother until he saw wobbly white bags "like the full udders of a cow" suspended from the ceiling, Ellison wrote:

> It was as though the mother's milk had turned acid, and with it the whole pattern of life that had produced the ignorance, cruelty, and fear that had fused with mother-love and exploded in the beating. It is significant

that the bags were of the hostile color white, and the female symbol that of the cow, the most stupid (and, to the small child, the most frightening) of domestic animals...And the significance is increased by virtue of the historical fact that the lower-class Negro family is matriarchal; the child turns not to the father to compensate if he feels mother-rejection, but to the grandmother, or to an aunt—and Wright rejected both of these. Such rejection leaves the child open to psychological insecurity, distrust, and all of those hostile environmental forces from which the family functions to protect it.[7]

The review of Wright's book turned the heads of many in the literary world. Howard University Professor Lawrence Jackson later said, "[The review] showcased Ellison's remarkable mental strength as well as his broad intellectual range. The essay also formally introduced his concept of the role of a blues ideology that was implicit in black life—a historically based collective subconscious that enabled blacks to face and triumph over adversity."[8]

Also in 1945, Ellison wrote "Beating That Boy," a review of *Primer for White Folks*, by Bucklin Moon, published in the October 22 edition of *New Republic*. In critiquing the collection of stories by and about black American writers, Ellison graphically described the race problem confronting the country:

For since 1876 the race issue has been like a stave driven into the American system of values, a stave so deeply imbedded in the American ethos as to render America a nation of ethical schizophrenics. Believing true democracy on one side of their minds, they act on the other in violation of its most sacred principles; holding that all men are created equal, they treat thirteen million Americans as though they were not.[9]

The racial situation "has become like an irrational sea in which Americans flounder like convoyed ships in a gale," Ellison wrote. He accused whites of being unable to think of sex, of economics, of "womenfolk," or of sweeping sociopolitical changes without "summoning into consciousness fear-flecked images of black men." That societal ill, Ellison said, resulted in misconceived ideas of black literary offerings. He said, "Thus when the literary artist attempts to tap the charged springs issuing from his inner world, up float his misshapen and bloated images of the Negro, like the fetid bodies of the drowned."[10]

As the small stipends for his essays and book reviews ran out, Ellison received the good news that his application had been approved by the Rosenwald Committee. He was awarded an $1,800 fellowship to work on his novel.

Still suffering from the after effects of the kidney infection, Ellison needed to rest. He and Fanny left New York to spend rest and recovery time at the farm of a friend in Vermont.

Birth of a Novel

CHAPTER 15

> *The nature of the American society is such that we are prevented from knowing who we are. It is still a young society, and this is an integral part of its development.*
>
> —RALPH ELLISON

The serene, pastoral setting of a Vermont farm seemed an unlikely place for Ellison to begin writing a novel that would have a lasting impression on the literary world. After all, Ellison's life experiences, the foundation of all his literary offerings, did not include any life on a farm. Possibly he needed the fresh air of John and Amelia Bates' farm in Waitsfield, Vermont, to regain his health—or maybe find solitude from the hustle and bustle of New York City and the constant interruptions of his work by friends and acquaintances.

In any event, Ellison worked in Bates' barn, pitching hay to the cattle, and caught up on his reading. He pored over *The Hero* by Lord Ragland and speculated on the nature of black leadership in the United States. He and Fanny enjoyed the relaxed atmosphere of the Vermont hills. They swam in a creek, attended a square dance at a community fair, and even won a quilt in a raffle.[1]

The calm days and restful activity restored Ellison's health. With a sound body and refreshed mind, he was ready to begin his promised novel. Several questions raced through his mind—Why did black leaders so often seem uncommitted to their black constituents? Why did they so often listen to their white patrons more than their black brothers? He was determined to write a novel about black identity and heroism.

One afternoon, sitting in the open barn looking at the peaks of the nearby Green Mountains, he took pen and paper and wrote a single line:

I am an invisible man.

Ellison had no idea what the words meant or where they came from. When he began to abandon them, he thought, "Well, maybe I should try to discover exactly what it was that lay behind the statement. What type of man would make that type of statement, would conceive of himself in such terms? What lay behind him?"[2]

The wild notion gave him hope. He searched for answers. Was it Lord Ragland's book he had been reading that caused him to speak of an invisible man? He recalled the many aspects of character that Ragland had assigned to his heroes—figures from religion and battlefields. He found "it would seem that the human imagination finds it necessary to take exemplary people, charismatic personalities, cultural heroes, and enlarge upon them." Real people often became mythical people, Ellison thought.[3]

Was it current events that resulted in the simple words, "I am an invisible man?" Ellison had closely followed newspaper accounts of blacks' quarrel with the federal government over segregation in the military and equal access to jobs in the

American war industries. He fretted over black leadership and wondered why that leadership "was never able to enforce its will."[4] It was no accident that the principal character in *Invisible Man* turned out to be hungry and thirsty to prove himself that he could become an effective leader.

Soon the Vermont vacation was over and Ellison and Fanny went back to New York City and their apartment at the Macedonia Baptist Church. As he began working seriously on the novel, he became aware of something else. In such a large and diverse country, he, as a writer, had to try to solve the complex social structure and conceive one character that accounted for all the people with their diverse social manners and their positions in the social hierarchy.

He discovered for himself that it was "necessary to work out some imaginative integration of the total American experience and discover through the work of the imagination some way of moving a young black boy from a particular area and level of the society" into a source of political power. Ellison wanted to write more than just a good, readable novel—he wanted to relate what he believed to be the important and abiding themes present in the best of American literature.[5]

Ellison found himself working tirelessly on his novel—trying to "build my fiction, trying to structure my 'lie' in such a way as would reveal a certain amount of truth." The "lie" Ellison spoke of was the American tradition of literature—telling the reader who he was, how he had grown, and where he was going.[6]

Ellison chose as his principal character in *Invisible Man* a young man who has "an infinite capacity for making mistakes," who in his passion for leadership and in his passion to prove himself within the limitations of a segregated society, blunders from one point to another "until he finally realized that American society cannot define the role of the individual, or at least not that of the responsible individual."[7]

The more Ellison wrote, the more he believed his novel was going nowhere. There was a sense of isolation—he thought he was not being inventive enough and the story could not possibly have any value to others. He silently wondered if the book would sell even a thousand copies.[8]

Ellison's greatest supporter during the seven years between the day in Vermont when the novel began, and its ultimate publication in 1952, was Fanny, whom he married in August of 1946. She earned sufficient money to provide for them a decent life. She also listened to him reading the day's efforts on the typewriter. As he moved from rough draft to finished product of a particular scene or chapter, Fanny typed the material into a more polished state.

Within a year, Ellison had an extensive outline of his entire novel and by the end of 1947, had a good idea of how the story would end. The idea of invisibility intrigued him—he spent long hours exploring his past in glimpses of his memory of insults and danger and adventure.

In early notes Ellison wrote during the "building" of the novel, he tried to explain, perhaps to himself, the concept of his story:

> First a couple of underlying assumptions: "Invisibility," as our rather strange character comes in the end to conceive it, springs from two basic facts of American life: from the racial conditioning which often makes the white American interpret cultural, physical, or psychological differences as signs of racial inferiority; and, on the other hand, it springs from a great formlessness of Negro life wherein all values are in flux, and where those institutions

and patterns of life which mold the white American's personality are missing or not so immediate in their effects. Except for its upper levels, where it tends to merge with the American whole, Negro life is a world psychologically apart. Its tempo of development from the feudal-folk forms of the South to the industrial urban forms of the North is so rapid that it throws up personalities as fluid and changeable as molten metal rendered iridescent from the effect of cooling air.[9]

In developing his invisible character, Ellison tried to paint a vivid picture of a man born into a tragic national situation who attempts to respond to it as though it were completely logical. His character accepted his identity handed down by the white South and the paternalism of northern philanthropy. Ellison said, "He sets out with the purpose of succeeding within the tight framework granted him by Jim Crow, and he blinds himself to all those factors of reality which reveal the essential inadequacy of such a scheme for the full development of personality."[10]

Ellison did not work fulltime on *Invisible Man*. He occasionally lectured to literature classes and reading clubs and wrote book reviews for *New Republic*. His days of association with leftist publications were in the distant past and he was recognized as a mainstream literary critic and author.

Concerned with Harlem's growing juvenile delinquency problem, Richard Wright and Ellison helped found a free psychiatric clinic for black youths suffering from the effects of prejudice. In March of 1946, the LaFargue Mental Hygiene Clinic opened in the basement of the parish house of St. Philips Church on West 133rd Street, largely due to Ellison's request to the bishop in charge.

In an unpublished essay describing the clinic, Ellison said it was the only center in the city where both blacks and whites could receive extended psychiatric care. He said, "Thus its importance transcends even its great value as a center for psychotherapy: it represents an underground extension of democracy."[11]

Ellison believed Harlem was overcrowded and exploited politically and economically and in great need of free psychiatric services for its people. He wrote in "Harlem is Nowhere:"

> Hence the most surreal fantasies are acted out upon the streets of Harlem: a man ducks in and out of traffic shouting and throwing imaginary grenades that actually exploded during World War I; a boy participates in the rape-robbery of his mother; a man beating his wife in the park uses boxing "science" and observes Marquess of Queensbury rules (no rabbit punching, no blows beneath the belt); two men hold a third while a lesbian slashes him to death with a razor blade; boy gangsters wielding homemade pistols...shoot down their rivals. Life becomes a masquerade; exotic costumes are worn every day.[12]

In the middle of 1946, Ellison and his wife moved into a ground floor apartment at 749 Nicholas Avenue. The back yard was large enough for dogs so the Ellisons bought two Scottish Terriers. Lawrence Jackson described the new haven for Ellison:

> From his steps he could look down into the valley of Harlem and check the pulse of the black United States,

while immediately to the east he could see the rise of City College. It was the quintessence of urban living, but over the years it exacted a high price. From the mid-through the late 1940s it became increasingly difficult for him to perform his daily labors at the typewriter when he had to wage war with berserk drunks who crowded the alleyway and the rear...of the apartment. His midday reverie at the typewriter was constantly interrupted by loud arguments, singing, and crying.[13]

Everywhere he went, Ellison thought about his novel. Ideas came to him on the subway and while walking his dogs. It was not uncommon for him to scribble a note on the back of an envelope or napkin at a restaurant. He then, in the privacy of his apartment, transferred the ideas onto long sheets of paper and eventually to a typewritten page.

In 1947, the first chapter of *Invisible Man* was published in the British journal, *Horizon*. American critics took note of the work and Ellison received invitations to submit materials to several periodicals. Even in Ireland, the literary world recognized Ellison's genius. Donat O'Donnell of Dublin's *Irish Times* said, "If the rest of Mr. Ellison's novel comes up to the level of the fragment published here...it will be one of the most important pieces of fiction for years."[14]

Ellison sought advice from old friends on how to organize and develop his novel. One close advisor was literary critic Kenneth Burke who had been instrumental in helping Ellison obtain the Rosenwald grant in 1945. Burke's writings, especially *A Grammar of Motives*, gave Ellison a formidable schematic on which to pace his own novel.

Also in 1947, Ellison's editors, Albert Erskine and Frank Taylor, moved to the publishing concern, Random House.

After extensive negotiations, Random House bought his contract and paid him an additional $500 advance. The new deal obligated Ellison to submit his novel to Random House before April 30, 1948.

Into the winter of 1947-1948 strode Ellison, adding to and taking from his story. He spent weeks at the Vermont cottage of Bea and Francis Steegmuller. The cold air unfroze his writing mind that had temporarily gone cold in the fall of 1947. Back in the City, Ellison supplemented his income by working as a photographer, writing movie and book reviews, and helping install audio systems once more. His interest grew in both photography and in electronic gadgets.

By early 1949, Ellison completed the second major section of *Invisible Man* and was working on the third. His manuscript had ballooned to nearly 800 pages. In January, 1950, Ellison believed he was nearing the end of his writing. He wrote fellow author Albert Murray, "Who knows, we might both have books during 1950."[15]

However, three months later, in a letter to Murray, "Book almost finished—I hope. There'll be rewriting to do but the main thing will be over. Right now it reads like a three-ring circus. All the anti-violence boys will blow their tops should it come their way."[16]

In April and May of 1950, Ellison was depressed after developing a high fever while trying to finish the novel. By June, he left his city apartment and tried to put the finishing touches on his work at the Westport, Connecticut, cottage of folklorist and critic Stanley Edgar Hyman whom Ellison called "an old friend and intellectual sparring partner."[17]

Ellison was worried over transitions in the story until he read the page proofs of a book written by Hyman's wife, Shirley Jackson. On June 6, Ellison wrote Murray, "then I read her page proofs and saw how simply she was managing her transitions and how they really didn't bother me despite their 'and-so-and-then-and-therefore'—and then, man I was on...I had chosen to recreate the world, but, like a self-doubting god, was uncertain that I could make the pieces fit smoothly together. Well, it's done now and I want to get on to the next."[18]

Working with his editor, Erskine, Ellison cut his mammoth manuscript down to 606 pages by June. The slowness of the process caused Random House to drop its plans to get the book to the printer by the end of the year.

Realizing the project had taken far too long, Ellison said, "With middle age staring me in the face [he was 36] I'm feeling the need to justify myself, or at least Fanny's working and my thinning hair."[19] He described his masterpiece-in-progress "a big fat ole Negro lie, meant to be told during cotton picking time over a water bucket full of corn, with a dipper passing back and forth at a good fast clip so that no one, not even the narrator himself, will realize how utterly preposterous the lie actually is."[20]

Ellison completed his writing of *Invisible Man* in the middle of 1951 and by December, had reviewed and corrected the page proofs. *Partisan Review* printed the prologue of the book. There was quite a bit of excitement at Random House as the requests for galleys of the forthcoming novel increased.

With the masterpiece behind him, Ellison told Murray, "I've been a tired, exhausted son of a bitch since I've finished and I want to feel alive again. It's an awful life, for years now I felt guilty because I was working on a novel for so long a time, and now I feel guilty that I'm no longer doing so. Fanny's after me to do some stuff on Negro culture and perhaps I shall."[21]

Little did Ralph and Fanny know what a shock wave *Invisible Man* would cause in the entire world within a few months.

A Classic

CHAPTER 16

> With the publication of Invisible Man, Ellison moved suddenly into the front ranks of American writers.
>
> —ROBERT G. O'MEALLY

From the moment *Invisible Man* arrived in the nation's bookstores in April of 1952, it was an American literary classic. Within three weeks it was number 14 on the *New York Times* best-seller list.

The finished novel was unique. Set in a 20-year period beginning in 1930, it is the story of the growth of an ambitious young black man from the South who migrates to college and then to New York City. He recognizes his "invisibility" when he is required to fight blindfolded in a battle royal with other black youths at a smoker attended by his hometown's leading white citizens. He is invisible because the whites see him as a buffoonish entertainer—not an individual or promise.

In New York City, the "invisible man," finds work in a paint factory, displays courage when making a moving speech at the eviction of an elderly Harlem couple, and hires on to

The cover of the original edition of *Invisible Man* in 1952. *Courtesy Random House.*

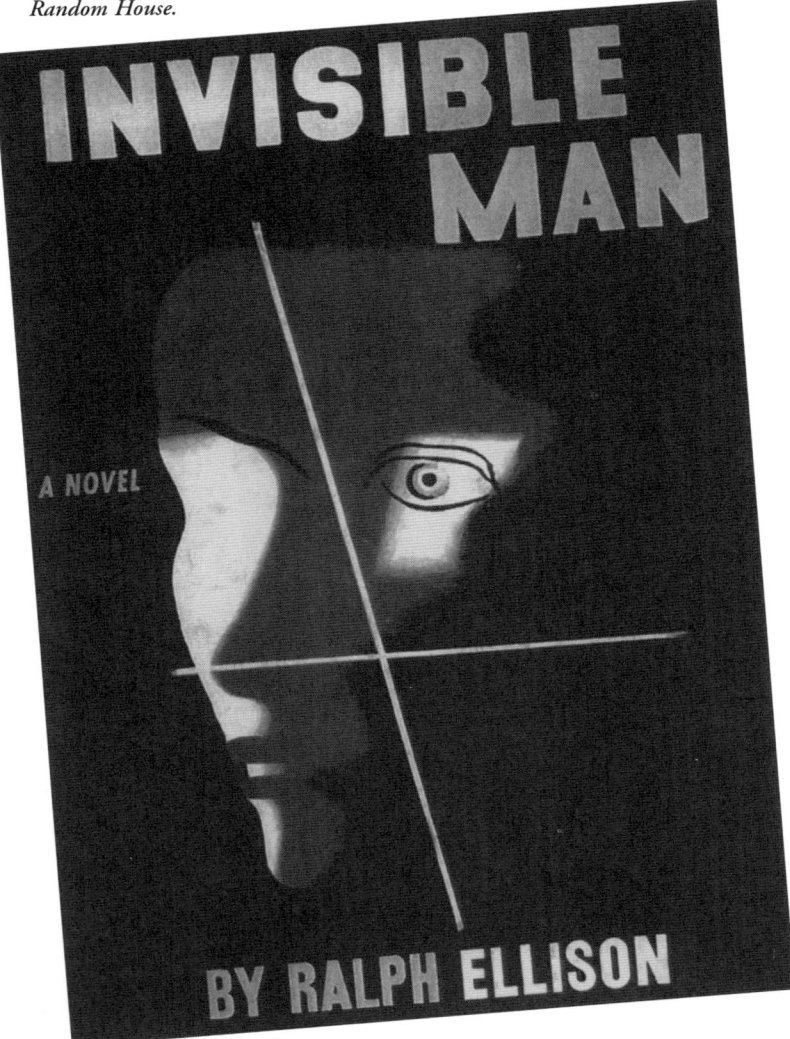

represent a predominantly radical political organization called the Brotherhood.

His stump speeches stir up the community in Harlem. A race riot erupts and invisible man falls down a manhole into

This solemn photograph of Ellison appeared on the back cover of the original printing of *Invisible Man*. The photo also was released to the nation's newspapers and magazines as a publicity shot of Ellison. *Courtesy Oklahoma Publishing Company.*

an abandoned cellar. There he fully realizes how society has betrayed him. He steals light from the power company and writes his memoirs in hibernation.

Ellison used the panorama of his life's experiences in *Invisible Man*. There are blues, spirituals, tales, bragging, sermons, and other examples of black folklore. Robert G. O'Meally said, "It is a benchmark black novel that seems aware of the entire tradition of African American letters. In it one overhears the black and white tricksters (slaves and slaveholders) of slave narrative locked in combat. One senses again the slaves' desperate yearning for education, mobility, and individual and communal freedom."[1]

Ellison combined his years of reading the classics of both white and black literature in *Invisible Man*. There were touches of Melville, Nathaniel Hawthorne, Hemingway, and

Twain. Symbolism and rhetorical richness surely flowed from Malraux, Joyce, Sigmund Freud, Homer, and Dostoevsky.

The influence of Ellison's introduction to jazz on Deep Deuce in his childhood in Oklahoma City shows through strongly in his classic novel. Trueblood, a sharecropper, who has faced his crime of incest, ends a portion of his place in the book with a song:

> Finally, one night, way early in the mornin', I looks up and sees the stars and I starts singin'. I don't mean to, I didn't think 'bout it, just start singin'. I don't know what it was, some kinds church song, I guess. All I know is I ends up singin' the blues. I sings me some blues that might ain't never been sang before, and while I'm singin' them blues I makes up my mind that I ain't nobody but myself and ain't nothin' I can do but let whatever happen, happen. I made up my mind that I was goin' back home.[2]

The invisible man, the hero, finally discovers much about American culture and history. He sees that he has been a fool for running the course that others have set for him. He goes underground and agrees with Trueblood, "I ain't nobody but myself...I made up my mind that I was goin' back home."[3]

Ellison completed his novel with the words, "Who knows but that, on the lower frequencies, I speak for you," a clear signal that everyone may be invisible, or as Albert Murray says, "It implies as a literary statement that nobody sees you the way you really want to be seen."[4]

Most critics liked what they read. Across the book review pages in newspapers of the land, it was called one of the definitive novels of the black experience and a definitive novel for all Americans.

William Barrett in *American Mercury* called *Invisible Man* "the first considerable step forward in Negro literature."[5] In *Commentary*, Saul Bellow called the novel a "brilliant individual victory" for Ellison and suggested that he displayed "the very strongest sort of creative intelligence."[6] Other excellent reviews were printed in *New Yorker*, *Time*, and the *New York Herald Tribune*.

However, not all reviews of *Invisible Man* were positive. Some leftist journals accused Ellison of selling out to the establishment and turning his back on his people. Somehow, Ellison was capable of tuning out the bad reviews—considering the source—and concentrating on the nice words the leading journals were giving him.

American readers lined up at bookstore checkout counters to buy the latest Random House release. By the end of April of 1952, more than 6,000 copies had been sold at the retail price of $3.50. After the first 5,000 sold, Ellison's contract provided that his royalty went from 12.5 to 15 percent. He cleared a profit of more than $3,000 in his first year, a tidy sum for an author in the middle of the 20th century. Ellison's friend Murray reported that there was a waiting list of 90 for the few copies of the book at the Tuskegee library. Ellison was elated at the appreciation of his book by mentors and students alike at his old college in the South.[7]

Ellison's popularity as a writer rose higher and faster than the red mercury in an old-fashioned thermometer on a hot, clammy Oklahoma summer day. He was invited to the most elegant parties in New York City and spoke to countless book review clubs and literary gatherings. At the end of each talk, he graciously sold books and meticulously inscribed them for his patrons. He became both a publicist and salesman.

Shortly after the publication of *Invisible Man* in 1952, work began on translating the best selling novel into other languages. This is the cover of the Japanese language edition of the book. *Courtesy Ralph Ellison Library.*

Basking in the glow of the flame of fame resulting from the success of *Invisible Man*, Ellison's views were sought on the greatest of the nation's ills. He was asked to write essays on race relations and also, in lighter substance, reviews of the latest jazz offerings and movies. He was invited to attend a prestigious lecture series at Princeton University in New Jersey.

Awards and honors began coming Ellison's way. He received the Chicago Defender Honor Roll of Democracy and the John B. Russwurm Award, a prize voted by the National Newspaper Publishers Association, made up primarily of black weekly newspapers.

But the greatest award came when Ellison won the National Book Award Gold Medal for fiction, presented at a January 27, 1953, gala at the Commodore Hotel in New York City. On the morning of the event, Ellison was interviewed on NBC's Today show. At a photography session at the Random House offices, he met for the first time his literary hero, William Faulkner.

The National Book Awards had been established in 1950 by a consortium of book publishing groups—its goal to

The first paragraph of *Invisible Man* in Portuguese. After the success of the novel in the United States, publishers in other lands vied for the rights to publish the book in a dozen languages.

Prólogo

Sou um homem invisível. Não, não sou um antasma como os que assombravam Edgar Allan Poe; nem um desses ctoplasmas de filme de Hollywood. Sou um homem de substância, de arne e osso, fibras e líquidos – talvez se possa até dizer que possuo uma ente. Sou invisível, compreendam, simplesmente porque as pessoas se cusam a me ver. Tal como essas cabeças sem corpo que às vezes são ibidas nos mafuás de circo, estou, por assim dizer, cercado de espelhos vidro duro e deformante. Quem se aproxima de mim vê apenas o que cerca, a si mesmo, ou os inventos de sua própria imaginação – na rdade, tudo e qualquer coisa, menos e enhance the public's awareness of exceptional books written by fellow Americans and to increase the popularity of reading in general.

Ultimately, the National Book Awards became the nation's preeminent literary prize and the annual awards dinner is the most important event on any author's literary calendar. In the 1950s, for example, winners of the award included William Faulkner, Herman Melville, Ralph Waldo Emerson, Bernard Malamud, Bruce Catton, and Saul Bellow.

While Ellison was the winner of the National Book Award for fiction, Bernard A. DeVoto was the non-fiction winner for *The Course of an Empire* and, in poetry, Archibald MacLeish's *Collected Poems* was the winner.

In his acceptance speech, Ellison attempted to explain his invisible man, "When I examined the rigid concepts of reality which informed a number of the works which impressed me and to which I owed a great deal, I was forced to conclude that for me and for so many hundreds of thousands of Americans, reality was simply far more mysterious and uncertain, and at the same time more exciting, and still, despite its raw violence and capriciousness, more promising."[8]

Ellison tried to reduce his conceived purpose of *Invisible Man* to simplest terms:

> We are fortunate as American writers in that with our variety of racial and national traditions, idioms, and manners, we are yet one. On its profoundest level American experience is of a whole. Its truth lies in its diversity and swiftness of change. Through forging forms of the novel worthy of it, we achieve not only the promise of our lives, but we anticipate the resolution of those world problems of humanity which for a moment

seem to those who are in awe of statistics completely insoluble.

Whenever we as Americans have faced serious crises we have returned to fundamentals; this, in brief, is what I have tried to do.[9]

Ellison told the glittering New York City audience why he chose a "rich babel of idiomatic expression" to tell the story of his nameless narrator. He said, "Our speech I found resounding with an alive language swirling with over three hundred years of American living, a mixture of the folk, the Biblical, the scientific, and the political. Slangy in one stance, academic in another, loaded poetically with imagery at one moment, mathematically bare of imagery in the next."[10]

When Ellison's picture appeared in the newspaper with the other book award winners, his friend, Murray, wrote, "Boy, I got a hell of a charge out of seeing you standing there in the picture with DeVoto and MacLeish."[11]

With the $1,000 cash prize for winning the National Book Award, Ellison and Fanny were able to move into a much nicer apartment on Riverside Drive, facing the Hudson River. In March, 1953, Ellison traveled to the South for the first time since the release of *Invisible Man*. He was the keynote speaker at the Bennett College Homemaking Institute in Winston-Salem, North Carolina, where he met numerous cousins and heard a story about his grandfather standing up in the streets of South Carolina and talking "a mob of mad crackers out of lynching one of his friends."[12]

Ellison was shocked back to his roots when he spoke at Vespers at Bennett. Dressed in a black robe, the organ blasted his arrival. He wrote, "My past hit me like a ton of bricks. I know all the hymns, and the whole order of service and in spite of everything the emotions started striking past my defenses, not a religious emotion, but that of *remembering religious feelings*...Once I heard my voice, it was as sad and gloomy a voice as I've ever heard; and I knew then why even the most sincere preacher must depend upon rhetoric, raw communication between the shaman and the group to which he's spiritually committed is just too overpowering. Without the art the emotion would split him apart."[13]

In July of 1953, Ellison returned home to Oklahoma City, his first visit to the world of his childhood since his college days at Tuskegee. For eight days he visited with long missed friends such as Jimmy Stewart, who promised to bring barbecue to Ellison on his frequent trips to New York City as a new member of the national board of the National Association for the Advancement of Colored People (NAACP).

Ellison's reception in his hometown was a grand affair. He thought the visit was "good medicine, as warm a return home as ever I've had."[14] Ellison described the charismatic journey home in a letter to Albert Murray:

> Not only were most people glad to see me and buddies now from way back, having bitten the nipples on the same breasts and bottles together, and shared the same adventures and loves and hates, they all wanted to tell me what kind of guy I was and the good things they predicted for me. And there were newspaper stories and receptions given by the city libraries, with some of the Negro clubs participating. And there were all the old teachers who many a rough day ago had wished me not only dead, but thronged with worms, now taking credit for having made me what I am today—whatever the hell that is![15]

Ellison found that Oklahoma City had expanded tremendously with blacks living all over town. He mused, "Well today Mose is living within spitting distance of the capital and the white folks are accepting our presence with a certain amount of grace."[16]

One of the highlights of his trip was a Sunday morning breakfast hosted by the Randolph-Slaughter-Rohne clan, the "family" from which he had become estranged as a teenager when one of the wives had accused her husband of being Ellison's father. Ellison recalled the breakfast, "There were some twenty of us, including several lively children, and we ate tons of chicken and drank gallons of coffee and just played havoc with the hot biscuits and looked over old photographs and relived old times well into the afternoon."[17] Of course, Ellison missed his mother and father, remembering every haunting, yet loving detail of their influence on his life.

Upon his return to Harlem, Ellison wrote a poem called "Deep Second," possibly because his extended family in Oklahoma City had told him his father always wanted him to be a poet—thus the name, Raldo Waldo Ellison. In the poem, Ellison wrote of the new Oklahoma City, in the shadow of the old town:

>...*Even in this Now, where derricks rise and engines throb upon our playing fields*
>
>*And young girls laugh and glide within the room wherein my father died*
>
>*And where my mother learned the grave transcendence of her pain—*
>
>*Would make their heroes and world-makers and world-lovers,*
>
>*And teach them the secret of that limping walk, that look of eye,*

A CLASSIC   **237**

That tilt of chin, the world-passion behind that old black-alley song
Which sings through my speech more imperious than trumpets or blue train sounds—
Yes, would heal the sick of heart and raise the dead of spirit
    And tell them a story
    Of their promise
    And their glory.
    Would sing them a song
    All cluttered with my love and regret
    And my forgiveness
    And tell them how the flurrying of their living shaped
    Time past and present into a dream
    And how they live in me
    And I in them.[18]

Professor in Residence

CHAPTER 17

> *I am a writer who sometimes teaches.*
>
> —RALPH ELLISON

The popularity of *Invisible Man* made it much easier for Ellison to have his essays and writings published in the 1950s. In late 1953, his essay, "Twentieth-Century Fiction and the Black Mask of Humanity," appeared in *Confluence*. Ellison tackled the complex and sensitive allegation that fiction written by whites left out the stories of Negroes as part of the American experience. Ellison wrote:

> Thus on the moral level I propose that we view the whole of American life as a drama acted out upon the body of a Negro giant, who, lying trussed up like Gulliver, forms the stage and the scene upon which and within which the action unfolds. If we examine the beginning of the Colonies, the application of this view is not, in its economic connotations at least, too far-fetched or too difficult to see. For then the Negro's body was exploited as amorally as the soil and the climate. It

was later, when white men drew up a plan for a democratic way of life, that the Negro began slowly to exert an influence upon America's moral consciousness.[1]

Ellison returned to his homeland—Oklahoma—sooner than expected. In October of 1953, he returned to Oklahoma City for the funeral of a cousin. From Monday to Friday, he spent time with his family. He felt rootless and frustrated, writing Albert Murray, "I was living in that earlier time, living in that old house where my cousin lived when we were young, hearing the old rain in the night, the old thunder, the old lightning, and in the morning the hens sang soft beneath my window."[2]

In a soul-searching letter, he talked of lecturing at Antioch College at Yellow Springs, Ohio, and going to see his mother's grave in Ohio. He said, "Perhaps this has been my life's pattern: Death, hunger, hunting, and death. If so, then I'll be true to the pattern."[3]

In 1954, Ellison published his short story, "Did You Ever Dream Lucky?" He also lectured in Germany and at the Salzburg Seminar in Austria and began making notes for a new novel. "I'm in my old agony again trying to write a novel," he wrote Murray, "I've got some ideas that excite me and a few scenes and characters, but the rest is coming like my first pair of long pants—slow as hell."[4]

Ellison was awarded the Prix de Rome by the American Academy of Arts and Letters in 1955. The prize financed a year's residency in the Italian capital. He and Fanny packed up their belongings in New York City, stored a few non-essentials,

In the 1940s, Ellison struck up a friendship with writer Albert Murray. Their letters were the focus of a book published a half century later after Ellison's death. Ellison took this 1947 photograph of Albert and Mozelle Murray and their daughter, Michele. *Courtesy Fanny Ellison.*

and headed to Italy aboard the ocean liner, *Constitution*. After stops in Spain, France, and Genoa, Italy, they landed at Naples and drove by car to Rome.

In Rome, they lived in a huge villa on Janiculine Hill with other Rome Fellows and Fulbright Scholars. He and Fanny

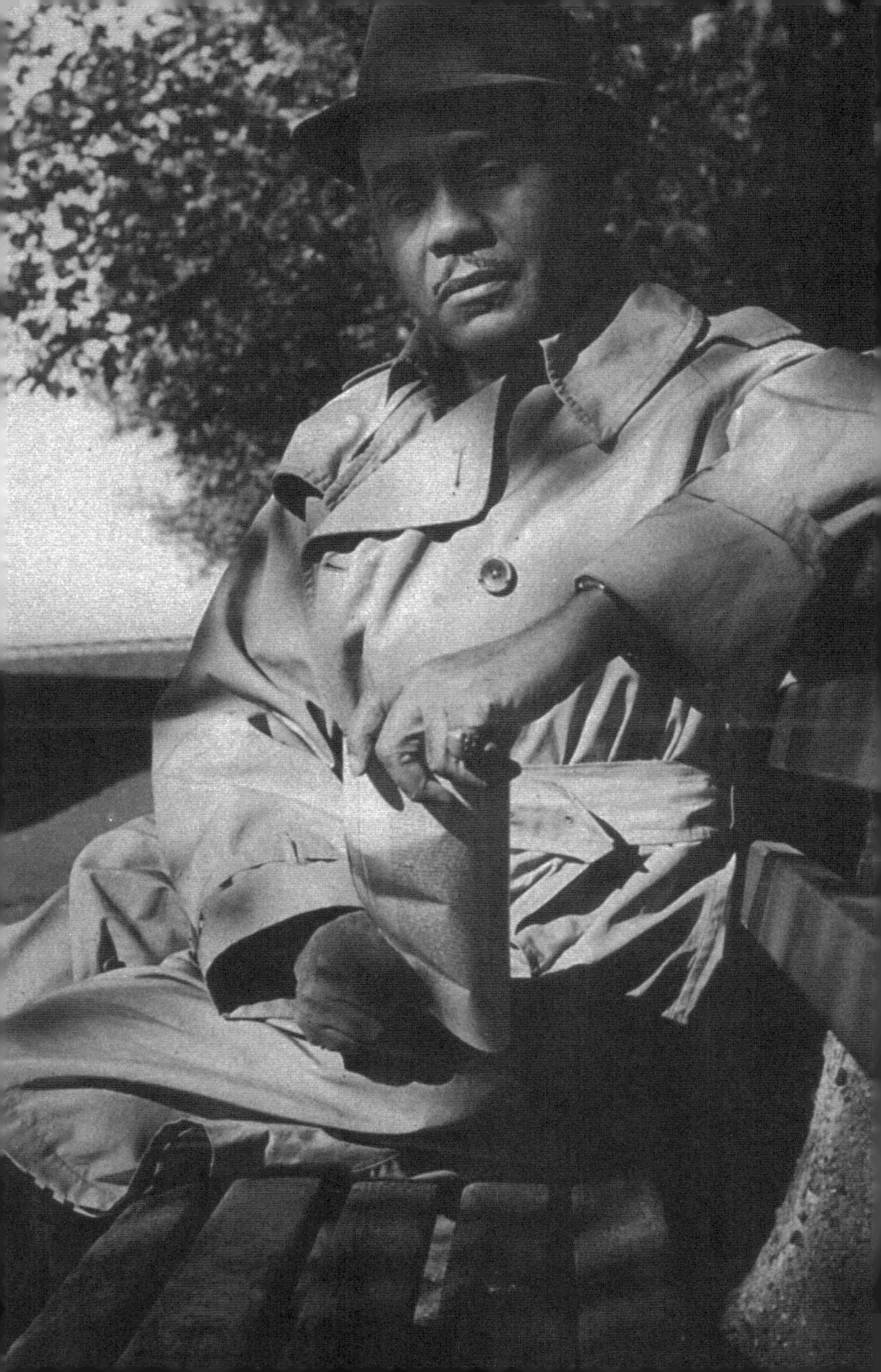

Ellison was home at his typewriter whether in Harlem or in Rome. However, when other authors were intrigued with living abroad, Ellison longed for home. He loved his country and sparred with magazines that tried to accuse him of wanting to live in foreign countries. *Courtesy Oklahoma County Metropolitan Library System.*

had a bedroom and a living room and a study in a one room cottage built against the old Aurelian Wall that surrounded the estate. His window faced the garden from which they harvested flowers and vegetables. He read constantly and listened to jazz tapes sent him by his friend Murray who was on active duty in the United States Air Force in Casablanca, Morrocco.[5]

While Ellison read and prepared for lectures, Fanny saw the sights of the Eternal City. Ellison cut his own hair, looked for unique restaurants, and did everything he could to avoid working on his new novel.

By January of 1956, he was tired of Rome. After Fanny had experienced an attack of appendicitis and he spent eight days in bed with bronchial pneumonia, he wrote Murray, "Right now, as far as I'm concerned they can give Rome back to the Etruscans. This whole joint is like a hospital most of the time. Americans don't seem to get the same energy from the food here and I'm told that it takes just about a year to adjust to the dampness of the climate and the germs that fill the air from the constant pissing on the streets, monuments, churches, cars, and anything else these studs can lean on and direct a stream against…The best of Rome remains in the past…"[6]

Ellison encountered very few blacks in Rome. He missed their camaraderie and more importantly, their food. "I'm homesick for some moses for one thing," he said, "and I got no way to get any corn bread and these Romans think a chittling is something to stuff a sausage into. There is very little

PROFESSOR IN RESIDENCE

whiskey I can afford, no sweet potatoes or yellow yams, a biscuit is unheard of…and their greens don't taste like greens."[7]

Fanny did find a source for pigs feet in Rome. However, Ellison could not complete his culinary project of preparing the delicacy because Fanny could not locate pickling spice in the Italian city. He refused to cook the pigs feet and spent the next day looking from shop to shop for pickling spice. He was shown everything from tomato paste to embalming fluid. Exasperated, he cooked the pigs feet in the spices available but threw most of them out. He said, "They weren't right!"[8]

Ellison wrote both fiction and critical prose while in Rome. Pieces included "Society, Morality and the Novel," written for *The Living Novel*, and "Living with Music," published in *High Fidelity* in December of 1955.

At the end of his first year in Rome, Ellison signed on for another 12 months of paid writing time. He and Fanny traveled to all points of Italy. He lectured in Paris, France, and Mexico, and returned to Harlem for a month to catch up on dental work and check out his apartment that had been abandoned by a renter. "She made a pig sty of the apartment," he reported to Murray, "Not only were things broken but she didn't replace a single light bulb…or dust a single piece of furniture."[9]

Occasionally, Ellison returned to his novel—struggling with organization and development of characters. When Fanny returned to Harlem and her job, Ellison was lonely. He wrote Murray that he was the only person he corresponded with on a regular basis. He said, "I tend to push people away from me and I don't want to waste time with unessentials."[10]

In November of 1957, Ellison returned to New York City, "dead tired, broke, and scrambled up inside."[11] He had spent two years in Rome but made little progress on his new novel.

However, he completed writing his response to Stanley Hyman's paper on black American writing, published as "Change the Joke and Slip the Yoke" in *Partisan Review*.

While in Rome, Ellison had been offered various teaching positions at American universities. He turned down $6,500 annually and academic status to teach literature at Brandeis University in Waltham, Massachusetts. However, he was intrigued by an offer to teach at Bard College at Annandale-on-Hudson, New York. In the fall of 1958, he began three years of teaching at Bard.

Bard College was founded in 1860 as St. Stephen's College by the leadership of the New York Episcopal church. In 1928, St. Stephen's became an undergraduate school of Columbia University and its name was charged to Bard College in 1934. Ellison joined other prominent intellectuals and writers on the Bard faculty—including Mary McCarthy, A.J. Ayer, F.W. Dupee, Franco Modigliania, Anthony Hecht, Dwight Macdonald, and Saul Bellow.[12]

For awhile, the Ellisons lived with the Bellows in a spooky house in Tivoli, New York, with the Catskill Mountains on the western horizon and the Hudson River in between. The house was two miles from Bard College. Fanny spent most of her time in Harlem where she was chief fundraiser for Gordon S. Seagrave, the Burma surgeon. Regularly, Fannie arrived from the city on Friday afternoon and returned to their New York apartment on Sunday afternoon.[13]

Bellow and Ellison, both being professional writers and leaning toward solitary times, often went days without speaking to each other, even though they lived in the same rambling house known as the Larrabee farm. They met each morning in the kitchen for breakfast—Ellison usually arrived in a Joseph's coat of many colors, a dressing gown from

Africa. While waiting for his coffee to brew, he engaged in a strange exercise. Bellow remembered, "He would occasionally massage his nose so strongly that you hear the crack of the cartilage. Perhaps the object was to expel the sleep from his face. I never asked him why it was only in the morning that he did it."[14]

When Ellison was not writing or preparing for his classes at Bard, he watered his African violets with a turkey baster or tinkered with his Chrysler engine in the driveway. Sometimes, he walked in the solitary woods behind the house with his black Labrador retriever.[15]

Ellison subjected himself to the discipline of isolation, did his own house work and laundry, and played around with French cooking "so as not to lapse into eating out of cans." He even made desserts and had wine for his meals that he ate alone.[16]

Ellison publicly read sections from his new novel to students at Bard. On one occasion, he reported to Murray, "at the end of two hours they were still in a trance." Old Hickman [the principal character in the novel that was published after Ellison's death as *Juneteenth*] had them, man...You would have laughed your ass off to see that old down home Moses rhetoric work."[17]

Ellison was a popular teacher at Bard but he expected much from his students. He said, "I wasn't nice at all. I hit them with their ignorance of the experience and their easy smugness towards the South, then tried to shake some of the shit out of their vague and inflated notions concerning the superiority of European fiction. I must say they took it well enough—once they found that they couldn't out argue me, and following the last class they caucused at the rear of the room then called my attention to something they'd written on the blackboard: "*You Were Right About the Damned Civil War.*"[18] Ellison's courses on American literature and the Russian novel were among the most popular electives on the Bard campus.

On Wednesday nights after teaching all day, Ellison sometimes ate dinner at a local bar where he had a few drinks and danced with the students. However, he was disappointed with the "mild swing" emanating from the jukebox. He remembered, "It's a sad substitute for the real thing and a real whiff of downhome funk would explode the joint."[19]

Ellison began writing magazine articles about jazz, beginning with a lengthy piece about the origin of bebop, "The Golden Age, Time Past," for a special jazz issue of *Esquire* in the spring of 1959.

He also wrote two articles for *Saturday Review* in 1958 which returned him to his childhood in Oklahoma City. In May, the magazine published "The Charlie Christian Story," with Ellison remembering the heart-warming days on Deep Deuce when Christian revolutionized the jazz guitar.

In July, "Remembering Jimmy," an article about the famous Oklahoma City blues singer, Jimmy Rushing, appeared in *Saturday Review*. Citing a recent renewal of interest in Rushing, especially in Europe, Ellison wrote, "Certainly this collection of discs will make us aware that the abiding moods expressed in our most vital popular art form are not simply a matter of entertainment; they also tell us who and where we are."[20]

After Ellison was enthralled with Mahalia Jackson at the Newport, Rhode Island, Jazz Festival in 1958, he wrote another article for *Saturday Review*, "As the Spirit Moves Mahalia." He described hearing the legendary gospel music artist at Newport:

Only the fortunate few who braved the Sunday-morning rain to attend the Afro-American Episcopal Church services heard Mahalia at her best...Many had doubtless been absent from church or synagogue for years, but here they saw her in her proper setting and the venture into the strangeness of the Negro church was worth the visit. Here they could see, to the extent we can visualize such a thing, the world which Mahalia summons up with her voice, the spiritual reality which infuses her song. Here it could be seen that the true function of her singing is not simply to entertain, but to prepare the congregation for the minister's message, to make it receptive to the spirit, and with effects of voice and rhythm to evoke a shared community of experience.[21]

By 1960, Ellison's new novel was far enough along for him to edit several episodes into a sequence called "And Hickman Arrives," published in *Noble Savage*, a new literary journal edited by Saul Bellow.

Ellison was pursued by English department heads at several colleges and universities. After carefully reviewing several offers, he accepted the post as Alexander White Visiting Professor at the University of Chicago in 1961. The following year he moved on to Rutgers University, the State University of New Jersey, as Visiting Professor of Writing, a position he held until 1969. He also was a Visiting Fellow of American Studies at Yale University from 1962 to 1964.

Rutgers' unique history as a colonial college was interesting to Ellison. It was chartered in 1766 as Queen's College, only the eighth institution of higher learning founded in the colonies before the revolution. It opened its door in New Brunswick with one teacher, one sophomore, and a handful of freshmen in 1771. In 1924, Rutgers assumed university status and was designated as the State University of New Jersey with campuses in Camden, Newark, and New Brunswick.[22]

Meanwhile, *Invisible Man* continued to be read and reread by the masses. John F. Callahan recalls beginning to read a friend's copy of the classic at eight or nine one night during his undergraduate days at Holy Cross College in 1960. He said, "I stayed up all night reading. When it was time to go to Latin class the next morning, I found I couldn't put it down. I just kept reading it."[23]

Callahan's response was similar to that of thousands of others across the land. He was an Irish Catholic at Holy Cross but felt like an outsider where he was supposed to feel at home. Legions of ordinary people—black and white—saw themselves as the Invisible Man—feeling no one truly saw them.

Jeanne M. Devlin wrote, "It was as if Ellison had named some new illness. It was almost as if he had single-handedly made cons of people visible simply because he had articulated what they felt in their respective souls. And by putting reality into words, Ellison's *Invisible Man* ultimately gave these same people hope."[24]

Shadow and Act

CHAPTER 18

> *The act of writing requires a constant plunging back into the shadow of the past where time hovers ghost-like.*
>
> —RALPH ELLISON

*I*n 1964, Random House published an excellent collection of Ellison's essays, *Shadow and Act*. It was a compilation of pieces he had written over the previous 22 years in New York City, Rome, and at Rutgers. One critic proclaimed the collection as Ellison's real autobiography.

Indeed, *Shadow and Act* contained several autobiographical essays such as "Remembering Jimmy," the story of singer Jimmy Rushing, and "The Charlie Christian Story," and "Harlem is Nowhere." In the Introduction to the book, Ellison described his metamorphosis from a jazz musician to a writer and how he had agonized piecing together some of the essays. He said, "One might say that with these thin essays for wings, I was launched full flight into the dark."[1]

Ellison explained why his upbringing in Oklahoma shaped his life and his writings:

Some literary critics believed that *Shadow and Act,* a 1964 collection of essays written by Ellison, was really his autobiography. The book contained many childhood memories of Oklahoma City. *Courtesy Random House.*

> Anything and everything was to be found in the chaos of Oklahoma; thus the concept of the Renaissance Man has lurked long within the shadow of my past, and I shared it with at least a half dozen of my Negro friends. How we actually acquired it I have never learned, and since there is no true sociology of the dispersion of ideas within the American democracy, I doubt if I ever shall. Perhaps we breathed it in with the air of the Negro community of Oklahoma City, the capital of the state whose Negroes were often charged by exasperated white Texans with not knowing their "place." Perhaps we took it defiantly from one of them. Or perhaps I myself picked it up from some transplanted New Englander whose shoes I had shined of a Saturday afternoon.[2]

The essays and magazine articles in *Shadow and Act* revealed the growth of Ellison as a writer. Some of the earliest pieces reflect the attitudes of a Marxist-oriented participant of the Federal Writers Project. The later works tell of a veteran writer who has matured and is more interested in art than injustice.

However, Ellison never lost his attraction to American politics. As a youth in Oklahoma City, he kept himself abreast of the current political climate—especially as it related to the struggle for equality for blacks. As a college student at Tuskegee, he consumed the daily newspaper and read the latest of political essays in a wide range of disciplines.

In the 1960s, a time of racial and political turmoil in the United States, Ellison had his ideas on what was right for the

SHADOW AND ACT

RALPH ELLISON

people and the land. He was concerned
that many black Americans succumbed to the idea that they
were locked in their sometimes existence in poverty and
unemployment. In a September, 1963 lecture at Bank Street

College of Education at Dedham, Massachusetts, on the subject of education for culturally different children, he said:

> It does me no good to be told that I'm down on the bottom of the pile and that I have nothing with which to get out. I know better. It does me no good to be told that I have no heroes, that I have no respect for the father principle because my father is drunk. I would just say to you that there are good drunks and bad drunks. The Eskimos have sixteen or more words to describe snow because they live with snow. I have about twenty-five different words to describe Negroes because I live principally with Negroes...Let's not play these kids cheap; let's find out what they have. What do they have that is a strength? What do they have that you can approach and build a bridge upon? Education is a matter of building bridges.[3]

In 1963, Ellison was invited to the White House Festival for the Arts as a guest of President John F. Kennedy and First Lady Jacqueline Kennedy. It was "an occasion of special significance" for the musician turned writer as the grandson of slaves and as a former student of Tuskegee Institute. He recalled a similar incident in 1901 when President Theodore Roosevelt provoked a national scandal by inviting Tuskegee's founder, Booker T. Washington, to a White House dinner to celebrate an anniversary of the signing of the Emancipation Proclamation.[4]

Ellison was a faithful supporter of and believer in the policies of President Lyndon B. Johnson who was elevated to the presidency by the assassination of President Kennedy on November 22, 1963. Ellison loved to quote Johnson, "Your art is not a political weapon, yet much of what you do is profoundly political, for you seek out the common pleasures and visions, the terrors and cruelties of man's day on this planet."5

Ellison saw Johnson as sympathetic to the cause for equality and believed the President's admonition to artists to refrain from using art as a political weapon as an "expression of hope."6

Ellison's defense of Johnson and his references to the segregationist tendencies of certain intellectuals and Northern Liberals caused a few of his white friends to say he had "changed" or had sold out to the "establishment." In fact, he lost a few friends because of his mild stance.

In "The Myth of the Flawed White Southener," part of a McGraw-Hill book, *To Heal and to Build*, published in 1968, Ellison further defended Johnson's presidency. He recognized that Johnson was a political genius but stood in the shadow of his predecessor, the legendary leader of Camelot, and that Johnson must be "a man who manipulates power and involves himself in the muck and mire out of which great political parties are composed."7

Ellison praised Johnson for supporting civil rights and voting rights legislation and appointing blacks to high positions in the federal government. He said, "When all the returns are in, perhaps President Johnson will have to settle for being recognized as the greatest American President for the poor and for the Negroes."8

Practicing his advice to black Americans to be politically involved, Ellison was a member of the Committee of One Hundred, an arm of the legal defense committee of the National Association for the Advancement of Colored People (NAACP). He tried to be a good citizen. He told an interviewer in 1963, "I try to vote responsibly. I contribute whenever I can to efforts to improve things."9

Ellison split with several of the nation's civil rights leaders who preached defiance as the way to win concessions in the

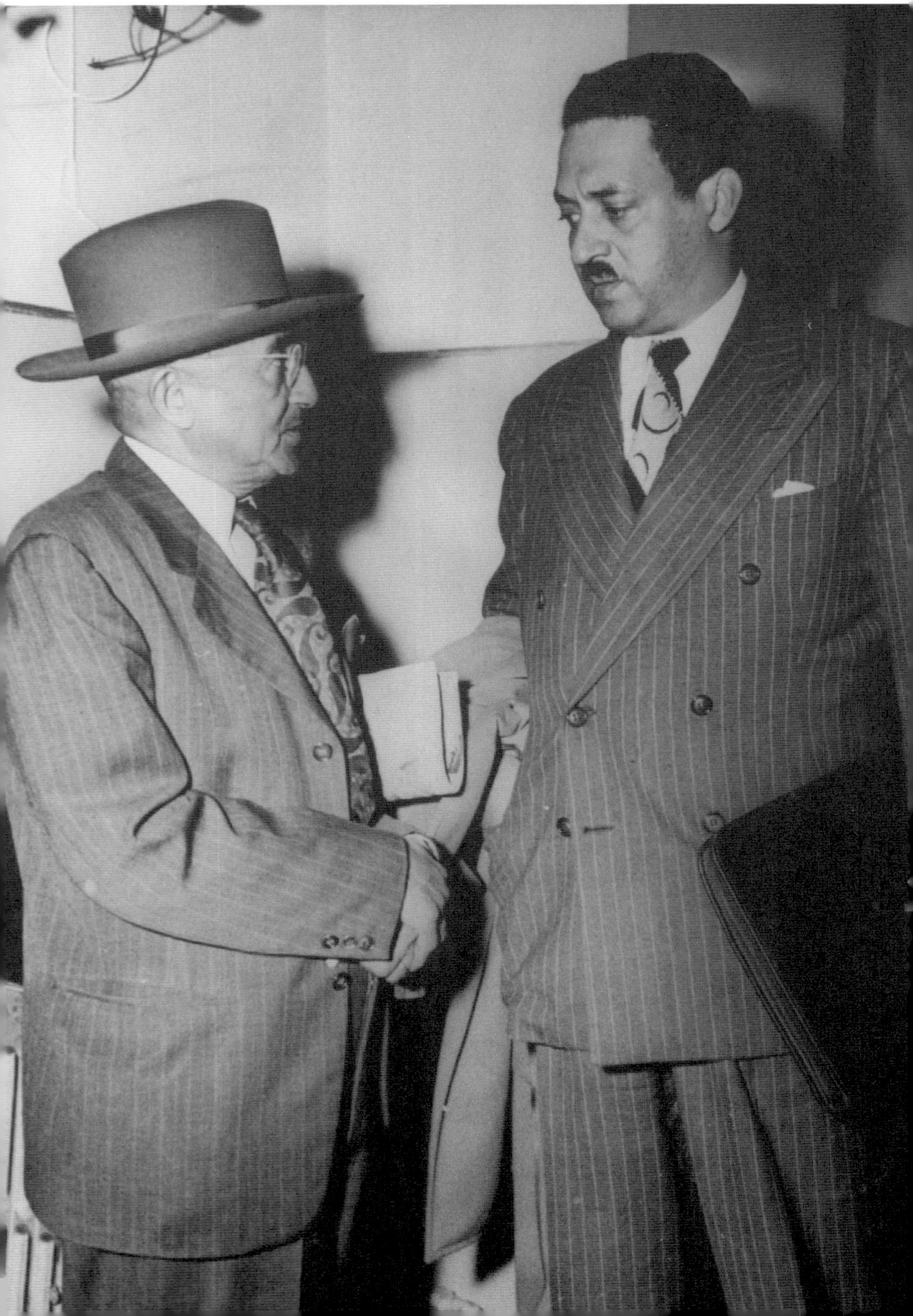

ABOVE: Ellison supported efforts in his hometown of Oklahoma City to integrate eating establishments. In this photograph, demonstrators wait at the door of Bishop's Restaurant in downtown Oklahoma City on August 5, 1960. *Courtesy Oklahoma Publishing Company.*

LEFT: Ellison faithfully kept up with civil rights struggles in Oklahoma City. He subscribed to *The Black Dispatch* which gave him a weekly update of legal and logistical battles for equal rights. In this photograph, editor Roscoe Dunjee, left, congratulates NAACP lawyer, and later United States Supreme Court Justice Thurgood Marshall, on another successful civil rights courtroom victory. *Courtesy Oklahoma Publishing Company.*

Clara Luper, left, was a civil rights activist in Oklahoma City who led the nation's first sit down demonstrations in the South in the 1960s. Ellison was proud of the fact that civil rights leaders in his hometown made a statement for equality before the sit down events began in Mississippi and Alabama. In this photograph, Luper and State Representative John White, right, led a support rally for striking sanitation workers in 1969. *Courtesy Oklahoma Publishing Company.*

struggle for equal rights. He said, "It's a more complex problem than that of simply thrusting out your chin and saying 'I'm defiant.' That's all right, but defiance has to have some real role." Ellison believed one of the big problems facing the country, especially his black people, was to prepare to take advantage of the breakdown in the old segregated system. He

A 1960s parade for civil rights in Oklahoma City. The signboard on top of the car urged lawmakers to do away with ancient laws which mandated separate waiting areas in train and bus stations for blacks and whites.
Courtesy Oklahoma Publishing Company.

thought one of the great failures of black education was its failure to prepare the black student to understand the "functioning of the larger American society."[10]

"It is not enough," Ellison said, "that the barriers to complete freedom and opportunity for black Americans go down." To an interviewer's question, "Why shouldn't the barriers go down quicker?" Ellison replied:

> I want them to go down quicker but it isn't that simple. Simply to take down a barrier doesn't make a man

free. He can only free himself and as he learns how to operate within the broader society, he learns how to detect the unwritten rules of the game...Why shouldn't it be easier for the Negro? The reason is because it's political, because there's a great deal of fear involved. Should it be changed? Yes. When? Today. The question is how.[11]

Ellison was an avowed non-violent and often avoided talking about personalities in the civil rights movement of the 1960s. He admired Martin Luther King, Jr., for "adapting a very old Negro tradition," but wondered if "once the struggle is moved from the streets into the elaborate process of politics, his [King's] framework restrains him." King's "framework" spoken of by Ellison was the civil rights leader's background as a churchman.[12]

Cautioning against black leaders who simply "ranted" against discrimination, Ellison opined, "This is still a racist society; but just recognizing this and having the ability to bring crowds into the street is no guarantee that a leader will know how to guide his followers or that he has any real power. Real power comes from the master of political technique."[13] One example of an effective leader, in Ellison's eye, was Harlem black Congressman Adam Clayton Powell.

Ellison's mild ideas and call for political, rather than rhetorical leadership in black America, sometimes caused him to be called "Uncle Tom." He cast off the aspersions to his loyalty to his race. Leon Forrest observed, "Ralph Ellison is one of the most river-deep militant race men I have ever met. His very soul is anchored to black pride and excellence. He is as likely to use the word 'Negro' as "black.' Yet his pride-filled pronunciation for the Afro-American is Nee-GROW."[14]

"I am novelist, not an activist," Ellison often replied to critics, "but I think that no one who reads what I write or who listens to my lectures can doubt that I am enlisted in the freedom movement."[15] Ellison believed in integration—but integration without surrendering the unique identity of blacks as a people.

As a highly visible American writer, Ellison was sought after for book reviews, lectures, speeches, and appointment to boards and commissions. In the 1960s he became a charter member of the National Council of the Arts, was named to the Carnegie Commission on Educational Television, was vice president of the National Institute of Arts and Letters, received an Honorary Doctorate degree from Rutgers

In August, 1966, Ellison testified about racial problems in America's big cities before a United States Senate subcommittee in Washington, D.C. He was one of the first to call for the rebuilding of the nation's ghettoes. *Courtesy Oklahoma County Metropolitan Library System.*

University, and honorary degrees from the University of Michigan and Grinnell College.

He even was asked to testify as an expert on urban problems before a United States Senate subcommittee. He said there was a crisis in American cities and lawmakers would be making a mistake if they believed blacks wanted to simply break out of Harlem and other black ghettos. "They want to transform it," he said, "into the Harlems of their country."[16]

Ellison's voice was an early call to rebuild the inner cities of America. He told Senators, "These places are precious to them. These places are where they have dreamed, where they have lived, where they have loved, where they have worked out life as they could…A slum like Harlem isn't just a place of decay. It is a form of historical and social memory."[17]

Ellison's closest friends in the 1960s were spread out over the globe—Albert Murray in Harlem, Stanley Hyman in Vermont, Robert Penn Warren in France, and Jimmy Rushing in Queens, New York. His frequent visits with Rushing, the singer he idolized on childhood nights overhearing the happenings on Deep Deuce, kept him close to his Oklahoma roots. Over a drink, the two would discuss the latest in jazz and belly laugh when they recalled the characters of Deep Deuce.

Ellison and his wife lived in an eighth-floor apartment on Riverside Drive. From his window, he often used high-powered binoculars to watch boys playing basketball in an expansive park that lay alongside a railroad track between the apartment building and the Hudson River.[18] Ellison enjoyed his place of abode. In fact, he compared it to Oklahoma City where he also lived by a river and near a park and railroad.

Ellison liked to show visitors his enormous collection of thousands of books, hundreds of photographs he had taken of his wife, friends, and children in Central Park, his collection of Kachina dolls from the Zuni and Hopi Indians, self-designed furniture, pieces of sculpture, paintings, African violets, and a mass of hi-fi equipment crammed into a closet. On a good day, Ellison would bring out some of his favorite jazz recordings and let the deep, rich sounds of the music fill the air.

Everywhere in the apartment, it seemed, there were deep drawers and filing cabinets which contained thick sheaves of notes and manuscripts on present and past writing projects. In a study just off the Ellison living room sat a huge desk covered with books, an electric typewriter, and tape recorders. There was a well-worn leatherstrap chair that Ellison used to gaze out the window at the Hudson and beyond.[19]

In 1965, *Invisible Man* was selected as the Best American Novel in the post-World War II era in a *Book Week* poll of leading American critics. The publicity surrounding the announcement of the results of the poll increased requests for Ellison to appear publicly and talk about art—and politics. By 1970, *Invisible Man* had gone through 20 paperback printings.

When not teaching classes or speaking about his works, Ellison continued the tedious process of finishing his second novel. He read sections of the work on public television and college campuses. Increasingly, there were rumors in the literary world that the National Book Award winner's new novel was imminent. Interestingly, Ellison himself contributed to the rise of rumors, sometimes promising interviewers that the book would be released shortly. Even Fanny entered the debate over the release of the book. She was overheard telling a friend, "I hear him in his study at night turning the pages and laughing to himself. I think he enjoys the book so much that he isn't in a hurry to share it with the public."[20]

Once when an interviewer, James Alan McPherson, spent an evening with Ellison in 1969, Ellison thumbed through the large manuscript of the new novel and began to read. McPherson recalled:

> He chuckles as he reads, stops to explain certain references, certain connections, certain subtle jokes about the minister whose sermon he is reading. And in those sermons his voice becomes that of a highly sophisticated black minister, merging sharp biblical images with the deep music of his voice, playing with your ears, evoking latent memories of heated southern churches and foot-stomping and fanning ladies in long white dresses, and sweating elders in the front row. And suddenly the sermons are no longer comic, and there is no writer reading from his work. You see a minister, and you feel the depth of his religion, and you are only

Lifelong friend Jimmy Stewart often brought barbecue ribs to Ellison from Oklahoma City on his frequent visits to the Apple where he served as a member of the board of directors of the NAACP. Ellison and Stewart would stay up until the wee hours of the morning discussing old times in Oklahoma City. *Courtesy Oklahoma Natural Gas Company.*

ABOVE: Ellison is honored by Oklahoma Governor Henry Bellmon in a ceremony at the State Capitol in Oklahoma City in 1963. *Courtesy Oklahoma Publishing Company.*

RIGHT: Left to right, Fanny Ellison, Ralph Ellison, and Clyde Kemery at an Oklahoma City library reception in November, 1966. *Courtesy Oklahoma Publishing Company.*

one soul in a huge congregation of wandering souls hearing him ask, over and over: "Oh Yes, Yes, Yes, Yes, Yes. Do you love, Ah Do you love?[21]

One good reason that the novel was not published in the 1960s came from the fateful afternoon of November 29, 1967, when flames from a fire in his Plainfield, Massachusetts, summer home in the Berkshires destroyed more than 300 pages of the Hickman manuscript. Fanny had to be restrained from the burning home by volunteer firemen who arrived too late. She told John Callahan later, "I wish I'd been able to break the window and pull out Ralph's manuscript. I knew right where it was."[22]

Ellison had to rethink and rewrite much of the story that had occupied his writing effort over the previous decade. Three more excerpts from the novel appeared in print as short stories in the 1960s—"The Roof, the Steeple, and the People," "Juneteenth," and "Night-Talk."

Taking the High Road

CHAPTER 19

> He was the first black American writer to be taken seriously by critics.
>
> —JOHN O'BRIEN

*I*n 1969, Ellison received the highest award an American president can bestow on a citizen—the Medal of Freedom. In a gala ceremony at the White House, Ellison and Fanny, dressed "to the nines," were wined and dined by President Lyndon Johnson and First Lady Ladybird Johnson.

The year 1970 was a watershed year in Ellison's career. More awards came his way, including the Chevalier de L'Ordre des Artes et Lettres, presented by Andre Malraux, Minister of Cultural Affairs in France. He received an honorary doctorate from Williams College in Williamstown, Massachusetts, and published "A Song of Innocence" in *Iowa Review*. And, he became Albert Schweitzer Professor of the Humanities at New York University (NYU) in New York City.

Founded in 1831, NYU is one of the nation's largest private universities. One of its original faculty members was inventor

Samuel F. B. Morse. The university is spread out over six major centers in Manhattan—although its center is its Washington Square campus in the heart of Greenwich Village.[1]

In April, 1970, Ellison wrote for *Time* magazine an essay titled "What America Would Be Like Without Blacks." He traced the sordid history of the notion of purging America of blacks. He quoted fellow Oklahoman and noted black historian John Hope Franklin who had proved that even the great emancipator, President Abraham Lincoln, had once suggested that blacks might be better off colonized and separate from whites in the United States.[2]

Ellison toyed with the idea of what America would have been like had not slaves ever been brought to work on Southern plantations. He slammed a recent writing of Daniel Patrick Moynihan, who insisted that the American melting pot did not melt because our white ethnic groups had resisted all assimilative forces that appear to threaten their identities. Instead, Ellison, wrote, "The problem is that few Americans know who and what they really are."[3]

Ellison believed that without the presence of blacks, America's political history would not be the same. He said, "No slave economy, no Civil War, no violent destruction of the Reconstruction, no Ku Klux Klan, and no Jim Crow system. And without the disenfranchisement of black Americans and the manipulation of racial fears and prejudices, the disproportionate impact of white Southern politicians upon our domestic and foreign polices would have been impossible."[4]

Ellison became friends with librarian Hannah Atkins of Oklahoma City. Atkins later became the first black woman to serve in the Oklahoma legislature and was appointed Oklahoma Secretary of State. *Courtesy Oklahoma Publishing Company.*

In the 1970s, Ellison continued to receive honorary doctorate degrees—from Adelphi University in Garden City, New York, Long Island University in Brentwood, New York, The College of William and Mary in Fairfax, Virginia, Harvard University, Wake Forest College in Winston-Salem, North Carolina, Bard College, and Wesleyan University in Middletown, Connecticut—quite an accomplishment for a man who liked to brag he was a college dropout.

He was vice president of the National Institute of Arts and Letters; a member of New York's Century Club and the American Academy of Arts and Sciences; and a trustee of the John F. Kennedy Center for the Performing Arts in Washington, D.C.

In 1972, John K. Crane and Daniel Walden of Pennsylvania State University in State College, Pennsylvania, conducted a survey of leading American critics. The result—*Invisible Man* was named as the "most likely to endure" of the two dozen or so novels published between 1945 and 1972.

The following year, Ellison published "Cadillac Flambe," a section of his novel-in-progress. However, when pressed by interviewers about the publication date for the entire novel, he simply said, "I don't know."

During the 1960s and 1970s, Ellison delivered a number of commencement addresses. At William and Mary in 1972, he challenged graduates to make their mark of change on the future:

> We do not bury the past, because it is within us. But we do modify the past as we live our own lives. And because of this we are now able to resuscitate in all its boldness, and with great sophistication, that conscious and conscientious concern for others which is the essence of the American ideal. I would remind you, however, that we are a nation that plays it by ear. We are inventive both

in creating sublime visions and in copping out on them. These too are part of the human response.[5]

Oklahoma City black newspaper editor Roscoe Dunjee was the subject of a speech that Ellison delivered to the 1972 Black Perspective Conference in New York City. Ellison confessed his debt to Dunjee who influenced him long before he ever thought about being a writer. He recalled his days of peddling *The Black Dispatch* on foot and from his bicycle, remembering, "We shouted their headlines through the black community for hours until we had either lost our voices or had all the money we could make."[6]

Ellison heaped praise on his childhood hero, Dunjee:

> Roscoe Dunjee understood what it has taken me many years to understand. He understood that not only were the American people a revolutionary people, but that in the shedding of blood, the sacrifice, the agony, and anguish of establishing this nation, all Americans became bound in a covenant. [He] was a constitutionalist…and launched sit-ins before they occurred in North Carolina…From the beginning he understood intuitively and consciously that the English language had to be made our own before we could unlock the secret of other Americans, before we could understand how we were different from Englishmen or Europeans, before we could come to grips with the new possibilities or individualism in those sermons preached by Thoreau, Emerson, and yes, by Melville and Hawthorne.[7]

Ellison wrote an essay in 1974 for the United States Bicentennial Society, in preparation for the 200th birthday of the nation in 1976. His essay was about a slave and little known hero of the American Revolution, James Armistead Lafayette. Born as James Armistead, the black spy took the name of the Frenchman, Marquis de Lafayette, to whom Armistead was assigned by his black master during the Revolutionary War.

In 1975, Ellison was elected to the American Academy of Arts and Letters and received news from his hometown that the Oklahoma County Libraries System wanted to place his name on a branch library on Northeast 23rd Street. Ellison was overwhelmed. When a reporter asked him his reaction, he said, "My God! I'm very flattered, but it's a terrible burden being put on my poor name."[8] Ellison later called the naming of the library for him one of the greatest honors of his life.

The honor for Ellison was not without controversy. The City Council of Oklahoma City officially adopted the name after an emotional plea from Ellison's longtime friend Jimmy Stewart. Minister Theodore G.X., who had suggested the name of Elijah Muhammed for the library, agreed to the Ellison name "in the interest of solidarity in the black community." The city council vote was 6-1—one white city councilman, Nelson Keller, opposed Ellison's name gracing the new library because he understood that *Invisible Man* was not suited for reading by children.[9]

The Ralph Ellison Library was dedicated on June 21, 1975. Oklahoma City Mayor Patience Latting, State Representative Hannah Atkins, and former Oklahoma City City Councilman A.L. Dowell presided over the ceremonies at the sparkling new facility that housed 40,000 volumes.

Ellison and his wife, Fanny, shook hands with many of the crowd of 400 that saw the unveiling of a bronze sculpture of

Ellison, in a moment of reflection, during the dedication of the library named for him in Oklahoma City in 1975. Beside him is Hannah Atkins. *Courtesy Oklahoma Publishing Company.*

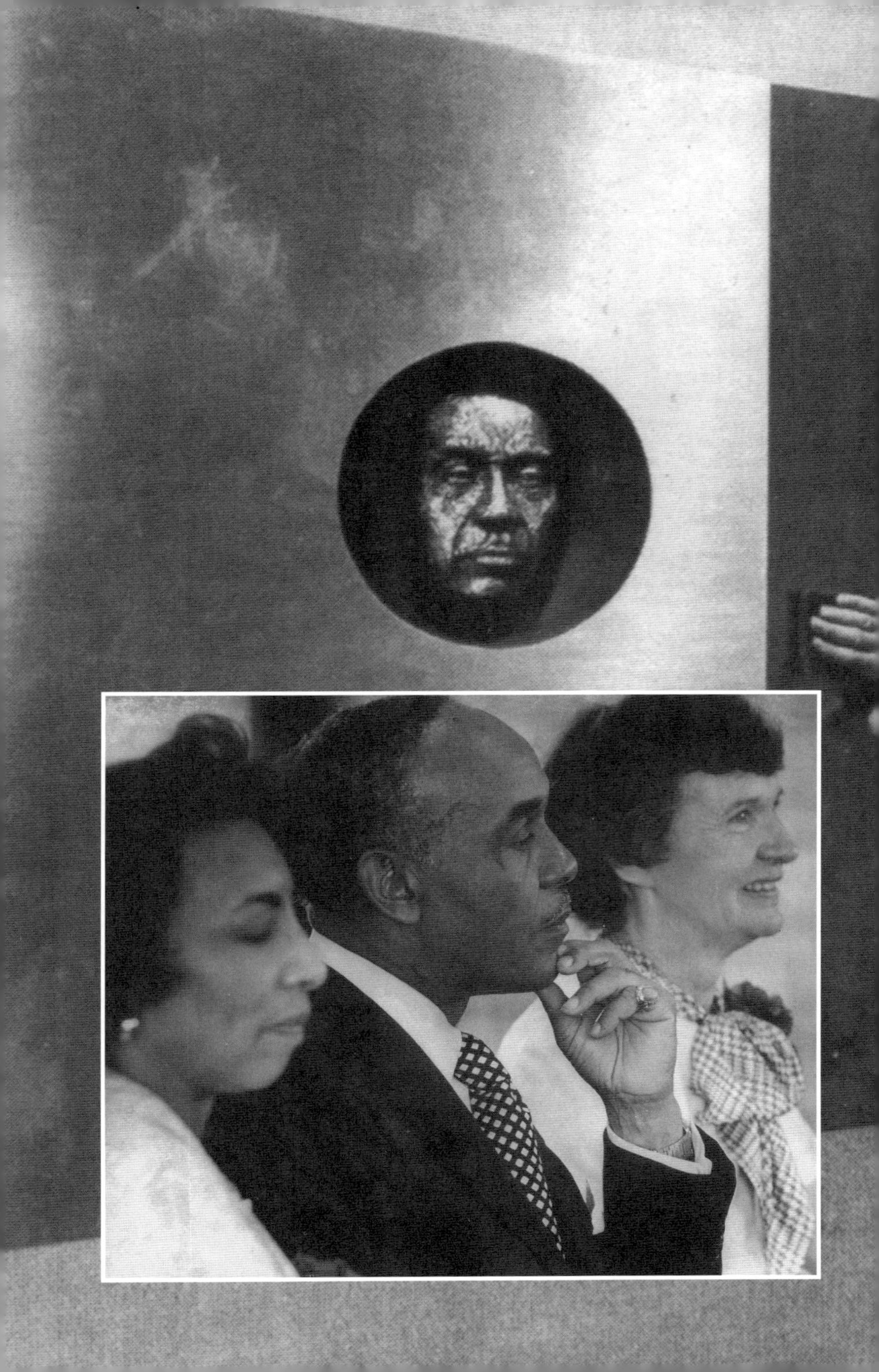

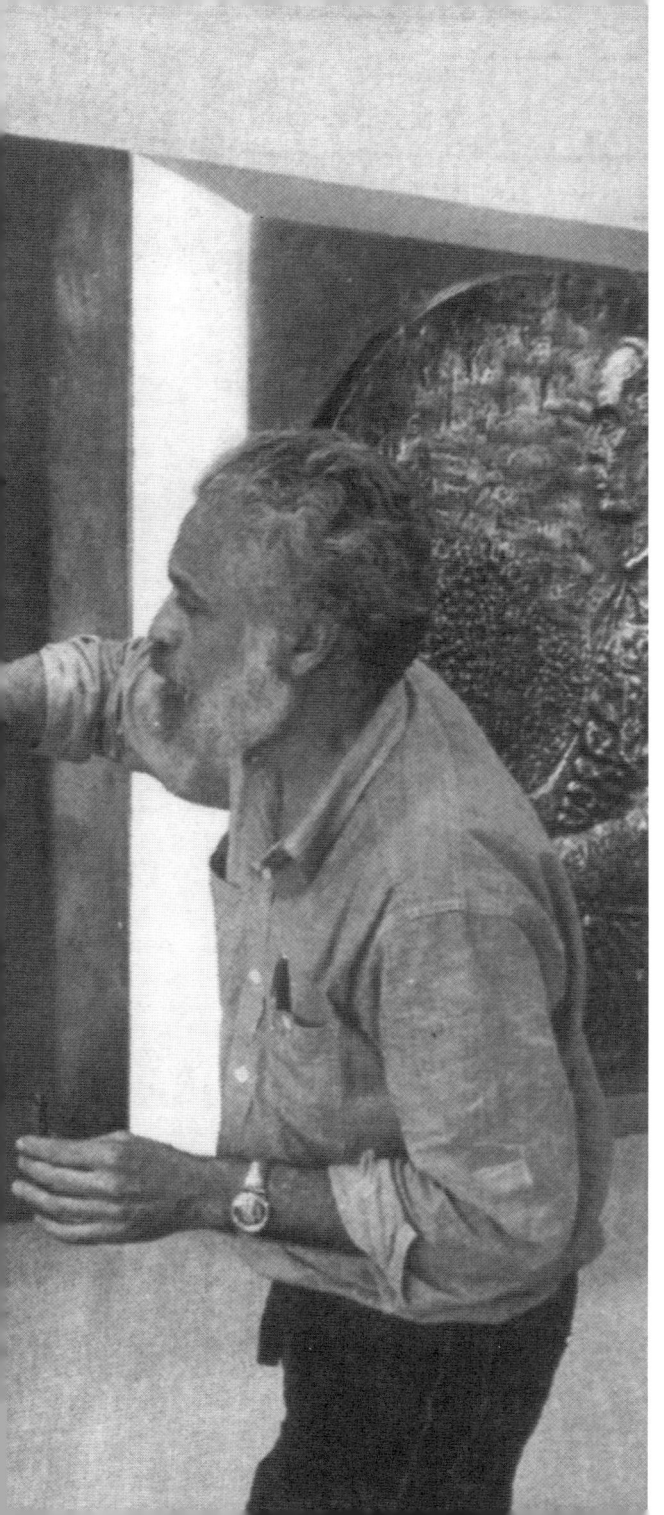

LEFT: New York sculptor Edward Wilson polishes his stainless steel and bronze sculpture of Ellison in time for the dedication of the Ralph Ellison Library on June 21, 1975. *Courtesy Oklahoma County Metropolitan Library System.*

INSET: Ellison, center, listens to his friends and Metropolitan Library System executive director Lee Brawner laud Ellison's contributions during the 1975 dedication ceremony of the Ralph Ellison Library. At left is State Representative Hannah Atkins. At right is Oklahoma City Mayor Patience Latting. *Courtesy Oklahoma Publishing Company.*

The Ellison Library sign at the corner of Northeast 23rd Street and Martin Luther King, Jr. Avenue in northeast Oklahoma City. *Courtesy Eric Dabney.*

Ellison, completed by Edward N. Wilson, a friend of Ellison and professor of art at New York State University.

When handed the microphone, Ellison told of the Catholic priest and Roscoe Dunjee who had done so much to make possible a library for black children of Oklahoma City. He applauded the original librarian, Athena Young, and those who followed her, for transforming young lives, quickening imaginations, and broadening the perspective of young blacks like him.[10]

Ellison looked to the future, "I have no doubts that within these walls, other writers—black, white, Indian—will emerge. And if so, it will be because the library is a place where a child or an adult can make a connection between the rich oral tradition which we have inherited from the past."[11]

284 RALPH ELLISON: A BIOGRAPHY

In 1977, John F. Callahan wrote a paper, "Historic Frequencies of Ralph Waldo Ellison," arguing that the essays of Ellison were a roadmap to understand *Invisible Man* and American literature in general. After the paper was published in a journal, Callahan boldly decided to send a copy to Ellison. Two months later, Callahan received a single-spaced letter back. After praising the essay, Ellison concluded the letter:

> *Dear Mr. Callahan, I really liked your piece…if you should ever be in New York, Mrs. Ellison and I would be glad to see you…*[12]

A few months later, Callahan took Ellison up on his offer. He appeared late one afternoon at the Ellison apartment on the West Side of Manhattan and sat in the presence of the literary master for an hour. When Callahan felt to the need to leave, Ellison slapped his hand on the table and said, "Well, John, would you like a drink?" Callahan remembered, "I needed one, so I answered right away, 'Yes, Mr. Ellison.'" Ellison gently scolded Callahan for not calling him "Ralph" and returned in a few moments from the kitchen with a bottle of Jack Daniels and a glass for himself and a bottle of Irish whiskey for Callahan.[13]

From 1977 to 1980, Ellison was Secretary of the National Institute of Arts and Letters. Upon the awarding of the group's Gold Medal for Fiction to Bernard Malamud, Ellison delivered a stirring address which portrayed his long-standing belief that American fiction and the democratic ideal were somehow connected. He said, "Not that it is the novelist's role to 'create the uncreated conscious' of his group or nation, for that was in motion long ago; rather it is to sensitize the nation's ever-floundering conscience by making us conscious of the strengths in our weaknesses and the triumphs in our failures."[14]

Ellison retired from his fulltime job as a professor at New York University in 1980 and accepted a Professor Emeritus status in 1982. He served as a trustee of the Colonial Williamsburg Foundation in Virginia and was awarded the National Medal of Arts in 1985.

In 1982, Random House published a thirtieth anniversary edition of *Invisible Man*. In a protracted introduction to the edition, Ellison explained the birth and life of the classic. In his gentle and humble manner, he looked back:

> My highest hope for the novel was that it would sell enough copies to prevent my publishers from losing their investment and my editor from having wasted time....this has always been a most willful, most self-generating novel, and the proof of this statement is witnessed by the fact that here, thirty astounding years later, it has me writing about it again.[15]

In the 1980s, Ellison continued to draft and redraft sections of his novel in progress. He liberally granted interviews to any number of publications, including *Playboy*, in 1982. After deftly rebuffing questions about when his latest novel would appear in bookstores, he was asked about President Ronald Reagan. In a scorching answer, Ellison said, "Reagan is dismantling many of the processes and structures that made it possible for me to go from sleeping on a park bench to becoming a writer. And he is assuring people, in the most cunning way, that this is good for us."[16]

Without the government's ready assistance, Ellison suggested that a key to overcome the conditions that held back

Ellison at his desk—with his typewriter, African art, and African violets in the background. The photogenic Ellison was sought after for lectures on the American novel. *Courtesy Oklahoma County Metropolitan Library System.*

young blacks with aspirations was to read, "use the libraries, move into some of the important areas of today's culture."[17]

Ellison worked with editors at Random House to publish *Going to the Territory* in 1986. It was a collection of two decades of Ellison's lectures, personal reminiscences, interviews, and essays. Nearly all the 16 pieces were written after the publication of *Shadow and Act* in 1964. The longest selection is "An Extravagance of Laughter," written especially for *Going to the Territory.*

The title to Ellison's new book came from the title he ascribed to an address delivered at the Ralph Ellison Festival at Brown University in Providence, Rhode Island, in 1979. The new collection was rich and varied, with interesting titles such as "The Myth of the Flawed White Southerner," "If the Twain Shall Meet," "Homage to Duke Ellington on His Birthday," The Novel as a Function of Democracy," and "The Little Man at Chehaw Station."

Also in 1986, Ellison returned to the city of his birth to introduce his childhood friend, Jimmy Stewart, at Stewart's induction into the Oklahoma Hall of Fame, sponsored by the Oklahoma Heritage Association.

In 1990, author Charles Johnson dedicated his acceptance speech to Ellison upon winning the National Book Award for fiction for his third novel, *Middle Passage*. In the preface to the 1994 Modern Library edition of *Invisible Man*, Johnson said, "It seemed to me the very least I could do in the presence of an elder who forged a place in American culture for the possibility of the fiction I dreamed of writing. For a man who when the global list of the most valuable authors of the twentieth century is finally composed, will be among those at the pinnacle."[18]

On Ellison's 80th birthday, on March 1, 1994, Random House hosted a private dinner for the Ellisons. After several toasts from his closest friends, Ellison rose to his feet, looked around the table, and surveyed the faces. John Callahan remembered the moment, "He came to rest on Fanny's face. His eyes met hers, hers met his, and they looked at each other for a long time. Every woman and every man should be looked at that way. 'And Fanny,' was all he said, 'Fanny.'"[19]

Ellison and his wife had a wonderful relationship—with each other—and their friends. It was always painful to them that they never had children. However, they made over the children of others, especially the younger children of friends like John Callahan.

After a painful bout with pancreatic cancer, Ellison died at his Manhattan apartment on the morning of April 16, 1994,

The program announcing a memorial service at the Ralph Ellison Library. Civil rights leader Clara Luper talked of Ellison's "celebrated life." Jesse Jackson, Jr., read a poem and Jimmy Stewart, Helen Sutton, Mary Moulder, and Darlene McLeod recalled Ellison as a student and friend. *Courtesy Oklahoma County Metropolitan Library System.*

RALPH WALDO ELLISON
"A CELEBRATION OF HIS LIFE"
1914 – 1994

WEDNESDAY
APRIL 20, 1994
11:30 A.M.

RALPH ELLISON LIBRARY
2000 N.E. 23
OKLAHOMA CITY, OKLAHOMA

the silence punctuated by the hushed voices of those present. Ellison was 80 years old.

From the literary world came messages of condolence for Fanny—and from Oklahoma, came expressions of praise. Oklahoma City civil rights leaders Clara Luper said, "We have a lost a star in the sky of achievement." Luper remembered, "*Invisible Man* had a tremendous impact on my life. It made me see that you are invisible because of the circumstances into which you are born, but that you must try to become visible to others, for them to feel you and touch you." Jimmy Stewart said, "America has lost a great writer and Oklahoma has lost one of its most important contributors to our way of life."[20]

The Oklahoma legislature, when informed of Ellison's death, stopped its regular business and passed a concurrent resolution honoring his life and his accomplishments. It would have been a proud moment for Ellison's mentor, Jefferson Davis Randolph, who, as a black man, worked in the shadow of his white brothers at the State Capitol library six decades earlier.

Stanley Crouch wrote, "When Ralph Ellison saddled up the pony of death and took that long, lonesome rode into eternity…the quality of American civilization was markedly diminished." Crouch said, "He had always traveled on a ridge above the most petty definitions of race and has given us a much richer image of ourselves as Americans, no matter how we arrived here, what we looked liked, or how we were made."[21]

Ellison's funeral service was in New York City, at Trinity Cemetery on Riverside Drive above the Hudson River in sight of the George Washington Bridge. John Callahan felt Ellison's presence so strongly at the service that surely he had "turned into a seabird now swooping in from the bridges out beyond the Statue of Liberty to explore the river."[22]

In Oklahoma City, a memorial and tribute service was held at the Ralph Ellison Library where friends and acquaintances took the podium to sing Ellison's praises. An editorial in *The Daily Oklahoman* ended with the words:

> *Ralph Ellison's achievements transcend time and circumstance.*

Indelible Ink

CHAPTER 20

> indelible (in-del'-uh-bel) adj. 1. Leaving a mark not easily erased.
>
> —WEBSTER'S DICTIONARY

Shortly after Ellison's death in 1994, Fanny asked John F. Callahan, Morgan S. Odell Professor of Humanities at Lewis and Clark College in Portland, Oregon, to become the literary executor of her late husband's estate. The idea was to comb through the mountains of Ellison's writings and notes and piece together, and publish, the unfinished novel.

Fanny walked Callahan into Ellison's vacant study. Callahan recalled:

> As if to protest his absence, the teeming bookshelves had erupted in chaos over his desk, chair, computer table, and copying machine, finally covering the floor like a blizzard of ash. Anyone else might have given up, but Fanny Ellison persevered in her efforts to do the right thing by what her husband had left behind. She

Random House published
Flying Home and Other Stories in 1996. *Courtesy Random House.*

whetted my appetite by showing me stacks of printouts, scraps of notes, jottings on old newspapers and magazine subscription cards, and several neat boxes of computer disks.[1]

The process of Callahan continuing Ellison's literary legacy had actually begun the last time he saw Ellison alive in February of 1994. Ellison was still talking about finishing his novel but was more interested in publishing a series of his short stories. He directed Callahan to what Fanny called "the little room" where files containing Ellison's life's works were stored.[2]

From the thousands of pages of material, Callahan worked with The Modern Library in New York City to publish *The Collected Essays of Ralph Ellison* in 1995. The book contained previously uncollected and newly discovered reviews along with the essay collections of *Shadow and Act* and *Going to the Territory*. Nobel Prize winner Saul Bellow wrote the preface to the book.

Later, Fanny told Callahan about a box she had discovered under the dining room table. It contained old magazines, newspaper clippings, and a brown imitation-leather folder with RALPH W. ELLISON embossed in gold letters on the front. Inside, Callahan found a manila folder labeled "Early Stories."

It was a literary treasure of stories typed on paper browned and frayed from age and beginning to crumble. Many of the stories had never been published—even Fanny was unaware of some of the writings. That cache of stories "gave impetus and shape" to a marvelous collection of stories edited by Callahan and published by Random House in 1996 as *Flying Home and Other Stories*.

Of the 13 stories in *Flying Home*, six were published for the first time. Ellison drew on early experiences—his father's death, riding the freight train to Tuskegee, and his dreams of becoming a musician. *The Washington Post* said the collection of stories approached "the simple elegance of Chekhov."[3]

According to Ellison's wishes, 140 boxes of his papers, speeches, correspondence, and photographs were given to the Library of Congress in 1996. For more than 30 years, the institution had expressed interest in the papers and had "mounted a strong effort" to get them. Even before Ellison gave his first lecture at the Library, John C. Broderick, then the Library's cultural manuscript specialist, wrote to Ellison of the Library's interest. Later, fellow Oklahoman, Daniel J. Boorstin, became the Librarian of the Library of Congress and made known to Ellison that he also was interested in the acquisition.[4]

By 1997, the general public was able to view Ellison's working library which was displayed in the Great Hall of the Jefferson Building of the Library of Congress. Today, one can access nearly 1,000 Ellison-related writings on the Library of Congress Website.

In 1998, Random House released the results of a survey of its editors of the 100 most significant novels of the twentieth century. Ellison's *Invisible Man* was 19th on the list, following *Ulysses*, by James Joyce; *The Great Gatsby*, by F. Scott Fitzgerald; and others. Interestingly, *Invisible Man* was ranked higher than works by some of Ellison's mentors and his favorite authors.

Native Son, by Richard Wright, was number 20. *Invisible Man* was ranked above such classics as *Tender is the Night*, by Fitzgerald; *Animal Farm*, by George Orwell; *As I Lay Dying*, by William Faulkner; *Lord of the Flies*, by William Golding; *The Sun Also Rises* and *A Farewell to Arms*, by Ernest Hemingway; and *The Catcher in the Rye*, by J.D. Salinger.[5]

John F. Callahan faced a monumental task of taking thousands of pages of Ellison's notes to publish *Juneteenth*, Ellison's second novel. *Courtesy Random House.*

Ellison's *Shadow and Act* appeared on a similar list of the most significant non-fiction publications of the twentieth century. Ellison was the only author who appeared on both lists.

After *Flying Home*, Callahan turned his attention to Ellison's unfinished novel, to be called *Juneteenth*, symbolic of June 19, 1865, when Union soldiers brought word to Texas of Lincoln's signing of the Emancipation Proclamation. June 19 has long been celebrated as the unofficial independence day in the black community.

It was a monumental task to sort through more than 2,000 pages of Ellison's manuscripts. There were as many as 25 different versions of a single scene. "Many times I followed the twists and turns of Ellison's plot," Callahan said, "and his characters' movements through space and time; traced and retraced their steps as they moved to Washington, D.C., south to Georgia and Alabama, southwest to Oklahoma, back again to the nation's capital."[6]

Callahan was faced to choose one of two accepted ways of posthumously completing a novel. One way was to publish the works as the author left them. That is why F. Scott Fitzgerald's *The Last Tycoon* has no ending. The other method was to allow an editor to organize the fragments and publish a completed book. Callahan, knowing that he was opening himself up to potential criticism, chose the latter way—and he did so with Fanny's blessing.

Callahan and Fanny agreed that *Juneteenth* be intended for large audiences as a single volume, unlike the multi-volume manuscript that Ellison may have intended.

Especially helpful to Callahan's completion of the novel were the thousands of notes Ellison wrote from 1952 to 1994. The notes were sometimes illegible—written on backs of envelopes, bills, or any "scrap of paper close at hand." Other notes were carefully recorded in notebooks. With no order to the notes, Callahan spent countless hours deciphering them and finding what section of the novel in progress to which they related.[7] In the end, every word in the novel was Ellison's, carefully placed in a reasonable order by Callahan.

Because Ellison had tantalized the literary world for 40 years with comments about the progress of the novel, there was much anticipation as Callahan and Random House prepared to release *Juneteenth* in 1999.

Juneteenth is the story of a New England senator, Adam Sunraider, who is mortally wounded by an assassin's bullet while making a speech on the floor of the United States Senate. From his deathbed, Sunraider summons an old black minister and friend from the past, Alonzo Hickman. Their long, complicated relationship is revealed through flashbacks and interior monologues.

Sunraider, as a child in the South known as Bliss, toured from church to church with Hickman. He was either white, or fair enough to pass for white, and was the object of the protecting hand of Hickman. At each revival service, the terrified child was placed in a small coffin and was "raised from the dead" at the moment most appropriate to impress the congregation with Hickman's theory of rebirth.

Ann DeFrange, reviewing the book for *The Daily Oklahoman*, wrote:

> Signs of the novel's history are evident in its storytelling pages. It is a work similar to pieces of art patched together and encrusted with jewels. Editor Callahan must have toiled to make a whole piece of those episodes and essays and keep their integrity. Nevertheless, plot

and continuity are fragile. Many weaknesses must be forgiven. But how easy it is to forgive. Oh, those jewels that appear throughout![8]

Also in 1999, the Independent Television Service (ITS) produced the first screen adaptation of Ellison's "King of the Bingo Game." Directed by Elise Robinson and produced by Charlie Schroder, the unusual program that had a feel of a "Twilight Zone" episode, was part of a public television series that featured dramatic adaptations of American short stories.

In a scene from the PBS adaptation of Ellison's "King of the Bingo Game," the crowd at the bingo parlor anxiously awaits the results of Sonny's fateful spin. *Courtesy Eric Gran and PBS.*

The cover of *Trading Twelves* featured photographs of both Albert Murray and Ellison. *Courtesy The Modern Library.*

Ellison's work was the second installment in the "American Storytellers" series.[9]

In 2000, The Modern Library published *Trading Twelves*, a collection of letters traded by Ellison and Albert Murray between 1950 and 1960. The book was edited by Murray and Callahan, who described the collection in its Introduction:

> The letters between Ellison and Murray are the bounty of a rare and spontaneous friendship in which each taps into the deepest experience of the other. Spanning the fifties, their correspondence chronicles a friendship at the same time that it reveals the increasing active visibility of the Negro who issued one unexpected challenge after another to the often desperate conformities and complacency of postwar America...And although Ellison and Murray were friends on many levels, their correspondence is first and foremost a literary one in which literary aspiration is nourished by a parallel, almost proprietary interest in jazz. Indeed, like jazzmen, Murray and Ellison find their rhythm with each other and hit their stride on the page gradually.[10]

Oklahoma Today magazine created a list in 2000 of the 50 most influential Oklahomans of the 20th century. Humorist Will Rogers topped the list—Ellison was number 10. In between were politicians Carl Albert and Robert S. Kerr; Olympic athlete Jim Thorpe; folk singer Woody Guthrie; aviator Wiley Post; baseball star Mickey Mantle; oilman Frank Phillips; and Governor, United States Senator, and University of Oklahoma President David L. Boren.[11]

8. FRANK PHILLIPS

"Those of us who have been more fortunate have a debt to society which I believe can best be paid by training and educating the youth of the nation."

Frank Phillips was a savvy businessman long before he founded Phillips Petroleum in Bartlesville in 1917. Born in Cherry County, Nebraska, he honed his business skills first as a barber, then as a banker. In 1905, Frank and his brother, L.E., moved to Bartlesville to begin the adventure that would lead to Phillips Petroleum, an international giant of petroleum products. Phillips could also lay claim to becoming the only white honorary chief of the Osage Indian Nation. Woolaroc, his rustic retreat in Osage County, to this day continues the work that Phillips believed was so important—teaching future generations about history and nature. When Phillips died in 1950, he was buried at Woolaroc alongside his wife Jane.

9. DAVID BOREN

"Oklahoma has given me everything. You have seasons in your life. I'm at the point in my life when I can start giving back to Oklahoma."

David Boren, a Seminole native and Rhodes scholar, has had a distinguished political career as Oklahoma governor and U.S. Senator. As the youngest governor in the nation, Boren established several education programs between 1975 and 1979, including the first state funding for gifted and talented classes, the Scholar-Leadership Enrichment Program, and the Oklahoma Summer Arts Institute. By the time he left office for the U.S. Senate, he had been called "one of America's most promising young leaders" by *Time*. In Washington, Boren led the fight for congressional campaign finance reform and for legislation discouraging abuses of power by administration and congressional staff. The 1988 *Almanac of American Politics* called him one of the five most effective members of the Senate. Since retiring from politics in 1994, Boren has served as president of his alma mater, the University of Oklahoma.

10. RALPH ELLISON

"If the word has the potency to revive and make us free, it has also the power to blind, imprison, and destroy."

Born and raised in Oklahoma City, Ralph Ellison is widely thought to have written the greatest African-American novel of the century. In 1952, he published his only finished novel, *Invisible Man*, which took an arduous seven years to write. Winner of the 1953 National Book Award, *Invisible Man* was named the nineteenth most influential novel of the century by the Modern Library Association in 1999. In 1969, Ellison received the highest civilian honor, the Medal of Freedom, by President Johnson. Last summer, *Juneteenth*, his unfinished second novel was published posthumously to widespread attention.

11. EDWARD K. GAYLORD

"We can earn respect and compel admiration if we put forth all the ability of which we are capable."

Edward "E.K." Gaylord moved to Oklahoma in 1903 determined to own his own newspaper. At 29, with a $5,000 investment, he began a publishing odyssey that would have a lasting effect on the young municipality of Oklahoma City. With fearless news judgment and keen instincts, he took *The Oklahoman* from a local publication to a national media giant during the seventy years he edited and published it. He also led the Oklahoma Publishing Company into the forefront of broadcasting, making it one of the most influential newspapers in the region. Gaylord never stopped working: at 100 years of age, he addressed a joint session of the Oklahoma legislature, and a year later he died after a full day's work at the office.

12. WILMA MANKILLER

"I believe in the old Cherokee injunction to 'be of a good mind.' Today it's called positive thinking."

The first woman Principal Chief of the Cherokee Nation, Wilma Pearl Mankiller has conquered many hardships in reaching her success. Born in

---

Oklahoma Today magazine published a list in 2000 of the 50 most influential Oklahomans of the 20th century. Humorist Will Rogers topped the list—Ellison was number 10. *Courtesy Oklahoma Today magazine.* Copyright 2000 *Oklahoma Today.*

Ellison certainly would have loved the posthumous publication of his writings on jazz in 2001. *Living With Music* was published by The Modern Library and edited by Robert G. O'Meally, the Zora Neale Hurston Professor of Comparative Literature at Columbia University. O'Meally, a leading interpreter of jazz in the American culture, selected Ellison's works on music, especially jazz, written over a 50-year period. O'Meally called Ellison "perhaps the most important jazz analyst we have."[12]

In *Living With Music*, readers relive Ellison's portraits of his heroes—Duke Ellington, Jimmy Rushing, Charlie Christian, Mahalia Jackson, and others. Also included are fictional accounts laced with jazz overtones—"Keep to the Rhythm" and "Cadillac Flambe." Finally, O'Meally presents an interview with an Oklahoma City television station that Ellison gave in 1976 and the transcript of an interview that O'Meally conducted with Ellison the same year.

In the introduction to *Living With Music*, O'Meally quotes Ellison:

> Without the presence of Negro American style, our [U.S.] jokes, tall tales, even our sports would be lacking in the sudden turns, shocks and swift changes of pace (all jazz-shaped) that serve to remind us that the world is ever unexplored, and that while a complete mastery of life is mere illusion, the real secret of the game is to make life swing.[13]

As the 21st century began, Ellison's *Invisible Man* and other writings were still considered elite in the literary world. The December 2001 issue of *Esquire* magazine listed *Invisible Man* as reason number 67 in a list of "162 Reasons It's Good To Be An American Man."

In February, 2002, "Ralph Ellison: An American Journey," was broadcast on America's public television stations. The 90-minute documentary traced Ellison's Oklahoma upbringing, his education at Tuskegee, and his development in Harlem into one of the nation's greatest literary figures. The program was punctuated by powerful recreations of scenes from *Invisible Man* that featured actor John Amos as the college

In 2002, Sony Music Entertainment, Inc., released a CD entitled "Living With Music: Ralph Ellison." The CD contained Ellison's favorite jazz, including selections from Louis Armstrong, Duke Ellington, Hot Lips Page, Mahalia Jackson, and Jimmy Rushing. It also included Ellison's lecture on jazz delivered at the Library of Congress in 1964. The recording was intended as a companion to *Living With Music*, the book. *Courtesy Sony Music Entertainment, Inc.*

RIGHT: This interesting combination of photographs appears on the back of the dust jacket of the Polish edition of *Invisible Man*. Courtesy Ralph Ellison Library.

professor and Jacques C. Smith as the Invisible Man. Nobel Laureate Toni Morrison read from *Juneteenth* and viewers saw rare archival footage and never-before-seen photographs from Ellison's family albums.

The documentary was the work of award-winning producer/director Avon Kirkland who worked closely with Fanny Ellison and John Callahan. Oklahoma City historian, Paul Lee, provided much of the research for the project.

The Polish edition of *Invisible Man*. Courtesy Ralph Ellison Library.

The tribute to Ellison was part of an elaborate celebration in 2002 of the 50th anniversary of the publication of *Invisible Man*. In his hometown of Oklahoma City, the Metropolitan Library System officially declared the entire year as a celebration to include a one-man play, the development of an interactive compact disc about Ellison, a

308 RALPH ELLISON: A BIOGRAPHY

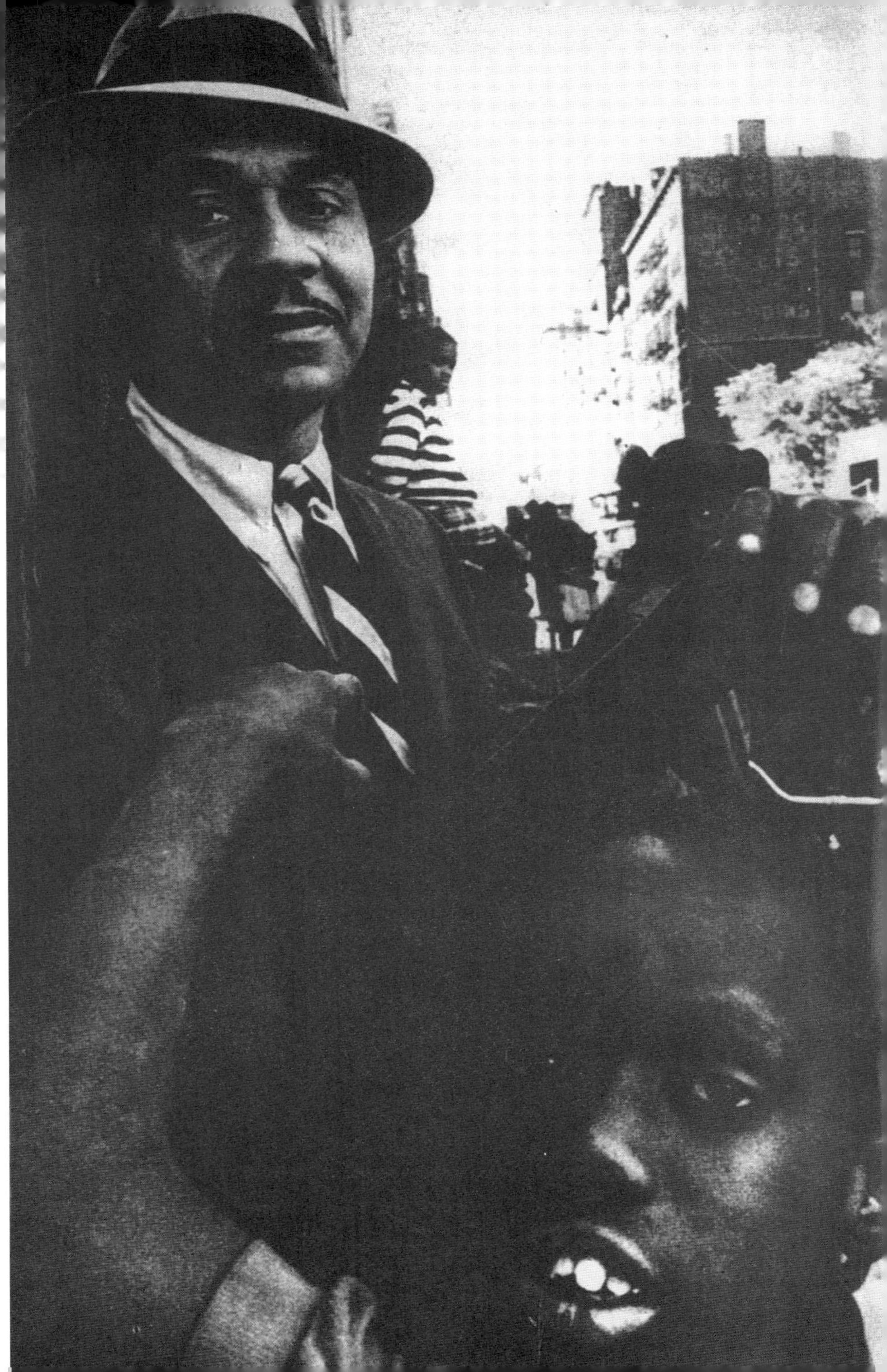

In February, 1997, the *Oklahoma Gazette* featured Ellison in a front page story. *Courtesy Oklahoma Gazette.*

Only the most popular books in the world are selected by the editors of *CliffsNotes* for publication of summaries for students. In the 2001 edition of *CliffsNotes*, Durthy A. Washington observes, "*Invisible Man's* humor, irony, and satire, as well as the narrator's fondness for wordplay, reveal Ellison's sensitivity to the nuances of the English language. The Prologue's references to 'the master meter,' the 'power station,' and 'free current' all relate to the underlying themes of power, freedom, and the legacy of slavery."
Courtesy IDG Books Worldwide, Inc.

John Callahan lecture, and other special events to mark the anniversary. The library system's monthly magazine, *Metro Library*, featured Ellison's life and work throughout the year.

Oklahoma City newspapers lauded Ellison's life. *The Daily Oklahoman* said, "Too many have ignored Ralph Ellison for too long."[14] *The Oklahoma Gazette* featured Ellison in a February 21, 2002, cover story:

> Ralph Ellison is Oklahoma's invisible man. Ellison…is virtually unknown in his hometown of Oklahoma City. There has been no stamp. There is no museum at his home. There is no statue of Ellison in any city park. Oklahoma City doesn't host an annual Ralph Ellison Day.

There are only a handful of artifacts and places, including the Ralph Ellison Library, to tell the average tourist that Oklahoma City is the place one of the most important authors of the past century considered home.[15]

Oklahoma made a giant step toward righting its sin of nonrecognition when Ellison was inducted into the Oklahoma Hall of Fame in November of 2002. Induction into the Hall of Fame is the highest honor the Sooner State can bestow upon one of its own.

The Hall of Fame honor was long overdue—after all, Stanley Crouch dubbed Ellison the Oklahoma Kid. Crouch said, "I sometimes thought of him as riding tall into the expanses of the American experience, able to drink the tart water of the cactus, smooth his way through the Indian nations, gamble all night long, lie before the fire with a book, distinguish the calls of the birds and the animals from the signals of the enemy, gallop wild and wooly into the big city with a new swing the way the Count Basie band had, then bring order to the pages of his work with an electrified magic pen that was both a warrior's lance and a conductor's wand."[16]

John Callahan, who, besides Fanny, probably knew Ellison best in his final 16 years on earth. To summarize the great writer's life, Callahan remembered:

> There was no politics with Ellison. He lived on a frequency of fraternity that simply went beyond matters of what one's background or gender or race was. The boy who aspired to being a Renaissance Man became a man who knew many things. He knew guns, football, electronics (he could take a radio apart and put it back

The Oklahoma City Community Foundation provided funds in 2002 for distribution of copies of *Invisible Man* to thousands of Oklahoma high school students. Here, Denyvetta Davis, right, prepares to distribute copies of the novel to students at Millwood High School in Oklahoma City.

together). He played the trumpet and studied musical theory. He knew jazz and literature. He was comfortable in the backwoods of Oklahoma and at the world's most sophisticated addresses. He was tough. Elegant. Gentle, dreamy, and tender one moment; he could be defiant, opinionated, and welcoming.

He was a guy who lived with his senses. He loved good food, birds, flowers, and he loved the quality of Fanny's martinis. He knew how to enjoy himself. He was a good storyteller. He knew what he thought about most things, and what kind of life he wanted to live. He was beholden to none.[17]

Invisible Man's cover for the German edition of *Invisible Man*. *Courtesy Ralph Ellison Library.*

The Portuguese edition of the best selling novel. *Courtesy Ralph Ellison Library.*

Conversations with RALPH ELLISON

Edited by Maryemma Graham and Amritjit Singh

Conversations with Ralph Ellison is typical of literary books published on the writings of Ellison since his death. In the introduction to the book published in 1995 by the University Press of Mississippi, editors Maryemma Graham and Amritjit Singh refer to Ellison as one of the few figures in American cultural history who "have engaged their sense of Americanness in the fullest possible measure." *Courtesy University Press of Mississippi.*

Ralph Ellison—The Invisible Man.

Ralph Ellison's influence on musicians, essayists, poets, and novelists will be felt for generations to come. Centuries from now, readers will relive his stories, cringe at the segregated conditions, and marvel at how a college dropout could make such an indelible mark on the literary heritage of his homeland and of the entire world.

Bibliography

Newspapers

Harlow's Weekly, Oklahoma City, Oklahoma.

New York Times, New York, New York.

Oklahoma City Advertiser, Oklahoma City, Oklahoma.

Oklahoma Gazette, Oklahoma City, Oklahoma

Oklahoma City Times, Oklahoma City, Oklahoma.

Oklahoma Journal, Midwest City, Oklahoma.

The Black Dispatch, Oklahoma City, Oklahoma.

The Black Chronicle, Oklahoma City, Oklahoma

The Daily Oklahoman, Oklahoma City, Oklahoma.

The Sunday Oklahoman, Oklahoma City, Oklahoma.

Tuskegee Messenger, Tuskegee, Alabama

Washington Post, Washington, D.C.

Washington Star, Washington, D.C.

Magazines and Periodicals

American Scholar
Antioch Review
Atlantic Monthly
Confluence
Delta
Esquire
Harper's
High Fidelity
New Leader
New Masses
New York Times Magazine
Reporter
Saturday Review
Time

Collections

Black Chronicles Collection
Ralph Ellison Library
Oklahoma City, Oklahoma

Jimmy Stewart Papers
Ralph Ellison Library
Oklahoma City, Oklahoma

Ralph Ellison Papers
Manuscript Division
Library of Congress
Washington, D.C.

Ralph Ellison Vertical File
Oklahoma Historical Society; Oklahoma City, Oklahoma

Books

Aldrich, Gene. *Black Heritage of Oklahoma*. Edmond: Thompson Book and Supply Company, 1973.

Arnold, Anita. *Charlie and the Deuce*. Oklahoma City: Black Liberated Arts Center, Inc., 1994.

Burke, Bob and Angela Monson. *Roscoe Dunjee: Champion of Civil Rights*. Edmond: University of Central Oklahoma Press, 1998.

Butler, Robert. *The Critical Response to Ralph Ellison*. Westpoint, Connecticut: Greenwood Press, 2000

Callahan, John F., ed. *The Collected Essays of Ralph Ellison*. New York: Modern Library, 1995.

Ellison, Ralph. *Flying Home and Other Stories*. New York: Random House, 1996.

Ellison, Ralph. *Going To The Territory*. New York: Random House, 1986.

Ellison, Ralph. *Invisible Man*. New York: Random House, 1952.

Ellison, Ralph. *Juneteenth: A Novel*. New York: Random House, 1999.

Ellison, Ralph. *Living With Music*. New York: Modern Library, 2001.

Ellison, Ralph. *Shadow and Act*. New York: Random House, 1963.

Franklin, Jimmie Lewis. *The Blacks in Oklahoma*. Norman: University of Oklahoma Press, 1980.

Franklin, Jimmie Lewis. *Journey Toward Hope*. Norman: University of Oklahoma Press, 1982.

Franklin, John Hope. *Race and History*. Baton Rouge: Louisiana State University Press, 1989.

Books *(continued)*

Gates, Henry Louis, Jr. *Figures in Black*. New York: Oxford University Press, 1987.

Graham, Maryemma and Amritjit Singh, eds. *Conversations With Ralph Ellison*. Hattiesburg: University of Mississippi Press, 1995.

Jackson, Lawrence Patrick. *Ralph Ellison: Emergence of Genius*. New York: John Wiley & Sons, 2002.

Lambert, Paul F., Kenny A. Franks, and Bob Burke. *Historic Oklahoma*. Oklahoma City: Oklahoma Heritage Association, 2000.

Miles-Lagrange, Vicki and Bob Burke. *A Passion For Equality: The Life of Jimmy Stewart*. Oklahoma City: Oklahoma Heritage Association, 1999.

Murray, Albert and John F. Callahan, eds. *Trading Twelves: The Selected Letters of Ralph Ellison and Albert Murray*. New York: Modern Library, 2000.

O'Meally, Robert G. "Ralph Ellison," in *African American Writers*, Valerie Smith, Lea Baechler, and A. Walton Litz, eds. New York: Collier Books, 1991.

Patterson, Zella J. Black. *Langston University: A History*. Norman: University of Oklahoma Press, 1979.

Peplow, Michael W. and Arthur P. Davis. *The New Negro Renaissance: An Anthology*. New York: Holt, Rinehart and Winston, Inc., 1975.

Savage, William W., Jr. *Singing Cowboys and All That Jazz*. Norman: University of Oklahoma Press, 1983.

Stewart, Roy P. *Born Grown*. Oklahoma City: Fidelity Bank, 1984.

Teall, Kaye M. *Black History in Oklahoma—A Resource Book*. Oklahoma City: Oklahoma City Public Schools, 1971.

Tolson, Arthur L. *The Black Oklahomans*. New Orleans: Edwards Printing Company, 1975.

Watts, Jerry Gafio. *Heroism and the Black Intellectual*. Chapel Hill: University of North Carolina Press, 1994.

Notes

Prologue

1. Jimmie Lewis Franklin, *The Blacks in Oklahoma*, (Norman: University of Oklahoma Press, 1980), p. 4.
2. Ibid., p. 5.
3. Ibid.
4. Zella J. Black Patterson, *Langston University: A History*, (Norman: University of Oklahoma Press, 1979), p. 3.
5. Ibid., p. 6.
6. Ibid., p. 9.
7. Franklin, *The Blacks in Oklahoma*, p. 8.
8. Paul F. Lambert, Kenny A. Franks, and Bob Burke, *Historic Oklahoma*, (Oklahoma City: Oklahoma Heritage Association, 2000), p. 101.
9. Bob Burke and Angela Monson, *Roscoe Dunjee: Champion of Civil Rights*, (Edmond: University of Central Oklahoma Press, 1998), p. 15.
10. Ibid., p. 16.
11. Ibid.
12. Franklin, *The Blacks in Oklahoma*, p. 16.
13. Burke and Monson, *Roscoe Dunjee: Champion of Civil Rights*, p. 21.
14. Ibid.
15. Ibid., p. 22.
16. Ibid., p. 24

Chapter 1:
Meager Beginnings

1. Roy P. Stewart, *Born Grown: An Oklahoma City History*, (Oklahoma City: Fidelity Bank, 1974), p. 12.
2. Ibid.
3. Ibid., p. 9-10.
4. Ibid.
5. Ibid., p. 13.
6. Vicki Miles-LaGrange and Bob Burke, *A Passion For Equality: The Life of Jimmy Stewart*, (Oklahoma City: Oklahoma Heritage Association, 1999), p. 16.
7. Ibid., p. 17.
8. Jeanne M. Devlin in "50 Years of the Invisible Man," *Metro Library* (Oklahoma City, Oklahoma), January, 2002, an excellent collection of facts about the life of Ralph Ellison printed in the official publication of the Oklahoma County Metropolitan Library System.
9. Some historians have written that Ellison was born March 1, 1913, because of muddled school and military records. However, in a 1971 interview, Ellison said he was two and a half years old when his father died in 1916—thus our conclusion that Ellison was born in 1914. Maryemma Graham and Amritjit Stingh, eds., *Conversations With Ralph Ellison*, (Jackson: University Press of Mississippi, 1995), p. 209.
10. Devlin, "50 Years of the Invisible Man."
11. Graham and Stingh, eds., *Conversations With Ralph Ellison*, p. 209.
12. Miles-LaGrange and Burke, *A Passion for Equality*, p. 35.
13. *Conversations With Ralph Ellison*, p. 209.
14. John F. Callahan, ed., *The Collected Essays of Ralph Ellison*, (New York: Modern Library, 1995), p. 35.
15. Devlin, "50 Years of the Invisible Man."
16. Ralph Ellison, *Shadow and Act*, (New York: Quality Paperback Book Club, 1994), p. 5.
17. *The Black Dispatch* (Oklahoma City, Oklahoma), October 3, 1919.
18. Callahan, ed., *The Collected Essays of Ralph Ellison*, p. 823.
19. Ibid., p. 824.
20. Ibid.
21. Ellison, *Shadow and Act*, p. 6.
22. Ibid.
23. *The Daily Oklahoman*, January 11, 1992.
24. Miles-LaGrange and Burke, *A Passion For Equality*, p.9.
25. Ibid., p. 19.
26. Ibid.

27. Ibid.
28. Ellison, *Shadow and Act*, p. 151.
29. Ibid., p. 4.
30. Ibid., p. 4-5.
31. Graham and Stingh, eds., *Conversations With Ralph Ellison*, p. 276.
32. Ibid., p. 277.
33. Ibid., p. 152.
34. Ibid.
35. Ibid., p. 153.

Chapter 2: Music and Books
1. Ralph Ellison, *Living With Music*, (New York: The Modern Library, 2001), p. 16-17.
2. Graham and Stingh, eds., *Conversation With Ralph Ellison*, p. 277.
3. Ellison, *Living With Music*, p. 17.
4. Ralph Ellison, *Going to the Territory*, (New York: Random House, 1986), p. 231.
5. Ibid., p. 136.
6. Ibid., p. 135.
7. Ibid., p. 137.
8. Ibid.
9. Ellison, *Living With Music*, p. 17.
10. Ibid., p. 260.
11. Ibid.
12. Ellison, *Shadow and Act*, p. 192.
13. Ibid.
14. Ibid.
15. Ibid., p. 191.
16. Ibid., p. 192.
17. Ibid., p. 191.
18. Ellison, *Living With Music*, p. 268.
19. Ibid., p. 20; Interview, James Edward "Jimmy"

Stewart, August 13, 1995, hereinafter referred to as Jimmy Stewart interview, Archives, Oklahoma Heritage Association, Oklahoma City, Oklahoma, hereinafter referred to as Heritage Archives.
20. Ellison, *Living With Music*, p. 197.
21. Ibid.
22. Ibid., p. 28.
23. Ibid., p. 29.
24. Ellison, *Going to the Territory*, p. 220.
25. Ibid.
26. Ibid., p. 221.
27. Ibid.
28. Ibid., p. 218.
29. Ellison, *Living With Music*, p. 198.
30. Ibid., p. 258.
31. Ibid., p. 155.
32. "The Dunbar Branch Library," an unpublished paper found in the files of the Oklahoma County Metropolitan Library System, Oklahoma City, Oklahoma.
33. Ellison, *Shadow and Act*, p. 156.
34. Callahan, ed., *The Collected Essays of Ralph Ellison*, p. 832.
35. Ibid.
36. Graham and Stingh, eds., *Conversations With Ralph Ellison*, p. 66.
37. Ibid.
38. Albert Murray and John F. Callaham, eds, *Trading Twelves: The Selected Letters of Ralph Ellison and Albert Murray*, (New York: Modern Library, 2000), p. 215.
39. Ibid., p. 216.
40. Ibid., p. 215.

41. Callahan, ed., *The Collected Essays of Ralph Ellison*, p. 6.

Chapter 3: Searching for a Father Figure
1. Jimmy Stewart interview.
2. Burke and Monson, *Roscoe Dunjee: Champion of Civil Rights*, p. 15.
3. Ibid., p. 17.
4. Ibid., p. 54.
5. Ibid.
6. Ibid., p. 64.
7. Callahan, ed., *The Collected Essays of Ralph Ellison*, p. 273.
8. Ralph Ellison, *Juneteenth*, (New York: Random House, 1996), p. 47.
9. John F. Callahan in "Ralph Ellison and the Law: A Covenant of Blood and the Word," *Oklahoma City University Law Review*, Fall 2001, Vol. 26, No. 3, p. 842.
10. Burke and Monson, *Roscoe Dunjee: Champion of Civil Rights*., p. 83.
11. Ibid., p. 24-25.
12. Ibid., p. 25.
13. Callahan, ed., *Collected Essays of Ralph Ellison*, p. 189.
14. Ellison, *Going to the Territory*, p. 322.
15. Ibid.
16. Ibid.
17. *Juneteenth*, p. 319.
18. Ellison, *Going to the Territory*, p. 122.
19. Ibid., p. 117.
20. Ibid., p. 118.
21. Ibid.
22. Ibid.
23. Ibid.
24. Ibid.

25. *The Daily Oklahoman,* August 4, 1995.
26. Ellison, *Going to the Territory,* p. 55.
27. Miles-LaGrange and Burke, *A Passion For Equality,* p. 19.
28. Jimmy Stewart interview.
29. Ralph Ellison, *Flying Home and Other Stories,* (New York: Random House, 1996), p. 18.
30. Ibid., p. 21.
31. Callahan, ed., *The Collected Essays of Ralph Ellison,* p. 42.

Chapter 4: The Influence of Deep Deuce
1. Miles-LaGrange and Burke, *A Passion For Equality,* p. 27.
2. Anita G. Arnold, *Charlie and The Deuce,* (Oklahoma City: Black Liberated Arts Center, Inc., 1994), p. 4.
3. William W. Savage, Jr., *Singing Cowboys and All That Jazz,* (Norman: University of Oklahoma Press, 1983), p. 25-28.
4. Kaye M. Teall, *Black History in Oklahoma,* (Oklahoma City: Oklahoma City Public Schools, 1971), p. 200.
5. Ellison, *Shadow and Act,* p. 235.
6. *Saturday Review* (New York, New York), May 17, 1958.
7. Ellison, *Shadow and Act,* p. 237.
8. George O. Carney, "Oklahoma Jazz Artists," *The Chronicles of Oklahoma,* Vol. 56, p. 17.
9. Ibid.
10. Ellison, *Shadow and Act,* p. 236.

11. Ibid., p. 239.
12. Miles-LaGrange and Burke, *A Passion For Equality,* p. 31.
13. Graham and Singh, eds., *Conversations With Ralph Ellison,* p. 306.
14. Ibid., p. 30.
15. *Saturday Review,* July 12, 1958.
16. Ibid.
17. Ibid., p. 242.
18. Ibid., p. 243.
19. Ibid.
20. Ibid.
21. Ibid., p. 244.
22. Jimmy Stewart interview.
23. Teall, *Black History in Oklahoma,* p. 200..
24. Miles-LaGrange and Burke, *A Passion For Equality,* p. 33.
25. *The Black Dispatch,* August 16, 1952.
26. Ibid.

Chapter 5: Finishing High School
1. Graham and Singh, eds., *Conversations With Ralph Ellison,* p. 199.
2. Ibid., p. 89.
3. Ibid.
4. Ibid., p. 370.
5. Jimmy Stewart interview.
6. *The Black Dispatch,* May 21, 1931.
7. Official class records of Douglass High School, Classes of 1931 and 1932, Heritage Archives.
8. *The Black Dispatch,* May 28, 1931.
9. Ibid., June 18, 1931.
10. Ibid., July 2, 1931.
11. Ibid.
12. Ellison, *Going to the Territory,* p. 57.

13. Jimmy Stewart interview.
14. Ibid.
15. www.tusk.edu, the official Web site of Tuskegee University.
16. www.biography.com
17. Ibid.
18. Ibid.

Chapter 6: Leaving Home
1. Graham and Singh, eds., *Conversations With Ralph Ellison,* p. 249.
2. Ibid.
3. Ibid., p. 250.
4. Ibid.
5. *New Yorker* (New York, New York), April 29, 1996.
6. Ellison, *Going to the Territory,* p. 324.
7. Ibid.
8. Ibid.
9. Ibid., p. 325.
10. Ibid.
11. Ralph Ellison file, Office of the Registrar, Tuskegee University, Tuskegee, Alabama.
12. Ralph Ellison, *Flying Home and Other Stories,* (New York: Random House, 1996), p. 83.
13. Ibid.
14. Graham and Singh, eds., *Conversations With Ralph Ellison,* p. 198.
15. Jimmy Stewart interview.
16. www.tusk.edu, the official Web site of Tuskegee University.
17. Graham and Singh, eds., *Conversations With Ralph Ellison,* p. 308.
18. Ibid.
19. Ibid., p. 309
20. Cleveland W. Encas, *Tuskegee Ra! Ra! An*

Autobiography of My Youth, (Nassau: Commercial Print Works, 1986), p. 29.

21. David L. Johnson, "The Contributions of William Dawson to the School of Music at Tuskegee Institute and to Choral Music," (Ph.D. dissertation, University of Illinois Press, 1987), p. 125.

22. Callahan, ed., *The Collected Essays of Ralph Ellison*, p. 436.

23. Ibid.

Chapter 7: Polishing the Trumpet

1. Graham and Singh, eds., *Conversations With Ralph Ellison*, p. 199.

2. Ibid., p. 308.

3. www.co.gloucester.va.us/moton

4. Robert R. Moton, *Finding a Way Out*, (Garden City, New York: Doubleday, 1922), p. 5.

5. Graham and Singh, eds., *Conversations With Ralph Ellison*, p. 308-309.

6. Ibid., p. 308-309.

7. Ibid., p. 337.

8. www.biography.com

9. Ibid.

10. Ibid.

11. Graham and Singh, eds., *Conversations with Ralph Ellison*, p. 337.

12. *Tuskegee Messenger* (Tuskegee, Alabama), December 9, 1933.

13. Ellison, *Shadow and Act*, dedication page.

14. Ellison, *Going to the Territory*, p. 70.

15. Ibid., p. 71.

16. Ibid., p. 168.

17. Ibid., p. 171.

18. Ibid., p. 172.

19. Ibid.

20. Ibid., p. 173.

21. Ibid., p. 3.

22. Ibid., p. 4.

23. Ibid.

24. Ibid., p. 5.

25. Ibid., p. 15.

Chapter 8: Separate but Not Equal

1. Ellison, *Shadow and Act*, p. 160.

2. Ellison, *Flying Home and Other Stories*, reproduction of Ellison manuscript on back cover of dustjacket.

3. Ibid., p. 160.

4. Ibid.. 136.

5. Graham and Singh, eds., *Conversations With Ralph Ellison*, p. 88.

6. Ibid., p. 89.

7. Ibid., p. 90.

8. *Oklahoma City University Law Review*, Vol. 26, No. 3, Fall 2001, p. 853.

9. Graham and Singh, eds., *Conversations With Ralph Ellison*, p. 276.

10. Burke and Monson, *Roscoe Dunjee: Champion of Civil Rights*, p. 40.

11. Ibid., p. 41.

12. Ibid., p. 143.

13. Ellison, *Going to the Territory*, p. 65.

14. Graham and Singh, eds., *Conversations With Ralph Ellison*, p. 240.

15. Ellison, *Shadow and Act*, p. 19.

16 Ibid.

17. Ibid., p. 20.

18. Graham and Singh, eds., *Conversations With Ralph Ellison*, p. 346.

19. Jimmy Stewart interview.

20. Ellison, *Going to the Territory*, p. 259.

Ch.apter 9: Discovering the Wasteland

1. Ellison, *Shadow and Act*, p. xx.

2. Ibid., p. xxi.

3. Ibid., p. xx.

4. Ibid., page 307-308.

5. Ibid., p. 308.

6. Graham and Singh, eds., *Conversations With Ralph Ellison*, p. 10.

7. Ellison, *Shadow and Act*, p. 306.

8. Ibid., p. 160.

9. Ibid., p. 168.

10. Ellison, *Going to the Territory*, p. 39.

11. Michael W. Peplow, *The New Negro Renaissance: An Anthology*, (New York: Holt, Rinehart and Winston, Inc., 1975), p. xix., 372.

12. Ibid., p. 53.

13. Ibid., p. 153.

14. Ibid., p. 275.

15. Ibid., p. 358.

16. Ibid., p. 374.

17. Graham and Singh, eds., *Conversations With Ralph Ellison*, p. 104.

18. Murray and Callahan, eds, *Trading Twelves*, p. 170.

19. Interview with Albert Murray. www.jerryjazzmusician.com

20. Robert G. O'Meally in "Ralph Ellison," *African American Writers*, eds. Valerie Smith, Lea Baechler, and A. Walton Litz, (New York: Collier Books, 1991), p. 84.

21. Ibid.

Chapter 10: Heading North

1. O'Meally, *African American Writers*, p. 84.

2. Graham and Singh, eds., *Conversations With Ralph Ellison*, p. 292.

3. Ibid.

4. Ellison, *Going to the Territory*, p. 201.

5. Ibid., p. 199.

6. Ibid., p. 202.

7. Ibid.

8. Graham and Singh, eds., *Conversations With Ralph Ellison*, p. 293.

9. Ibid.

10. Ellison, *Going to the Territory*, p. 163.

11. Ibid., p. 147.

12. Ibid., p. 222.

13. Ibid., p. 222.

14. Ibid., p 223.

15. Ibid., p. 166.

16. Ibid., p. 186.

17. Ibid. p. 187.

18. Ibid., p. 188.

19. Ibid., p. 197.

Chapter 11: Detour to Ohio
1. O'Meally, *African American Writers*, p. 86.

2. *Metro Library*, January, 2002.

3. Ibid.

4. Ibid.

5. Ibid.

6. O'Meally, *African American Writers*, p. 87.

7. Graham and Singh, eds., *Conversations With Ralph Ellsion*, p. 133.

8. Ralph Ellison, "A Party Down at the Square," *Flying Home and Other Stories*, (New York: Random House, 1996), p. 5.

9. Ibid., p. xii.

10. Ellison, *Flying Home and Other Stories*, p. 114-115.

11. Ibid., p. 97.

12. Ibid., p. xiv.

13. O'Meally, *African American Writers.*, p. 86

14. Graham and Singh, eds., *Conversations With Ralph Ellison*, p. 294.

15. Ibid., p. 295.

16. Ibid., p. 294

17. Ibid., p. 295.

18. Ibid.

19. Ellison, *Going to the Territory*, p. 293.

20. Ibid., p. 294.

21. Ibid., p. 296

22. Ellison, *Living With Music*, p. 282.

Chapter 12: Perfecting His Craft
1. Graham and Singh, eds., *Conversations With Ralph Ellison*, p. 181.

2. Lawrence Jackson, R*alph Ellison: Emergence of Genius*, (New York: John Wiley & Sons, 2002), p. 215-216.

3. Ralph Ellison, "Judge Lynch in New York," *New Masses*, August 15, 1939.

4. Ibid.

5. Ellison, *Flying Home and Other Stories*, p. 80.

6. Ibid., p. 61.

7. Jackson. *Ralph Ellison: Emergence of Genius*, p. 228.

8. Ralph Ellison, "A Congress Jim Crow Didn't Attend," *New Masses*, May 14, 1940.

9. Ibid.

10. Ralph Ellison, "The Birthmark," *New Masses*, July 2, 1940.

11. Ellison, *Flying Home and Other Stories*, p. 23.

12. O'Meally, *African American Writers*, p. 89.

13. Ellison, *Shadow and Act*, p. 232-233.

14. Ibid., p. 233.

15. Ibid., p. 295-296.

16. Ibid., p. 296.

17. Ibid., p. xi.

Chapter 13: Master Storyteller
1. O'Meally, *African American Writers*, p. 91.

2. Jackson, *Ralph Ellison: Emergence of Genius*, p. 283.

3. Ellsion, *Flying Home and Other Stories*, p. 60.

4. *New York Post* (New York, New York), August 2, 1943.

5. Graham and Singh, eds., *Conversations With Ralph Ellison*, p. 300-301.

6. Ellison, *Flying Home and Other Stories*, p. 127.

7. Ibid., p. 151-152.

8. Ibid. p. 171.

9. *Oklahoma City University Law Review*, Vol. 26, No. 3, Fall 2001, p. 957.

10. Ibid., p. 953.

11. Ibid., p. 927.

12. Ibid., p. 928.

13. Ellison, *Flying Home and Other Stories*, p. xxiv-xxv.

14. Heather Forest, *Wisdom Tales from Around the World*, (Little Rock: August House Publishers, Inc., 1996), p. 9.

15. Ellison, *Flying Home and Other Stories*, p. 50.

16. Ibid., p. 48.

Chapter 14: Cooking on the High Seas
1. John Scott Douglas and Albert Salz, *He's In The Merchant Marine Now*, (New York: Robert McBride and Company, 1943), p. 11.

2. Ellison, *Flying Home and Other Stories*, p. 138.

3. Jackson, *Ralph Ellison: Emergence of Genius*, p. 299.
4. Callahan, ed., *The Collected Essays of Ralph Ellison*, p. 349.
5. Ibid.
6. Ellison, *Shadow and Act*, p. 79.
7. Ibid., p. 85.
8. Jackson, *Ralph Ellison: Emergence of Genius*, p. 313.
9. Ellison, *Shadow and Act*, p. 99.
10. Ibid. p. 100.

**Chapter 15:
Birth of a Novel**
1. Jackson, *Ralph Ellison: Emergence of Genius*, p. 318-319.
2. Ellison, *Going to the Territory*, p. 42.
3. Ibid. p. 44.
4. Ibid.
5. Ibid., p. 45.
6. Ibid. p. 46.
7. Ibid. p. 49.
8. Ibid., p, 53.
9. Callahan, ed., *The Collected Essays of Ralph Ellison*, p. 343.
10. Ibid., p. 344.
11. Ellison, *Shadow and Act*, p. 295.
12. Ibid. p. 297.
13. Jackson, *Ralph Ellison: Emergence of Genius*, p. 333.
14. *Irish Times* (Dublin, Ireland), October 25, 1947.
15. Murray and Callahan, eds., *Trading Twelves*, p. 9.
16. Ibid., p. 10.
17. Ibid., p. 19.
18. Ibid.
19. Ibid., p. 21.
20. Ibid.
21. Ibid., p. 25.

Chapter 16: A Classic
1. O'Meilly, *African American Writers*, p. 95-96.
2. Ibid., p. 97.
3. Ibid., p. 98.
4. www.jerryjazzmusician.com
5. *American Mercury* (New York, New York), June, 1952.
6. *Commentary* (New York, New York), June, 1952.
7. Jackson, *Ralph Ellison: Emergence of Genius*, p. 440.
8. Ellison, *Shadow and Act*, p. 104.
9. Ibid., p. 106.
10. Ibid., p. 103-104.
11. Murray and Callahan, eds., *Trading Twelves*, p. 39.
12. Ibid., p. 43.
13. Ibid., p. 42-43.
14. Ibid., p. 49.
15. Ibid., p. 50.
16. Ibid., p. 51.
17. Ibid., p. 52.
18. *Metro Library*, April, 2002.

Chapter 17: Professor in Residence
1. Callahan, ed., *The Collected Essays of Ralph Ellison*, p. 85.
2. Murray and Callahan, eds., *Trading Twelves*, p. 61.
3. Ibid.
4. Ibid., p. 67.
5. Ibid., p. 98.
6. Ibid., p. 103-104.
7. Ibid., p. 118.
8. Ibid., p. 124.
9. Ibid., p. 149.
10. Ibid., p. 172.
11. Ibid., p. 181.
12. www.bard.edu

13. Callahan, ed., *The Collected Essays of Ralph Ellison*, p. x.
14. Ibid., p. xi.
15. Ibid., p. x.
16. Murray and Callahan, eds., *Trading Twelves*, p. 204.
17. Ibid.
18. Ibid. p. 205.
19. Ibid., p. 226.
20. Callahan, ed., *The Collected Essays of Ralph Ellison*, p. 277.
21. Ellison, *Living With Music*, p. 93.
22. www.rutgers.edu
23. *Metro Library*, January, 2002.
24. Ibid.

**Chapter 18:
Shadow and Act**
1. Ellison, *Shadow and Act*, p. xi.
2. Ibid., p. xii-xiii.
3. Ellison, *Going to the Territory*, p. 66.
4. Ibid., p. 78.
5. Ibid., p. 76.
6. Ibid.
7. Ibid., p. 83.
8. Ibid., p. 87.
9. Graham and Singh, eds., *Conversations With Ralph Ellison*, p. 85.
10. Ibid., p. 85.
11. Ibid., p. 86.
12. Ibid., p. 105.
13. Ibid.
14. Ibid., p. 220.
15. *Metro Library*, March, 2002.
16. Graham and Singh, eds., *Conversations With Ralph Ellison*, p. 106.
17. Ibid.

18. Ibid., p. 173.
19. Ibid., p. 185.
20. Ibid., p. 187.
21. Ibid., p. 188.
22. Ellison, *Juneteenth*, p. xii.

Chapter 19: Taking the High Road
1. www.nyu.edu
2. *Time* (New York, New York), April 6, 1970.
3. Ibid.
4. Ibid.
5. Callahan, ed., *The Collected Essays of Ralph Ellison*, p. 413.
6. Ibid., p. 451.
7. Ibid., p. 455.
8. *Oklahoma Journal* (Midwest City, Oklahoma), October 25, 1972.
9. Ibid.
10. Text of Ellison's acceptance speech at dedication of the Ralph Ellison Library, June 21, 1975, Oral History Collection, Oklahoma Historical Society, Oklahoma City, Oklahoma.
11. Ibid.
12. *Metro Library*, January, 2002.
13. Ibid.
14. Callahan, ed., *The Collected Essays of Ralph Ellison*, p. 466.
15. Ibid., p. 485.
16. Graham and Singh, eds., *Conversations With Ralph Ellison*, p. 385.
17. Ibid.
18. Ralph Ellison, *Invisible Man*, (New York: Modern Library, 1994), p. xii.
19. Robert J. Butler, ed., *The Critical Response to Ralph Ellison*, (Westpoint, CT: Greenwood Press, 2000), p. 207.
20. *The Daily Oklahoman*, April 17, 1994.
21. Butler, ed., *The Critical Response to Ralph Ellison*, p. 195.
22. Ibid., p. 199.

Chapter 20: Indelible Ink
1. Ellison, *Juneteenth*, p. xiv.
2. Ellison, *Flying Home and Other Stories*, p. xx.
3. Ibid., dustjacket.
4. Library of Congress Information Bulletin, April 1, 1996, Heritage Archives.
5. *The Daily Oklahoman*, August 2, 1998.
6. Ellison, *Flying Home and Other Stories*, p. xiv-xv.
7. Ibid., p. 351.
8. *The Daily Oklahoman*, June 27, 1999.
9. Ibid., November 20, 1999.
10. Murray and Callahan, eds., *Trading Twelves*, p. viii-vix.
11. *The Daily Oklahoman*, January 30, 2000.
12. Ellison, *Living With Music*, dustjacket.
13. Ibid., p. ix.
14. *The Daily Oklahoman*, March 10, 2002.
15. *Oklahoma Gazette* (Oklahoma City, Oklahoma), February 21, 2002.
16. Butler, ed., *The Critical Response to Ralph Ellison*, p. 195.
17. Web site of Black Oklahoma Today, www.blackoklahoma.com

Index

25th U.S. Colored Infantry 20

***A Grammar of Motives* 221**
"A Hard Time Keeping Up" 173
"A Song of Innocence" 275
Abbeville, SC 20, 24
Adams, Lewis 104
Adelphia University 278
"Afternoon" 185
Albert, Carl 304
Aldridge Theater 45-49, 80-81, 88
American Academy of Arts and Sciences 242, 278
American Mercury 231
American Writers Congress 182
American Writing 185
Ammons, James 75-76
Amos, John 307
An American Dilemma 147, 208
"An Extravagance of Laughter" 130
"And Hickman Arrives" 250
Anderson, Buddy 82
Anderson, Sherwood 135
Antioch College 242
Antioch Review 208
Arban, Jean Baptiste 124
Armstrong, Louis 51-53, 86-87, 307
Atchison, Topeka, and Santa Fe Railroad 18
Atkins, Hannah 8, 83, 276, 281, 283
Avery Chapel AME Church 25, 36, 38-39, 43-44, 124-125
Ayala, Stephanie Graves 7
Ayer, A.J. 247

Babb, Sanora 182
Bach, Johann Sebastian 45, 131
Baltimore, MD 88
Bank Street College of Education 258
Bard College 247-249, 278
Barrett, William 231
Barthe, Richmond 162-163
Basie, Count 82-83, 87
Bates, Amelia 215
Bates, John 215
"Beating the Boy" 211
Bellmon, Henry 270
Bellow, Saul 231, 234, 247-249
Bennett College 235
Benny Goodman Orchestra 87
"Between the World and Me" 159
Bibbs, Tia Jones 8
Bishop's Restaurant 261
Black Boy 210
Black Dispatch (The) 26, 63-66, 94, 100-102, 138-139, 261, 279
Blue Devils 88-89, 141
Blue Front Grocery 30
Book Week 268
Booker T. Washington Park 66
Boorstin, Daniel J. 298
Boren, David L. 304
Botkin, B.A. 176
Bowen, Hilliard 102
Brandeis University 247
Breaux, Zelia N. 44-52, 71, 103, 105, 125
Brentwood, NY 278
Broderick, John C. 298
Brooks, James "Doebelly" 95
Brotherhood of Sleeping Car Porters 186
Brown University 287
Brown, Sterling A. 151
Buffalo Soldiers 20
Bunche, Ralph 126
Burke, Kenneth 221
Butler, Adrienne 8

"Cadillac Flambe" 306
Caldwell, Erskine 164-165
Callahan, John F. 7, 67-68, 198, 251, 271, 285, 288, 290, 295-302, 308, 311, 316
Callaway, Cab 87
Campbell, George W. 104
Campbell, Gini Moore 7
Carnegie Commission on Educational Television 266
Carnegie Hall 132
Carney, George O. 87
Carter, Scott 8
Caruthers, Melecia 7
Carver, George Washington 126-128
Casablanca, Morrocco 245
Catskill Mountains 247
Catton, Bruce 234
Central Park 268
Century Club 278
Challenge 160
Chaney, Lon 100
"Change the Joke and Slip the Yoke" 247
Charlie Christian Jazz Festival 83
Chattanooga, TN 20
Chehaw Station 131-132
Chestnut, James, Jr. 73
Chevalier de L'Ordre des Artes et Lettres 275
Chicago Defender Honor Roll of Democracy Award 233
Chicago, IL 112, 147
Chicago, Rock Island, and Pacific Railroad 25
Christian, Charlie 82-88, 306

Christian, Clarence 84
Christian, Edward 84
Cincinnati, OH 169
Civil War 9, 71, 104, 147, 276
Clark, David Draper 8
CliffsNotes 311
Clinton, Bill 73
Cobb, Rufus Willis 104
College of William and Mary 278
Columbia University 150, 306
Columbus, GA 117, 129
Commentary 231
Commodore Hotel 233
Common Council for American Unity 194
Common Ground 194
Confluence 241
Conversations With Ralph Ellison 315
Coughlin, Charles E. 182-183
Count Basie Band 90-91, 312
Cowen, Chester 7
Cox, Dorothy 100
Cox, Ida 50
Crane, John K. 278
Crime and Punishment 135
Crouch, Stanely 290, 312
Cullen, Countee 56, 149

Dabney, Eric 7
Dabney, Shelley Irby 7
Daily Oklahoman (The) 100, 291, 301, 311
Daily Worker (The) 160
Davis, Denyvetta 313
Davis, George 8
Davis, Henry Bowman Otto "Hoolie" 36
Davis, Marcia 8
Davis, Miles 87
Davis, Ralph 146
Davis, Richard Harding 17
Davison, Robin 7
Dawson, William L. 118-119, 139
Days of Wrath 158
Dayton, OH 169-174
Death in the Afternoon 145
Debussy, Claude 131
Decatur, AL 113
Dedham, MA 258

Deep Deuce 79-95, 110, 125, 141, 230, 267
DeFrange, Ann 301
Denver, CO 101-102
Devlin, Jeanne 8, 251
Devoto, Bernard 234
Dewey, George 33
"Did You Ever Dream Lucky?" 242
Direction 177
Dostoevsky, Fyodor 172, 230
Douglass Elementary School 25
Douglass High School 44-46, 71-72, 90, 101, 289
Douglass, Frederick 33
Dowell, A.L. 280
Drye, Frank 106, 117, 123-125
Dunbar Branch Library 56-57, 59
Dunbar, Paul Laurence 56
Dunjee, Roscoe 13-14, 63-69, 94, 101-102, 138-139, 261, 279, 284
Dupee, F.W. 247

East St. Louis, MO 112
Eliot, T.S. 137, 148-149
Ellington, Duke 53-55, 87, 163-164, 290, 306-307
Ellison, Alfred 20, 24
Ellison, Fanny McConnell Buford 207-210, 215-218, 235, 242-247, 270, 280, 288, 295-298
Ellison, Harriet 20
Ellison, Herbert Maurice 21-23, 36-37, 39, 74-75, 99, 138, 170-171
Ellison, Ida Milsap 20-26, 30-33, 36-37, 67, 138, 169-170
Ellison, Lewis Alfred 20-24, 75-76
Ellison, Ralph Waldo childhood 15-38; high school 41-105; at Tuskegee Institute 109-153; mother's death 167-178; Merchant Marines 191-210; writing *Invisible Man* 213-223; as professor 239-265
Ellison, Rose Aramita Poindexter 181-186

Emancipation Proclamation 9, 300
Emerson, Ralph Waldo 33, 234
Erskine, Albert 221
Esquire 142, 152, 249, 306
"Extravagance of Laughter" 165

Fairfax, VA 278
Fairlawn Cemetery 7, 23-24
Faulkner, William 182, 233-234, 299
Federal Writers Project 175-178, 181-183, 256
Fitzgerald, F. Scott 135, 299-300
Five Civilized Tribes 9
Flying Home and Other Stories 198, 297
"Flying Home" 196-197
"For a Lady I Know" 149
Ford, Ford Maddox 135
Forest, Heather 199
Forrest, Leon 265
Franklin County, VA 104
Franklin, Jimmie Lewis 12
Franklin, John Hope 276
Franks, Kenny 7
Freud, Sigmund 141, 230
Frissell, Hollis Burke Library 117, 132

G.X., Theodore 280
Gallatin, TN 69-70
Garden City, NY 278
Gargoly 31
Garvey, Marcus 58
Gary, IN 67
Geer, Will 165
Gehrig, Lou 185
George Washington Bridge 290
Gillespie, John "Dizzy" 117
Going to the Territory 71, 287, 297
Golding, William 299
Goodman, Benny 83, 87
Graham, Maryemma 315
Great Depression 55, 93, 105, 175
Green Mountains 216
Greenwich Village 162
Grinnell College 267
Guinn v. United States 13
Guthrie, OK 18
Guthrie, Woody 304

Hall, Shorty 117-118
Hamlin, Albert Comstock 12
Hamlin, Eva 152
Hampton Institute 104
Hampton, Lionel 87
Handel, George Frederic 44-45, 119
Harcourt Brace 208
Hardin, Mary 7
Harlem 157-167, 220-222, 246
"Harlem is Nowhere" 255
Harlem Renaissance 149
Harlem YMCA 158, 161
Harper, Michael S. 127
Harpers 17
Harris, Rodger 7
Harrison, Hazel 125, 131-132, 158
Harry, Billie 7
Harvard University 278
Hassman Park 66
Hawthorne, Nathaniel 229
Hayer, Melissa 7
Haywood, William 43-44
Hebestreit, Ludwig 50
Hecht, Anthony 247
Hemingway, Ernest 135, 142, 145-146, 172, 182, 229, 299
Henry, Pat 7
Herman, Woody 87
"Hidden Name and Complex Fate" 57
High Fidelity 246
Hines, Earl "Fatha" 51, 53
Hirt, Al 118
Hobbs, Steven H. 193, 197-198
Holy Cross College 251
Homer 230
Horizon 221
Hound and Horn 176
Howard University 211
Hubbard, Anna 7
Huckleberry Finn 113
Hudson River 235, 247, 290
Hughes, Langston 56, 150, 158-159, 164-165, 177
Huntington Hall 118
Hyman, Stanley Edgar 222, 247, 267
"Hymie's Bull" 115, 162

"I Have Seen Black Hands" 159
Ideal Orchestra 88
"In a Strange Country" 206
Independent Television Service 302
Indian Territory 9-11
Indinola, IA 126
International Literature 176
Introduction to the Science of Sociology 146
Invisible Man 217-241, 268, 278, 288, 298, 306, 308-309
Iowa Review 275
Iowa State University 126
Irby, Mike 7-8
Irish Times 221

Jackson, Jesse, Jr. 289
Jackson, Lawrence 211, 220-221
Jackson, Mahalia 249-250, 306-307
Jackson, Shirley 222
James Europe Post 101
James, Henry 176
James, Jesse 57
Jenkins Music Company 106
John B. Russwurm Award 233
Johnson, Charles 288
Johnson, David L. 118
Johnson, Jack 33
Johnson, Ladybird 275
Johnson, Lyndon B. 258-260, 275
Journal of the American Folklore Society 177
Joyce, James 172, 230, 299
Jude the Obscure 135
"Judge Lynch in New York" 182
Julius Rosenwald Fellowship 290-210
Julliard Conservatory of Music 103
Juneteenth 68, 70, 248, 299-302
"Juneteenth" 271

Kansas City Times 10
Kansas Territory 126
"Keep to the Rhythm" 306
Keller, Nelson 280
Kemery, Clyde 270
Kennedy Jacqueline 258

Kennedy, John F. 258
Kerr, Robert S. 304
"King of the Bingo Game" 195-196, 302
King, Martin Luther, Jr. 265
Kirkland, Avon 308
Knights of Pythias 58
Ku Klux Klan 276

L & N Railroad 112-113
LaFargue Mental Hygiene Clinic 219-220
Lafayette, James Armistead 280
Lane v. Wilson 14
Langston University 71, 100-103
Langston, OK 10-12
Last of the Mohicans (The) 76
Latting, Patience 280
Le Havre, France 209
League of American Writers 175
Lee, Paul 308
Lewinsohn's Clothing Store 103
Lewis and Clark College 295
Library of Congress 298
Lincoln University 150
Lincoln, Abraham 9, 276
Literary Digest 55
Living With Music 306
Locke, Alain 149, 158
Logan Hall 117
Long Island University 278
Luper, Clara 262, 289-290
Lynn, Linda 7

Macdonald, Dwight 247
Macedonia Baptist Church 217
MacLeish, Archibald 234
Macon County, AL 104, 109, 173
Malamud, Bernard 234, 285
Malraux, Andre 158, 176, 230, 275
Man's Fate 158
Mantle, Mickey 304
Marshall, Thurgood 69, 261
Marx, Karl 141, 159
Massachusetts Review 127
McAlester, OK 74-75
McCabe, Edward P. 10-11
McCann, Fred 8
McCarthy, Mary 247
McCorvey, Morris 56

INDEX **329**

McFarland, Lamonia 55-56
McGraw-Hill 259
McGrew, Dan 57
McKay, Claude 56
McLeod, Darlene 289
McPherson, James Alan 269
Meade, Frank 57-58
Meade, Joseph 43
Medal of Freedom 275
Melville, Herman 136, 151, 229, 234
Mendelssohn, Felix 131
Metro Library 311
Metronome All-Stars 87
Michener, Judith 7
Middle Passage 288
Middletown, CT 278
Midway Café 81
Miles-LaGrange, Vicki 8
Miller, Marilyn 7
Millinder, Lucky 87
Mills Brothers 53
Mississippi River 112-113
"Mister Tousan" 186, 199
Mitchell, Abbie 124
Moby Dick 151-152
Modigliania, Franco 247
Montgomery, AL 117
Moon, Bucklin 211
Moore, Bill 7
Morrison, Toni 308
Morse, Samuel F.B. 276
Moton, Robert Russa 105, 124, 145
Moulder, Mary 289
Moynihan, Daniel Patrick 276
Mt. Zion Baptist Church 68
Muhammed, Elijah 280
Murray, Albert 152, 222, 230, 235-236, 242, 245-247, 267, 303-304
Murray, Michele 242
Murray, Mozelle 242
Murray, William H. "Alfalfa Bill" 11, 68, 138
"Must We Then Meet as Strangers" 128
Myrdal, Gunnar 147, 208

National Association for the Advancement of Colored People 13, 236, 259, 269
National Book Award 233-234, 268, 288

National Council of the Arts 266
National Institute of Arts and Letters 266, 285
National Maritime Union 193
National Negro Congress 185-186
National Newspaper Publishers Association 233
Native Son 185, 187, 299
Negro Digest 208
Negro Folk Symphony 118
Negro Quarterly 177, 188-189, 193
Neill, Debbie 7
New Challenge 160, 162, 177
New Masses 158, 177-178, 182-183, 185-188
New Negro Renaissance 149
New Republic 211, 219
New York Herald Tribune 231
New York Post 195
New York Times 10, 67, 227
New York University 275-278, 286
New York Yankees 185
New Yorker 231
Newport, RI 249
Nicar, Amy Burke 7
"Night-Talk" 271
Noble Savage 250
Norman, McHenry 100
North Canadian River 31, 82, 102

O'Donnel, Donat 221
O'Mealy, Robert G. 227, 306
Oberlin College 103
Oklahoma Baptist Convention 22
Oklahoma City Board of Education 51
Oklahoma City Community Foundation 313
Oklahoma City Diner's Club 184
Oklahoma City Golf and Country Club 103
Oklahoma City Zoo 27
Oklahoma County Libraries System 280
Oklahoma County Metropolitan Library System 200

Oklahoma Department of Libraries 7
Oklahoma Gazette 310-311
Oklahoma Hall of Fame 288, 312
Oklahoma Heritage Association 7, 288
Oklahoma Historical Society 7
Oklahoma 88
Oklahoma Medical, Dental, and Pharmaceutical Association 94
Oklahoma Publishing Company 7
Oklahoma Station 18
Oklahoma Supreme Court 138
Oklahoma Territory 9-11, 18, 69
Oklahoma Today 304-305
Onie Allen v. Oklahoma City 138
Orchard Park Elementary School 31
Orwell, George 299
Oxford University 100

Page, Inman 63, 71-73
Page, Oran "Hot Lips" 51, 307
Page, Walter 90, 92
Paris, France 246
Park, Robert E. 146-147
Parker, Charlie 87
Partisan Review 222, 247
Patterson, Frederick 145
Pennsylvania State University 278
Perry, Ezelle W. 21-22
Phenix City, AL 129, 164, 172
Phillips, Frank 304
Phillips, Mary 7
Pittman, Kitty 7
Pittman, Portia 125
Plainfield, MA 270
Playboy 286
Plessy v. Ferguson 11
Portland, OR 295
Post, Wiley 304
Pound, Ezra 135
Powell, Adam Clayton 265
Primer for White Folks 211
Princeton University 233
Prix de Rome 242

Prokofiev, Sergey 125
Providence, RI 287

Queen's Colelge 250

Ragland, Lord 215-216
Rainey, Ma 50
Ralph Ellison Festival 287
Ralph Ellison Library 280, 283-284
Randolph, A. Phillip 186
Randolph, Jefferson Davis 21, 63, 69-71, 290
Randolph's Drug 34, 57, 102
Random House 221-224, 231, 233, 255, 287-288, 296-299
Ratcliffe, Richard 7
Reader's Digest 208
"Recent Negro Fiction" 187
Reese, Jeff 7
"Remembering Jimmy" 249, 255
Revolutionary War 205
Rhine River 209
"Richard Wright's Blues" 210
Richardson, Hallie 94
Riley, Fletcher 138
Riverside Park 66-67, 138, 235, 267, 290
Robinson, Elise 302
Rockefeller Hall 118, 126
"Rodelinda" 188
Rogers, Will 304-305
Rome, Italy 242-247
Roosevelt, Franklin D. 33, 175
Roosevelt, Theodore 11, 258
Roseman, Andrew Fletcher 124
Rover Boy 113
Ruby's Grill 81, 88
Rushing, Jimmy 82, 88, 89-93, 267, 306-307
Rutgers University 250-251, 266

S.S. *Sun Yat Sen* 206
Saint-Jacome, Louis A. 124
Salinger, J.D. 299
Sand Town 19
Sandy Bend 31
Saturday Review 84, 249
Savage, Augusta 152-153, 162
Savage, William W., Jr. 83
Schroder, Charlie 302
Schubert, Franz 51
Scottsboro, AL 113-114
Seagrave, Gordon S. 247
Shadow and Act 27, 37, 127-128, 155-157, 287, 297, 300
"She of the Dancing Feet Sings" 149
Simpson College 126
Singh, Amritjit 315
Slaughter Hall 53-54, 81, 88, 93-94
Slaughter, W.H. 94
Slick 174, 181-182, 184
"Slick Gonna Learn" 182
Small's Paradise Bar 163
Smith, Bessie 85
Smith, Clara 50
Smith, Jacques C. 308
"Society, Morality and the Novel" 246
Soldier Field 147
"Song for a Banjo Dance" 150
Sony Music Entertainment, Inc. 307
South Town 19
Spanish American War 58
Sprague, Morteza 127-128, 148
St. Louis, MO 112
St. Philips Church 219
St. Stephen's College 247
State University of New Jersey 251
Statue of Liberty 290
Steegmuller, Bea 222
Steegmuller, Francis 222
Stein, Gertrude 135, 172
Stepto, Robert 127
Stewart, James Edward "Jimmy" 17, 31-33, 54, 84, 93, 141, 236, 234, 269, 280, 288-290
Stokes, William O. 173
"Strong Men" 151
Sugar Hill 163
Sullivan, Harry Stack 164
Sunraider, Adam 301

Tabernacle Baptist Church 21, 30, 103
Taylor, Frank 221
Taylor, Steven 8
Tchaikovsky, Pytor 131
Tender is the Night 299
"That I Had Wings" 194, 199-200

"The Birthmark" 186
"The Black Ball" 173
"The Charlie Christian Story" 249, 255
The Collected Essays of Ralph Ellison 297-298
The Crisis 149
The Great Gatsby 299
The Hero 215
The Last Tycoon 300
The Living Novel 246
The Modern Library 297-299, 306
"The Myth of the Flawed White Southerner" 259
"The Negro speaks of Rivers" 150
"The Roof, the Steeple, and the People" 271
"The Waste Land" 148-149, 159
"The Weary Blues" 150
These Low Grounds 162
Thomas, J.R. 128
Thorpe, Jim 304
Thrasher Hall 117
Time 231, 276
Tivoli, NY 247
To Heal and to Build 259
Tobacco Road 164-165
Tolson, Melvin 100
Tomorrow 206
Topeka, KN 52
Tourgee, Albion 100
Trading Twelves 303-304
Trinity Cemetery 290
Tulsa, OK race riot 67-68
Tulsa, OK 67-68
Turpin, Edward 162
Tuskegee Airmen 196
Tuskegee Chapel 118
Tuskegee Messenger 128
Tuskegee University 103-106, 109, 114-119, 123-132, 258
Twain, Mark 136, 176, 230
"Twentieth-Century Fiction and the Black Mask of Humanity" 241

U.S. Air Force 245
U.S. Bicentennial Society 279
U.S. Merchant Marine 193-201, 205-209
U.S. Senate 266-267
Ulysses 299

Unassigned Lands 9
Uncle Tom's Children 161
United States Military
    Academy 73
Universal Negro
    Improvement Association
    58
University Hospital 22
University of Alabama
    School of Law 197
University of Chicago 146
University of Michigan 267
University of Oklahoma 304
University Press of
    Mississippi 315

***Vanity Fair* 24, 55**
Victoria Temple 101
Volkening Library Agency
    201
Volkening, Henry 201,
    207-208

Waitsfield, VT 215
Wake Forest College 278
Walden, Daniel 278
Walnut Grove 19
Waltham, MA 247
Warren, Robert Penn 267
Washington Post (The) 298
Washington, Booker T. 33,
    104-106, 124-126, 148,
    258
Washington, D.C. 71, 185,
    300
Washington, Durthy A. 311
Welch, Sandi 7
Welge, Bill 7
Well's Chili Parlor 90
Wesleyan University 278
West Town 19, 31
Western League Baseball
    Park 31, 44
Westport, CT 222
"What America Would be
    Like Without Blacks" 276
Wheeler Park 19
White Oak, GA 20
White, Alexander 250
White, John 262
Whittaker, Johnson
    Chestnut 63, 73
Wichita, KN 52, 112
Wilberforce College 147
Wiley College 100

Williams College 275
Williams, Alonzo 100
Williams, B.J. 8
Williams, Slick 182
Williams, Walter 132
Williamstown, MA 275
Wilson, Edward 283-284
Winston-Salem, NC 235,
    278
*Wisdom Tales From Around
    the World* 198
World War I 33, 58, 84
World War II 34, 186, 205,
    268
World's Fair 112-113
Wright Field 172
Wright, Richard 158-162,
    169-170, 175-177, 182,
    185, 187, 209-211, 219,
    299
Wuthering Heights 135

Yellow Springs, OH 242
Young, Andrew 31
Young, Athena 284
Young, Charles 33
Young, Lester 87